WHEN YOU DEAD, YOU DEAD

Guy Martin

BOOKS

3 5 7 9 10 8 6 4 2

Virgin Books, an imprint of Ebury Publishing,
20 Vauxhall Bridge Road,
London SW1V 2SA

Virgin Books is part of the Penguin Random House group of companies
whose addresses can be found at global.penguinrandomhouse.com

Penguin
Random House
UK

Copyright © Guy Martin 2015

Guy Martin has asserted his right to be identified as the author of this
Work in accordance with the Copyright, Designs and Patents Act 1988

First published by Virgin Books in 2015
This edition published by Virgin Books in 2016

www.eburypublishing.co.uk

A CIP catalogue record for this book is available from the British Library

ISBN 9780753556672

Printed and bound in Great Britain by Clays Ltd, St Ives PLC

Penguin Random House is committed to a sustainable future for our
business, our readers and our planet. This book is made from Forest
Stewardship Council® certified paper.

MIX
Paper from
responsible sources
FSC
www.fsc.org   FSC® C018179

Contents

Introduction – When you dead, you dead   7

1. I wasn't whoopin' or hollerin', but I was chuffed   11

2. Best shit of my life   29

3. Only boys in the sheep game know that   45

4. 65 storeys up, looking the shitehawks in the eye   53

5. Brian the Chimp   79

6. No one cares who I am. I loved that   90

7. You can afford it   105

8. My farts could be one of your five a day   124

9. I had the confidence that my brain was cleverer than I was   139

10. I don't want any regrets when I finally do
    stop racing   153

11. Steam-cleaning muck from under trucks   173

12. When Francis smacked the dog   183

13. Waiting for a dickhead like me   196

14. The Maws are my default setting   206

15. It'll only get messy if it barrel rolls   213

16. Racing in my anorak. Not very corporate   225

17. Fair play to him, he gave me a cup of cold coffee
    with ice cubes in it   235

18. Bored to back teeth of riding through bloody
    chicanes   252

19. Blacking out is going to be the only problem   261

20. Turning down the biggest job in TV   268

21. If he says pork scratchings are the fuel of
    champions, I'm listening   276

22. I don't want another podium   287

23. I don't have time to be having a week off work
    with a broken back   305

Index   316

When you dead, you dead

My second go at writing a book followed my first pretty quickly because 2014's *My Autobiography* went down so well. You might be thinking I'd struggle to fill this one, considering that book covered the first 30-odd years of my life and this one concentrates on just 12 months. I thought the same for a while. To be honest, I still hadn't got my head around anyone wanting to read about me in the first place, so it wasn't an easy decision to write another. In the end, I had no bother filling another book because this has been the maddest year of my life. And previous years had been full-on, so that's saying something.

The book starts at a race that made a big impression on my life, Pikes Peak International Hill Climb of July 2014, and finishes just after one that made an even bigger impression, the Ulster Grand Prix of August 2015. I talk about winning and losing, successes and almighty fuck-ups. It'll let you know a bit about my decision-making process, that sometimes only I can understand. I describe how and why I do stuff and the opportunities I've turned down. It also covers the day-to-day routines that have made me who I am. I'll also introduce you to people I work with and mates I spend time with.

There have been a couple of big additions to my life who don't really get a proper introduction in the book, but were there through all of it.

When I started writing the book I was a bit lonely. Every morning I was getting up at daft o'clock in the morning, working in the truck yard on my own, only going into the office for a brew and some passive smoking with Mick Moody every three or four hours. Then I'd come home to an empty house, because Nick, my cousin who lodges with me, doesn't come home till late most nights.

One day, not long after getting home from Pikes Peak, I was on a pushbike ride with Jason Miles, who crops up regularly in the following chapters. I was telling him I'd love a dog, and when he said his mate's sister's cousin knew about a litter of Labradors that were due, I told him to put my name down for one. There wasn't any big decision about this breed or that breed, but Labradors are a bit like Retrievers and the Lancasters had them on their farm when I lived there.

It wouldn't be possible for me to own a dog if it wasn't for my sister Sal, so we decided we'd share one, her looking after the dog when I was away. So in August 2014, me, Sal and her boys George and Louie went over to Manchester to see this litter of Labradors. There were only a couple to choose from, because most of them had already been picked, but as soon as I saw them I thought they were the best things ever. I'd eaten some bacon Frazzles on the drive over and one pup I picked up started licking my chops straight away. I thought, Right, you're my man. He was the smallest of the survivors. There had been a smaller pup, but that one had died. I didn't bother having his back end checked – Labs are notorious for having dodgy hips, but I wasn't bothered because I was having him whatever.

We named him Nigel, after Mad Nige, the late Mad Nige, my mate from the Isle of Man. He causes loads of grief, tries to eat everything and disappears for hours, but I just put that down to him showing a bit of character.

The other big change in my home life is the fact that Sharon moved in. She's from Dublin, and we've been together for most of the time I was writing the book. I first met her at a charity moped race at Mondello race track in February 2014. Sharon is a mate of people I know out there because she was involved with the Loughshinny Motorcycle Club, who organise the Skerries and Killalane road races. She was invited out for a meal with a group of us and I got talking to her a bit that night and then again at the race the next day, quizzing her about a load of stuff. She said she liked that and even though she promised herself she'd never go out with a road racer we ended up together.

For most of the time covered by this book I would go over and visit her for the odd weekend I had off and every time I was racing, testing or doing anything in Ireland, but she moved over to England after the 2015 TT and it's great. In the past, I've dragged jobs out because I'd get whinged at when I came home, but Sharon doesn't whinge about anything. She gives me a cup of tea, we have a yarn and then I go into the shed or we do something. We're well suited.

It's important to point out that I've written this book as I've gone along, so you're reading what I thought at the time. Even if I end up contradicting myself later I haven't gone back and changed it, so you can see what I was thinking, and hopefully why, then follow the process of me changing my mind. So you might know the ending, but I certainly didn't when I started writing the book or even when I thought I'd finished it. My life has a habit of going off the rails every now and then, and it happened so late in the day this time that I had to rewrite the last chapter.

And if you're wondering about the book's title, it comes from a saying my mum's dad would repeat to me when I was a little kid. There was no doubt in Voldemars Kidals's mind, and he'd seen plenty in his life. I wasn't even ten years old, but he let me have it straight and made sure I knew that he believed, 'When you dead, you dead.' With that thought never far from my mind I make sure I pack a lot in.

CHAPTER 1

I wasn't whoopin' or hollerin', but I was chuffed

I have been road racing for over 12 years and for the last few years I've been slowly but steadily realising I want to do different stuff. Call it a bucket list or a do before you die list or whatever you like, but I just want my eyes opening and I know there's more to motorbike racing than what I have been doing. I also think the arse has been kicked out of road racing for the last few years. There are too many people who are only there because it's the cool thing to do. I love motorbikes, but I sometimes forget it when I'm at certain races. People might think it's just talk when I say 'I just want to ride my motorbike', but I do. How long I was going to keep road racing was something I'd been thinking about a lot.

Those are just some of the reasons I ended up in Colorado at an oddball race called the Pikes Peak International Hill Climb. Pikes Peak is nicknamed, by the organisers at least, 'The Race to the Clouds', and it's the second oldest motor race in USA, after the Indianapolis 500.

It's a totally different kettle of fish to the Indy 500, though. For one thing, the Indianapolis 500 is just for cars, whereas Pikes Peak is for motorbikes, trucks, quads, trikes and all kinds of cars from classic to electric. Pikes Peak has more similarities to the Isle of Man TT than a short circuit race, because it's held on a toll road up a mountain, not a purpose-built racetrack. The mountain is like a national park and you have to pay to go up it with a vehicle. At the bottom there are log cabins built across the road where you drive up to a barrier, pay a park ranger a fee to get through and onto the two-way road. Then you can drive right up to the café and gift shop, 19 miles further on, at the very top of the mountain.

The mountain is named after the explorer Zebulon Pike Jr, and Pikes Peak is part of the Rocky Mountain range, in the west of the state of Colorado. Pike was so impressed by the mountain, when he first saw it in 1806, that he reckoned it would never be climbed by a human. He got that wrong, obviously. By 1888 there was a carriage track to the top. In 1915, a local entrepreneur, Spencer Penrose, paid for the building of the dirt road up it. He did it to attract tourists to nearby Colorado Springs. He is also the man who came up with the idea of running a motor race to promote the new road and the area. The race I entered, in the summer of 2014, was the 92nd running of the Pikes Peak International Hill Climb.

Colorado is at such a high altitude that the lowest point in the whole state is over 3,300 ft (1,000 m) above sea level. That means the lowest point of the whole state is higher than Scafell Pike, the highest mountain in the whole of England. The nearby city of Colorado Springs, where we stayed in for the week in a hotel, is on a plateau a mile above sea level, and the car park at the summit of Pikes Peak is 14,115 ft or nearly 2.7 miles (4,302 m) above sea level.

By comparison, that is over three times higher than Ben Nevis, and while Mont Blanc, the highest mountain in the whole of Europe, is just 500 m taller than Pikes Peak, at the top of the American mountain there's a shop selling fudge and cuddly Big Foot toys.

From the gravel car park at the top of Pikes Peak, it's said you can see five different states on a clear day and after you've had a look around you drive down the same way you went up. A cog railway carries tourists to the top and there are walking trails too.

I found out about the Pikes Peak race three or four years before from Paul Dunlop, my mate from Northern Ireland. I sometimes stay with him when I'm racing at the North West 200 and he's into rare stuff. He showed me the famous short film, *Climb Dance*, of Ari Vatanen driving his Peugeot 405 T16 rally car up the mountain in 1988. Back then, much of the road was still dirt, but now it's completely tarmac'd. *Climb Dance* planted a seed, then I heard about the Loeb thing, when Peugeot returned to Pikes Peak with the multiple World Rally Champion Sebastien Loeb. He raced his Peugeot WRC car there in 2013 and smashed the course record, though the first fully tarmac race was in 2012, and the new surface helped him lower the course record.

The Pikes Peak race was definitely in my mind when the TV lot were looking for new things to do. Well, they were looking for anything to do, but if we were going to carry on with the TV job I only wanted to be involved with new challenges. I'm not interested in repeating the same kind of programmes, that's why I stopped doing the history series, like *How Britain Worked*, even though I enjoyed them at the time.

We got talking about me racing Pikes Peak and them filming it. Their original thought was to race my TAS Suzuki superbike, but I wasn't interested in that. It seemed too easy. If I was going to do it, I reckoned I should do it on my Martek. Pikes Peak is one of the few races anywhere in the world where you can ride whatever you want, and I love that about it. Pretty much everywhere else they make you enter on a production bike, something based on a showroom bike and modified to very strict rules, or it's MotoGP – and even there the rules are tight and you can't run a turbo or supercharger, meaning all the bikes have ended up looking just like each other. Pikes Peak happily accepts, and attracts, all the weirdos and oddballs.

There was just one small problem: I bought the Martek in late 2009 and it had been in bits for most of the time I had owned it. It is a turbocharged special based on an early-1990s Suzuki GSX-R1100, but it has had so much work done to it, there's not that much Suzuki left. It was originally built by Mark Walker, one of the co-owners of Martek, a motorcycle chassis-building firm in Grimsby that has now stopped trading.

When I bought the bike I thought I'd change a few bits and pieces, and bring it all up to the same high standard, because there were a few areas that were letting it down. Then one thing led to another, and four years later it was an expensive pile of bits in the corner of my shed. I'd only ridden it a few times in all the years I'd had it.

Everyone involved agreed that racing the Martek would make a more interesting programme, but it meant I had to pull my finger out and get it finished. Instead of just bolting it all back together I planned to change loads more of it.

I bought a new BorgWarner turbo and TiAL wastegate. I needed to fit a scavenge pump to draw oil through the turbo, because the turbo was too low for the oil to flow by gravity alone. Racefit, in Derbyshire, made me a titanium exhaust system with a huge outlet you could lose a Jack Russell up.

Because the race climbs so many feet up the mountain, the fuelling changes as the air becomes thinner at altitude, and most bikes would lose power. My thinking was, I could change the turbo boost pressure as I climbed, so the motor would make a constant amount of power and wouldn't get breathless. Most engines make far less power at high altitudes because there isn't the density of air to mix with fuel. So I had an all-new, one-off wiring loom and electronics made for the bike by Track Electronics in Norfolk. This included a one-off ECU (the engine's brain). I could've got an off-the-shelf MoTeC ECU, like we use on the TAS bikes, but that would have meant I needed a separate boost controller for the turbo and I wanted it as neat as possible, so I had my own ECU made.

A mate was supposed to do some welding for me, but after weeks of my bike being at his workshop nothing had happened, so I brought it back home. To rub salt in the wound, the bike fell over in the van on the way home and put a big gouge in the petrol tank. Bugger. I bought myself a TIG welder so I could practise and make parts myself. I'm alright at welding steel, but I have next to no experience welding alloy, so it's much harder to be neat. It would take me years to get as good as the Martek boys, but I had a go.

The mechanical and engineering side of the project was never a worry, but one of the hardest things to get right was how the bike looked. At first I wanted a modern café racer style, but I couldn't get the right seat unit. I had the look in my head, but every seat I tried looked like it had been taken off something else and I didn't want that. In the end the bike became a mix of café racer and dirt tracker. The seat is a modified Harley-Davidson XR750 dirt track tailpiece with the back trimmed and blanked off. I fitted a dirt track number plate on the front with my number on it. The eight was made from the number three the American champion Gene Romero had on his bikes in the 1960s and 70s, but reversed and filled in to make it an eight. Again it would make more sense to have a full fairing, for aerodynamics and to keep the wind off at high speed, but I wanted this look and was happy to make the compromise.

The old Öhlins suspension that was fitted to the Martek when I bought it was changed for the latest Superbike-specification forks and rear shock from K-Tech, the British company that supply TAS and loads of other race teams. I also changed the front brakes to AP Lockheed Moto2 brake calipers. They are proper, money-can't-buy kit. Well, I bought them, but you try to find another set.

The Suzuki engine got a lot of attention. I found an MTC big-block, brand new. They are as rare as rocking horse shit too, but one was sat on Mark Walker's shelf five minutes from my work. What are the chances of that? This engine was five-speed as standard, but I set my heart on fitting a six-speed, close-ratio gearbox and a dry clutch from the 1980s Suzuki factory racing kit – the stuff race teams bought to convert road bikes for Superbike racing. This clutch was probably the rarest part I was hunting. They cost £25,000 in the late 1980s and anyone who has one now isn't selling it. Suzuki fit a dry clutch to the late-eighties GSX-R750RR homologation road bike, but it isn't the same as the factory one. And, of course, I wanted the real thing. Sometimes it's not what you know, it's who you know and the multiple TT-winning sidecar racer Dave Molyneux had one that he was willing to loan me to make a pattern from so I could get my own sand-cast, but then I found one through Goose at York Suzuki, the bloke who knows these older Suzukis inside-out. Again, one of the rarest parts and it was in the next county.

Paddy repainted the bike in a dead subtle metallic grey and silver with white stripes, repairing the tank while he was at it. Paddy is an old mate of mine, he lives locally and he's painted my helmets for years. He does them as barrow jobs, because he's a full-time brickie, and I worked with him when I left my dad's place in 2010. He's also a retained fireman, and the name he uses for his painting work, 3SIX2SEVEN, is his fireman's number. When I see Paddy he'll come out with words like 'prequel' and I have to ask, 'Paddy, have you been listening to Radio 1 again?'

He painted me an AGV helmet to match the bike, and Dainese made me some new matching leathers and they became my favourites straight away.

While all this was happening I was driving up and down the country, from Grimsby to the electronics man in Norwich or over to Racefit in Darley Dale, to get the Martek finished in time to do one quick test at Cadwell before the bike was packed in a crate and flown to America. I got the bike finished and it felt great going round Cadwell, much more nimble than a bike of this age and weight should've felt, and I was pretty impressed. The fuelling felt good as a starting point too. Then it was time to go.

My mate Cameron 'Cammy' Whitworth flew out with me to be the mechanic and a part of the TV show. Cammy has spannered for me at the TT and other races for years, on and off, but his day job is live cable jointing. He connects new buildings to the national grid, so he's normally down a hole when I'm trying to get hold of him.

We flew to Dallas, then caught another flight to Albuquerque, New Mexico. From there we picked up the Martek from a hotel, where it had been delivered after passing through customs, and went on a bit of a road trip. With the bike loaded into our rented U-Haul box van we headed off to meet an old boy called Robert 'Bobby' Unser. He is a Pikes Peak legend, having won the race 13 times. His brother Al won it and his son, Robby Unser, won it eight times. Bobby, who we met, won the Indy 500 and Daytona too.

He was very American, cool and had done very well out of racing. He seemed genuinely pleased to see us, and we spent a few hours at his place. He could tell I was interested in his shed and we had a good look around. He had built his own flow bench and that was impressive. It simulates air passing through an engine's cylinder head and was something special.

The whole visit only made about a minute of the finished programme, but meeting Bobby was a good experience.

The next day, while we were still in New Mexico, we went horse riding in Taos, an out-of-season ski resort, high in the mountains. The idea was to get us used to the altitude. It was a bit of TV bullshit really, the kind of thing we have to do to make the programmes flow and link from one bit to the other, and you couldn't get further away from a couple of hoss riders than me and Cammy, but it was still mint. After the riding we had a few beers and just had a dead relaxed time.

I couldn't feel the effects of the altitude while we were on the horses, but when I got off and had to walk up a banking I knew about it. I was out of breath a hell of a lot quicker, and any kind of exertion made my heart rate rise a lot sooner than it would at sea level.

I'd already done a bit of altitude training back in Lincolnshire, and that's about as difficult to do as you'd expect in a county that's barely above sea level. The highest point of my home county is only 550 ft (168 m) above sea level, so the TV lot arranged for a hypoxic chamber to be set up in a spare room at home. This is the opposite of the hyperbaric chambers that motorcycle racers sometimes use to help recover from injuries. A hyperbaric chamber is an environment that is very high in oxygen, and the hope is the oxygenated blood helps bones heal more quickly. The hypoxic chamber we set up in a spare room at my house was a great, big bubble attached to two pumps. One would pump out normal sea-level air, the other would pump in air with a reduced oxygen content. Air contains 21 per cent oxygen and it contains that at sea level or at the top of a mountain, it's just that there's less air to breathe at altitude, because the air is less dense in the atmosphere. The make-up of air is still the same, 21 per cent oxygen, 78 per cent nitrogen and a bit of argon and carbon dioxide. So, to get the effect of breathing thin air at sea level, you reduce the oxygen content in the air. We knew we'd reduced the oxygen level enough when a match wouldn't light in the hypoxic chamber. Then I'd get in and cycle as hard as I could on the turbo trainer.

To be honest, we only did it once, and that was for the cameras. I was too tight to have the pumps working for two hours to get the right oxygen content in the tent. The electricity bill would have gone through the roof.

After riding Daisy and Zeus, we drove to Colorado Springs, the town where we'd be based for the practice week and race day. The whole practice set-up is different to anything else in the racing world. They had stopped early morning practice at the TT before I first raced there, but I don't think it was ever as early as this. We had to be out of the hotel at half-three in the morning. If you're on the mountain much later than half-four you can't get up the toll road before they close it and you're buggered. The whole road is 19 miles long, but the race is held over the last 12.42 miles of it. For practice, that

FINISH

SUMMIT

COG CUT

BOTTOMLESS PIT

COVE CREEK

DEVIL'S PLAYGROUND

RAGGED EDGE

SUMP

GILLY'S CORNER

HEITMAN'S HILL

BROWN BUSH CORNER

ENGINEER'S CORNER

PIKES PEAK
INTERNATIONAL HILL CLIMB

LENGTH – 12·42 MI
TURNS – 156

ALTITUDE AT FINISH
– 14,110 FT

START

12-mile course is split into the three sections: bottom, middle and top. The race vehicles are split into three groups, with all the motorcycles and quads put together, and each group practises on a different section each morning.

On day one of practice the bikes were on the top section, Devil's Playground to the finish line. There are four days of practice so we did one section, the top, twice. Each day's practice session is over by nine in the morning so the road can open for tourists. The one and only time you get to ride the whole track at racing speed is on race day, and you only get one run at it. There is no practice on that day – it's shit or bust.

Unfortunately, right from the off the bike didn't behave itself. It felt like a fuelling problem, but the bike would cut out like it was electrical. The way the practice is run wasn't giving us much chance to experiment either. The man with the flag would set bikes off one at a time, with a 30-second gap in between. When the whole group, of well over 50 bikes, had all had a run and was at the top of the section, a couple of travelling marshals would ride up and guide us back down, in what was supposed to be an orderly line. Someone still managed to crash on the way down one morning, his bike flying off the side of the road, bouncing down the mountain and hitting another racer's bike on the road below. Luckily no one was hurt.

We heard from some of the racers, who been competing at Pikes Peak for a few years, that they used to set riders off a lot closer together. The organisers' thinking was it was safer to spread them out, but it meant that less experienced riders couldn't see the lines the fast lads ran and the quick fellas couldn't get used to new bikes because it took much longer to run right through the session. So we were up on the mountain for four and a half hours or more and only getting three or four runs at each section, because we had to wait for everyone to come through before we followed the marshals back to the temporary pits. Still, I was learning the track alright, even though there are 156 bends, with names including Brown Bush Corner, Engineer's, Sump, Ragged Edge, Devil's Playground and Bottomless Pit. I'd been watching onboard laps of it, like I used to with the TT, but we weren't getting much of a chance to experiment with bike settings.

In between each run, we plugged a laptop into the bike and James, the TV director who knows a lot more about laptops than me or Cammy, was helping me change the fuel maps. I'd tell him what needed doing and he operated the keyboard with short cuts I didn't know. James started calling us FITA Racing – Finger In The Air.

We thought we'd cured the problem, but every day it was more of the same. If I went above about 4,000 revs it would cut out and go dead, then come back to life. One of the other teams had a workshop with a rolling road dyno in Colorado Springs, where we were staying, so we arranged to see them. One night, me and Cammy worked on that till midnight. I was on the phone to John Ewals of Track Electronics back in England and he was dead helpful, but nothing he suggested worked.

The place we were at were turbo specialists and, even though it wasn't running right, they said the Martek made the most power they'd ever seen, 273 bhp at the rear wheel. We changed everything, plugs, coils, maps, everything except the ECU, and we couldn't solve the problem, so I thought it must be the ECU. I was kicking myself a bit. I built 80 per cent of the bike and the 20 per cent I trusted to someone else seemed to be where the problem was.

We went back to the hotel and set off up the mountain at four in the morning for the final day of practice, this time on the bottom section, below the treeline. Like the day before, we'd think we had cured the problem and didn't need to change anything, but the bike would then go back to how it was, spluttering and cutting out. It seemed like the problem was evolving to make sure the answer was out of our reach. We couldn't get on top of it and I just had to think, It is what it is, and get on with it.

After practice we'd go for breakfast at a café at the bottom of the mountain with a few other racers who were on a similar wavelength, like Travis and Carl from Colorado and Jimmy from Vermont. Later that day I rented a mountain bike and rode up most of Pikes Peak. I rented it from Manitou Springs, and it must be five miles of steep climbing from there before you even get to the start of the Pikes Peak toll road, so I didn't make it easy for myself, but I didn't want to. I had the World Cup 24-hour solo race coming up in October, and I was fit, but I wanted to keep on top of things. The ride was hard work and I felt I was going nowhere fast. I got to Devil's Playground, which isn't the end of the road, but it's higher than the top car park. From there the road goes up and down and round the houses, but doesn't actually get any higher. I turned round and headed back to the bike shop from there, because I had to get the bike back before they closed at five. They were locking the door as I got there. I was out for about four hours and really enjoyed being back on a pushbike. Then I went for something to eat and had an early night, because race day started even earlier than practice.

On Sunday morning, race day, the road opened to racers, their teams and helpers between 2 and 3am, before the public are allowed in at 4.30. The road closes, from the start line up, at 7am.

The Pikes Peak fans are hardcore. Loads were at the roadside at four in morning, five hours before the race starts, and they're trapped there until after 6pm when the race ends and the road reopens. Even then, they're stuck in a traffic jam to get off the mountain. That means they're there whatever the weather, and it regularly snows at the top of the mountain, even in June.

We set up our pit in a clearing in the woods. I say pit – we pulled the bike out of the truck and parked it on the dirt. I'm happiest working out of the back of a van anyway, so it didn't bother me, but some teams paid extra to be at the side of the road. Right near us was a Freightliner racing truck, parked on the back of a low-loader. It was wrecked, because it had driven off the side of the mountain during practice and ploughed through 50 yards of pine trees before grinding to a halt. The driver, a bloke called Mike Ryan, is a Hollywood stuntman and a regular at Pikes Peak, so the organisers let him enter on his Triumph Tiger 1200 road bike instead, just so he could have a race.

On race day the bikes go off first, after lining up on the road, one behind the other down the hill away from the start line. I wasn't nervous, just a bit disappointed that I had to keep the bike revving below 5,000 rpm and I wouldn't be able to do it or myself justice. Still, it could be worse.

The first bike set off close to nine o'clock and I was in the queue, 20-odd bikes back, tyre warmers on the soft, treaded tyres that Metzeler made for the Martek. All competitors are stranded at the top of the mountain until everything has run up, and there are over a hundred entries, so it takes all day, plus there are stoppages for crashes. Because the bikes are up there first, we're parked at 4,300 m above sea level, with only a small café and a stinking pumping station to hide in, while the car drivers can stay with their teams at the bottom till later in the day. I knew it was going to be a long day and I wanted something to read, so I stuck a paperback copy of George Orwell's *Animal Farm* down the front of my leathers.

When it was my time to race I set off and got in a rhythm, but wasn't really going for it. I didn't change anything for the race day, so I knew what I had. I couldn't rev the bike to more than 5,000 rpm, less than half what it would rev to. If I did it would go *ba-ba-ba-baarrrppp*. I wasn't going to have a hissy fit, because I knew it would get to the top, just not as quickly as I hoped. Still, the whole experience had been mint.

Sitting at the top, I thought this race was the best thing I've done in motorbiking, even with all the problems. If I'd have gone with my TAS superbike I'd have been battling for the win, but it would be, So what? Not one little bit of me wishes I had taken that option, even after the problems with the Martek.

I don't give a shit if people think my times weren't any good. It was going racing with a couple of mates and an oddball bike. That's what I wanted. If I was competing on something mass-produced I would just be a sheep following the next sheep. It wasn't until I got back to England that we found the problem was a quick-release joint in the fuel line. Bugger.

While I was reading about Napoleon, Snowball and Old Major, the race went sour right outside the café. A motorbike racer from Texas crossed the line, pumped his fist in the air, excited to have finished in one piece, but didn't concentrate on braking on the gravel of the car park. By the time his mind was on the job, he'd run out of room to slow down and he ran off the road into a field of boulders. I didn't see the crash, and stayed out of the way, but was told later he had died of his injuries. The way motorcycle racers are, within an hour of the accident, everyone was still telling their mates they were coming back next year, or sometime in the future.

My time was 11:32.558, while the fastest motorcycle time of the day was 9:58.687 set by Jeremy Toye, on the factory-supported Kawasaki ZX-10R. My time was enough to win the class I entered, the Exhibition class. I wasn't whoopin' or hollerin', but I was chuffed enough with that and the chequered flag they gave me as a class-winner.

Like a lot of the things I set off to do, I didn't have any preconceived ideas of what it was going to be, I just wanted to go there and ride my bike. I didn't know Pikes Peak was like this, but I was trying to find somewhere I could go back to just racing motorbikes. You go to the Isle of Man or Brands Hatch and it's all dick-swinging. It's all about numbers – how much are you earning? Who do you know? How many Twitter followers have you got? Fair play, get on with it. Here it's just, 'You've got a bike? What size is it? 1300 cc? With a turbo on it? Yeah, we'll find a class for you.' And I bloody love that.

CHAPTER 2

Best shit of my life

Filming *Speed* was my kind of TV, because I was doing stuff I was genuinely interested in, trying to break records and pushing myself in training and while we were filming. The first programme of the second, four-part series concentrated on me and Jason Miles trying to break the 24-hour distance record for pedalling a tandem. And we did, covering 565 miles in the time. The next was about Pikes Peak, and then I tried to break the 85 mph world speed record for hovercraft. That didn't go totally to plan, it flipped while I was attempting the record, but I did reach 79 mph, with a hovercraft that was built in a hurry and to a very small budget. The final episode, shown in the autumn of 2015, was based on an attempt to beat the world gravity racer speed record. It stood at 84.4 mph and was set by an American. The Americans call it downhill soapbox.

In America, soap powder used to be delivered in big wooden boxes. Right back as early as the 1930s, kids, or their parents, would fit pram and rollerskate wheels to these boxes to make cheap, DIY go-karts, so that's how they got the name, but I don't like the description soapbox, so I called it a go-kart. (Like I went sledging in the first *Speed* series, not tobogganing. We don't have toboggans or soapboxes in Lincolnshire. We have sledges and go-karts.)

The most important bit of information about this record is that no pedalling or power is allowed. After an initial push-off it's all gravity-assisted, so aerodynamics are important and, like everything, these karts had developed over the years. Even by the 1960s they were looking like mini land speed record cars and little streamlined Bonneville salt flat racers.

The record we were looking to break was set by an old boy in America. He had built a right fancy thing, a work of art, with wishbone suspension like a Formula One car. There are videos of him setting his record on a public road, with traffic on it, but the location was kept secret. The biggest thing with this job is finding a hill steep and straight enough to get up to speed. You need it as straight as possible, because any momentum you lose braking for the entry of a corner takes a lot of getting back on the exit of the corner. The American bloke achieved 84.4 mph for a split second and went to Guinness with the evidence, but there is no official record, because Guinness wouldn't recognise it. When we talked to the *Guinness Book of Records* people they told us we had to set the top speed as an average measured over 100 metres.

This American bloke hadn't done that, but his speed was the benchmark we set ourselves and we had our work cut out to beat it.

The researchers at North One, the TV production company, got on the case trying to find the ideal location. They looked all over the UK first but didn't find anything. Then they decided on Mont Ventoux in the Provence region of France. There was a place in Brazil that would've been better, but the production company had already spent too much going to Pikes Peak, so France it was.

I'd heard of Mont Ventoux through reading about and listening to the Tour de France. It's one of the classic climbs in that race. Chris Froome won the last stage that finished at the summit, in 2013, and Tom Simpson, the top British cyclist of his day, died climbing the mountain in the 1967 Tour. His death was blamed on exhaustion, dehydration and using amphetamines to keep going. He collapsed off his bike and couldn't be revived, so the mountain has become famous, or infamous, among cyclists.

Mont Ventoux is also famous for being bald near the top. Its landscape gets compared to the surface of the moon. They say it used to be covered in forest, but all the trees were cut down for shipbuilding and the weather is so wild and windy up there the trees have never grown back. Wind speeds up to 200 mph have been measured on the mountain, but we had two mint days. It couldn't have been any better.

After working all day Monday and up till dinner-time Tuesday at Moody's, I drove back home to load up the trick carbon-fibre go-kart, that had been built specially for the job, then set out to drive out to France. The go-kart wouldn't fit in my van, so we borrowed a medium-wheelbase Ford Transit.

Me and my mate Tim Coles headed off, driving pretty much non-stop, except for the Channel Tunnel, for the next 900 miles. We drove all through the night, me driving till about three in the morning and Tim doing the last couple of hours.

Tim is in his late forties and I see a load of him. We call him the beef farmer, but he's spread his wings and has about a thousand pigs as well now. He's a real good man to do a road trip with. I originally met him through the trucks and I like him because he's understated, he's not trying to be owt, he's just dead level. He loves his dirt track but doesn't race; he helps a load of folk out and he has a track on his farm that I ride at. And he has a really interesting view on the history of World War II.

We got to the hotel in Malaucène, the local town where all the film crew were staying, at five o'clock Wednesday morning. Sensibly, they'd all gone down the day before, but I genuinely couldn't because there was too much on at work. When we parked outside the hotel I climbed in the back of the van with the go-kart, while Tim stayed in the front and we had a couple of hours' sleep, before we had a pizza and a slice of custard pie for breakfast, then drove up the mountain to suss the job out.

The plan was to head onto the mountain at 8am for practice at nine. It had been arranged that, for the next two days, we could have the run of a certain section of road for 20 minutes in every hour between nine and five.

We met the folk who had built the go-kart. They were a team from Hallam University, Sheffield, made up of Alice, Heather, Christina and Terry. I think the TV lot had asked for this episode to have a bit more female focus than previous ones, and the women were all totally switched on, especially Heather; she was a doctor, a real clever lass. Terry was the fella on the team, and he'd done a lot of machining and fabricating of the go-kart.

While we were waiting to go I told the Hallam lot that I reckoned we'd know on the first run if we were going to break the record or not in the time we had. I wasn't being negative, but I thought if I'd only done 60 mph or thereabouts at the first attempt, there was no way we were going to find 25 mph in two days. On the section of road we'd chosen to concentrate on, there were a couple of corners that I had to get a good run out of to reach the target speed. We might find a couple of mph here and there, because I knew I'd get out of the corners faster after a couple of runs at them, but I was trying to be realistic when I said if we'd only done 60-odd, we weren't going to do it.

After weeks of preparation and all the effort that had gone into building this amazing go-kart, it was time to get in and see what we could do. It was built with loads of adjustment and variables, especially to the suspension and geometry. We could also change the tyres, change the tracking, castor and camber and try pushing off or not pushing off.

The first run felt smooth, but I only did something like 70 mph. Everything felt safe and the thing handled well, but even then I started to think we were going to struggle to break the record. Still, we had the mountain for two days, so there was nothing to do but keep plugging away.

As the day went on it was obvious the Mont Ventoux people in charge of closing the road for us were bloody brilliant. We didn't use the 20-minute slot in every hour because we were adjusting stuff, but then they'd let us have half an hour when we were ready to go.

The TV lot had employed Tag Heuer to officially time our record attempt and we kept adjusting the timed 100-metre section during the practice day, moving it further down the mountain so I could accelerate for as long as possible and brake right at the death before the corner at the end of our section.

By the end of Wednesday we'd done 82 mph. We had found 5 mph just swapping from treaded tyres to slick tyres. We had worked out straight away on the first day that there was no point in having the lasses give me a push-start. We had done some filming at the UK Olympic bobsleigh team's headquarters near Bath, to practise the running push-start, but when we got to the mountain, the section we decided to use had a corner just after the start, a tight right-hander, so there was no benefit from pushing. If I was given a hell of a push it meant I'd just have to brake harder to scrub off more speed to get around it safely. By just having a gentle push, I got to the corner at a good speed to make it through using the optimum line for the run down the long straight. I had learned the course a bit and ended up clocking a speed just 2.4 mph shy of the existing record. The plan all along was not to try to break the record on the Wednesday, but to use the first day to get a feel for the job. Still, we nearly broke it – even though I'd thought, after the first run of the day, we weren't going to do it.

We were all feeling pretty good when we drove back to the pretty town at the bottom of the mountain. Malaucène is very French, a bit run-down but with modern cafés, a real laid-back place.

That night I stayed in the Domaine des Tilleuls hotel, the place I slept outside previously. It was just a mile from the bottom of the mountain, posh as hell, really arty-farty. There was no television in the room, but *Time* and fascinating French magazines were lying around. I'd only slept for a couple of hours in the back of the van the night before, so I was feeling knackered, but we all went to a posh restaurant, and I had a couple of beers. It was the last night of filming for the whole series so it was good to just get out together.

I sat with the Hallam University lot, about a dozen of the film crew and a French lass called Hélène Schmit, who featured in the programme. She was the world street luge champion, an expert at racing what looks like a massive skateboard which you lie on, feet first, and hammer down mountains on. The TV lot got her involved to show how body position and the like affect the vehicle. It was more for TV than to actually help my record attempt. After 15 years of racing motorbikes, if I haven't worked out that moving around on the machine helps it go around corners by now there isn't a lot of hope for me. Still, it all adds to the programme and she wasn't hard to look at, so no harm done.

I'd enjoyed all the stuff we'd done for this series of *Speed*, but the filming was starting to get in the way of work. I also felt I had no time to myself. On Saturday or Sunday I'd be racing my pushbike or motorbike, or training for a race. On Monday morning I'd be up at five o'clock to bike to work. I tried to make Monday my night off, and I'd aim to get home from work and try to stay out of the shed, by just reading instead and planning to get an early night, but it hardly ever happened that way. I'd end up in the shed and the early night would be out of the window, or I'd call at my mates, the Maws, and still be there at 11. Tuesdays would normally see me cycling to work at five or five-thirty again. Then I'd leave at five or six o'clock and drive to wherever we were filming for Wednesday morning. I had been filming on nearly every Wednesday and Thursday from February till the middle of October.

I'd get home at daft o'clock on Thursday night, go to work at Moody's on Friday, bike home, then, if I'm not working Saturday, I'd be trying get caught up at home, building flat trackers, preparing the Martek for Pikes Peak, racing motorbikes or doing a training ride.

I'm not complaining, but it felt good to be finished with the filming, and by the end of the evening I was feeling a bit drunk. Not drunk, drunk, but on the way. I had an early night and was dead to the world, so I wasn't even going to start thinking about going to a bar late at night with a good-looking luge lady. I'm not saying she wanted humping, but I've learned my lesson from past mistakes and I was seeing a new girlfriend, Sharon.

As far as a timetable for day two on Mont Ventoux went, the plan was the same as the practice day – meet up on the mountain at eight for a nine start.

I had a proper French breakfast with some strong French coffee. I'm not much of a coffee drinker, but when in Rome. We drove to the mountain, parked up near the bottom of the run and I got into my race overalls to be ready. We all waited at the point the run finished and sussed a plan. We made some small adjustments to the go-kart, changing the castor and camber of the wheels. We knew if we added a bit more ballast we'd break the record on the first run, then we could spend the rest of the day trying different stuff to go faster still, because I didn't just want to break the record, I wanted to smash it if I could. Anyone who attempts a record like this is dealing with gravity, so if anyone was going to beat us, it would be by bugger all. No one was going to do 120 mph.

I was really looking forward to getting back in the go-kart, having the canopy clipped down and setting off for another run down the mountain, trying to get every corner entry and exit perfect. We just had to wait for the ambulance to arrive. You can't be doing these things by the seat of your pants any more, especially when the TV and timing officials and all that get involved. You have to get all the proper insurance and hire the correct medical cover. The TV lot even put crash barriers along sections of the roads and covered the metal Armco barriers with softer stuff in case something when wrong.

With time ticking on, me and Tim drove to the top of the section we were using. We got a message, telling us the ambulance was going to be another half an hour, but by now that strong French coffee had, as *Viz* comic puts it, greased the runway.

I asked Tim if he had any bog roll, because I was breaking my bloody neck for a shit. We had a look around and he found some kitchen roll. I said, 'Give it here, I've got a big job on.'

I'm not afraid of shitting outside, so I traipsed up this mountainside, right into the woods. We were on the lower slopes of the mountain. Higher up, where it is bald, white rock, the road wasn't suitable, because there were too many hairpins and I wouldn't be able to get a good run at it without having to brake for another sharp bend. We had settled on a 2 km section with a couple of kinks in it that was still surrounded by woodland.

After a few minutes' hiking I found a suitable spot. Then it entered my head that trying to drop the kids off at the pool while I was wearing my race overalls could potentially get messy, so I took them off and hung them from a tree branch. I took my undies off and hung them up too. Then I got straddled and leant against this tree. From there I was looking out across what looked like the whole of the south of France. I could see the Alps, the sun was just coming through the trees, I'd had a real good night's sleep after a few beers, I was pretty sure we were going to set a new world record, and it was a mint morning. I was feeling good.

Before anything even started moving I knew it was going to be a big moment in my life. I didn't want anything to spoil it. It was a bit of 'me time', that's why I made the effort to take my overalls fully off. Sitting like that – my back straight, against the tree trunk, like a bear scratching its back, my legs akimbo, bent at right angles – I would be able to see the fruits of my labour. When I'm at work and need the bog I'm not a read the paper man, but it's my time. I like to just relax. It was the same on the side of this French mountain, and I was propped against the tree for a good five minutes.

I'd rather have a good shit than a good shag, any day of the week. I told this to a mate and he said, 'You're obviously not shagging right.' And I told him, No, you're not shitting right. It's not about the actual shitting. It's about everything around it. You've got to be in the right frame of mind. And propped there, on the side of Mont Ventoux, was the ultimate shit.

I was thinking, I don't have a bad life. I got to drive a Transit to the south of France, and I love driving Transits. I had a bit of tea, a few drinks … Sometimes when I'm getting pulled from pillar to post I think, What's happening? I never question why I'm doing it, but I sometimes feel I need a bit more of my time back. Still, it's not a bad life.

After I walked back to the van I got out my diary and made a note: 'The Greatest Shit Ever'. It's very rare I put pen to paper about something like that, but it was a big moment.

By the time I got back to where the van was parked, the ambulance had just arrived. I got my helmet on and climbed in the go-kart, then went out and beat the record on the first run of the day, like we all thought we would. We did 85 mph, breaking it by about 1 mph, showing just how difficult it was to beat.

We did another two or three runs, gaining a tenth here and a tenth there, just by carrying more weight. We'd broken the record, so all the team and TV bods were dead happy, it was all champagne and blowjobs. North One had a helicopter there to film the two last runs, telling me to stay nice and safe while they filmed what they call drop-ins, a different angle of the action to cut to when they edit the programme. We loaded the go-kart into the back of the van and drove to the top again.

I had spoken to Alice, Heather, Christina and Terry, saying, 'We've broken the record, but I think we've got to go shit or bust.'

We'd been adding a couple of kilos every run, just filling up any space with bottles of water, but we'd run out of room for any more bottles. The only space we had left, in this very cramped, faired-in, teardrop-shaped, carbon-fibre go-kart, was under my bent legs. My idea was to fill my helmet bag with rocks, so me and Tim got as much weight in the bag as we could. We had some bathroom scales with us that had been used to weigh each corner of the go-kart to make sure it was balanced as well as possible, and found we had 20 kilos of stone in the bag.

In all the stages of adjustment up to that point we had added a kilo here and a kilo there; adjusted a millimetre here, a millimetre there. Then we were going into the unknown by adding 20 kilos. But all I was thinking was, Every time we add weight we go faster, so let's have it.

Heather had obviously read the same book as me, *The Chimp Paradox* by Dr Steve Peters, because she said, 'That's your chimp talking.' She knew chimp behaviour was just to say fuck it, without fully thinking of the consequences.

I even knew it was my inner chimp talking as the words

were coming out of my mouth, and I also knew if things went wrong the chimp would be stood there saying, 'I didn't say those rocks. I didn't say put them there. It's not my fault.'

Heather and I were laughing about the chimp thing and agreed, 'Right, this goes no further.' The TV lot didn't know about the 20 kilos and I said I'd take all the blame if it went wrong. I felt that no one needed to know, because it was my neck on the line and it was all my idea. I never did admit we had done anything different, and if North One are reading this book, it'll be the first time they're finding out about it. Sorry ...

As I set off, with this bag of rocks under my legs, my chimp was shouting, 'Yeah, we're going to smash the record! 90 mph! We'll have it!' Then, going into the first corner, still within sight of the start, I had to gently feel the brakes to get around the corner and even with a dab on the pedal the back-end came round on me. It made me think, Hell, this is going to be nasty.

The wise thing to do then would have been to feather the brake all the way down, so I could come to a controlled stop at the end, and get a feel for the job. The braking system, that was brilliantly designed by Hope, the mountain bike parts company in Barnoldswick, Lancashire, had big, ventilated, hydraulic, mountain bike type disc brakes on each of the four wheels. Hope had designed an adjuster with a knob I could twist to alter the bias of the brakes from front to back, meaning it could be tweaked so the fronts were doing more braking than the rears or the other way around. It was trick and could be set to compensate for changes to the front-to-back weight ratio and balance of the go-kart. Now that I'd put all this extra weight in the go-kart it meant I had too much brake bias to the front and the front brakes were biting hard, so the weight was transferring forward and making the back end light. With less traction and grip for the rear tyres, the back end came round when I braked because the back wheels were virtually off the floor.

We were way over-braked anyway. I just had to fart on the brake pedal and it would lock the wheels, but, previous to this run, we had it set up so all four brakes were biting evenly.

After getting so out of shape, I got out of the corner and into the 1.5 km-long straight run of steep stuff. Even before this run, by the time I got to the end of the 100-metre timed section and into the braking zone, I felt I needed every metre available to slow down before a proper tight hairpin loomed up. If I couldn't stop, or slow down enough to make the hairpin I'd head straight into the metal crash barrier.

So, while the sensible thing to do was coast down on the brakes, the chimp was telling me, 'Have it! Keep going. Worry about stopping at the end of the run.'

It was pretty unusual for me to listen to my inner chimp by this time in my life. If I had thoughts like that in a motorcycle race, and acted on them, I'd be dead, but this was only a go-kart. There's a time and a place to say fuck it, and it was probably then.

Looking back, I don't know what was going through my head. I just tried to blank any possible consequences out. My chimp had convinced me the first skid was just some dirt on the road and it would all be OK.

A few seconds later I went through the timed 100-metre

section at 90 mph, 5 mph faster than any other run I'd done, but for the record to stand I had to come to a controlled stop ...

As soon as I pressed the brakes the back end came straight round. I let go of the brakes and it came back into line. I got on the brakes again and the back end came round again, so I corrected it again. I'd probably got rid of 10 mph before I realised the barrier was coming up fast. I braked hard and the whole kart flicked sideways. The canopy came off as it started going end over end, barrel-rolling down the mountain. All I could see was sky-trees-sky-trees-sky-trees, before the go-kart ended up sliding, upside-down, into the red and white barrier at the side of the road. I can remember hearing my mint, pink and blue, Britten colours helmet scraping along the floor. Bastard.

Everything went quiet, but I kept still, because I didn't know if I was still in the air or what. I was expecting a big impact with the barrier, but then I realised I'd stopped and put my arms out.

I'd had to do something. If I hadn't have slammed on the brakes, causing the go-kart to spin out of control, I'd have gone head-on into the barrier at 80 mph. That would have been an ankle-breaker, no doubt about it. So I did the right thing. After doing the wrong thing.

The TV lot came over like it was Armageddon. I had to take my trainers off to get out because the bag of rocks was still in the way and my inner chimp had already started denying any involvement. The cameraman in the helicopter filmed the crash, but there wasn't going to be another run. Two of the wheels had been smashed off the go-kart and the other two were bent in half.

No one saw the bag full of rocks and I didn't feel bad about not telling the film crew about them, because the University lot were sort of with me and they'd built the thing I'd just demolished. I guess they would probably have preferred to build up to the 20 kilos a bit more slowly, but my inner chimp wasn't having it.

For some people that would have all added up to a bad day, but it was the most pleasant crash of the year. I wish I hadn't smashed up the beautiful bit of engineering, but I still drove home with a smile on my face. And I'd had the best shit of my life.

CHAPTER 3

Only boys in the sheep game know that

Part of the whole TV job involves me agreeing to do a couple of days' press when a new series or programme comes out. That meant I had to go to London to promote the new series of *Speed* that was about to start showing on Channel 4. Going to London for a load of interviews on telly and radio isn't my cup of tea, I'd rather be at work, but you take the money and make the choice.

Because the first interview was early on a Wednesday morning I went down on a Tuesday night and stayed in a nice hotel, a converted court in Great Marlborough Street called The Courthouse. It was where Mick Jagger was in front of the magistrates for possession of cannabis and, another time, his fellow Rolling Stone Keith Richards got fined for possession of heroin, marijuana, a revolver and an antique shotgun. Sounds like a quiet night in.

The hotel bar is made up of the old holding cells and you have breakfast in the courtroom – which still looks like a court, with all the wood panelling and red upholstery. I like it. Yes, I'd rather be at the truck yard, but I can go to London for a day or two and see everything and everyone as personal entertainment.

Andy Spellman came with me. He's not a manager, because I'm unmanageable when it comes to stuff like this, but he's an agent and adviser. He looks after the TV and business side of things for me, and my accounts and the Proper online shop that sells woolly hats and the like. Not much would get done without him. He comes from a TV background and has been working with me since 2010. He's involved with some of the racing side of things, but I still do deals with the TAS team on a handshake and a quick scribble before anyone's looked at the contract. This annoys the hell out of Spellman, because a contract will sometimes arrive saying I'll do this and that, but I didn't know anything about it, because I didn't bother reading it, and it's at odds with something he's trying to set up. I should just leave it up to him, but I want to keep control of the racing side of things.

I've said to Spellman, and only half-joking, that everyone in racing hates him, but that's because he's sorting things out for me and saying no to people. He knows what I can and can't and will and won't do. He knows what my diary looks like, most of the time, anyway, and it looks like a bomb's gone off with truck tests, motorbike races, sponsor stuff, mountain bike races and filming days scrawled in it.

Over the years I've got myself into trouble for either saying yes or, to be more accurate, not actually saying a straight no when I've been asked to do something. Sometimes I don't want to disappoint people when they ask me to go to this place or enter that race or hand these awards out, so I'll say something like, 'Maybe, maybe', when I'm really thinking no. And I do it because I don't want to seem rude, even though it isn't rude. I've said in the past that I like things in black and white, to know where I, and everyone else, stands, but sometimes I'm my own worst enemy because I haven't been blunt enough. So when I've said maybe, I haven't committed to anything, but the race organiser, or whoever, goes away thinking I've said yes and tells the world and his brother. That's when the problems start because it turns out I'm not going to their event and really had no plans to from the start. So Spellman does his best to stop things like that happening. It's not foolproof, because I'm still involved, but it's better.

He came down to London to make sure I got to everywhere I was supposed to on time and also to go with me to a meeting at North One, who make all the TV shows I've done.

That first night we went out for a Vietnamese – that's not something I say very often – and after the hot spice of the meal I wanted an ice cream, but the only place we could find that was open was a real fancy place and an ice cream cone cost £5. Five quid for an ice cream! I was so bloody gob-smacked I wanted to commemorate the moment with a photo of me and the bloke who sold me it.

All the interview appointments are arranged by the folk at Channel 4, and Spellman tells me they would like me to go to all sorts of events to nod, smile and agree with advertisers and the like. Jamie Oliver shows up for these kind of do's, but it isn't my thing so they set up the minimum amount of appointments they can get away with, fit it into the shortest possible time, and I do the best I can in front of the microphone. It's like a ram raid. If I wanted to try and earn more out of the TV job I'd have to do all that more corporate stuff, but I'm alright as I am. I don't do bad out of it.

The first interview of this visit to London was on Radio 4's *Midweek* show with Libby Purves. It's topical show that I listen to at work and Libby Purves has presented it for 30 years. She won an OBE for journalism, and was very professional, almost running through the interview before we went live on the radio, testing her lines and my reactions and answers. It was like me taking a gearbox out of a Scania. I take the retarder oil cooler off, even though I don't really need to, but it only takes ten minutes and it saves a lot of wangling. That's what she was doing, saving a bit of grief further down the line, showing her experience.

I was interviewed first, and I sat there, with my headphones on, while the other folk were interviewed. One guest was Sofka Zinovieff, an author. Another was Mark Bell, a theatre director. He was a Northerner with a stage show in London, and I was interested to hear what he said, because he was so passionate about what he did. I was interested in all the other guests, so it wasn't a bad way to spend an hour.

Next we went to see Steve Wright. Love the show, Steve. He's a big fella, I was surprised how big. He has a lot of passion, but manages to broadcast it without a lot of movement. From listening to him I thought he'd be jumping around and waving his arms about, but he barely moves. He just sat there, like the most passionate Stephen Hawking you've ever seen.

I used to listen to Radio 2 a lot, because it was the compromise I came to with my dad when we worked together. We decided on Radio 2 after I threatened to petrol bomb Lincs FM if he made me listen to it for another day. I've listened to hundreds of hours of Steve Wright and thought the studio would be bunged up with people, but there was just him and one other bloke. When they clap a guest or something they've heard, it sounds like a room full of people on the radio, but it's just two of them. The weather girl came in, and Sally Traffic too, then they leave. It's interesting to see all this, but it makes me appreciate my life even more.

After the radio interviews we had to go to North One for a meeting and I thought it would be a good idea to go on a rickshaw. I was impressed by the 'engine'. He could pedal, even with me and Spellman in the back. Then we got stuck on Oxford Street, probably the busiest street in the whole of London. It got embarrassing when someone recognised me and took a photo of me and Spellman in the back of this rickshaw.

Next we went off to meet my big sister Sal who had got the train down from Lincolnshire for the day. She met us at the Tower of London, where the poppy memorial was all laid out at the time. We went for something to eat, and all through it *The One Show* people from the BBC kept ringing Spellman to get me there earlier.

They told him they wanted me to arrive on a motorbike with the woman presenter on the back, or ride in on a pushbike, because the *Speed* series had the tandem thing in it, or do a wheelie or something at the beginning of the programme, but Spellman knows me well enough to not even pass the question on for an answer. He knows I'm not keen on doing stuff like that.

We got to the BBC TV centre at about six, just about the last minute. When you turn up there you sign in, get met at reception, then go downstairs into the Green Room, that isn't green, it's just a room full of *Good Housekeeping* magazines. A make-up lady came in and asked if I wanted make-up on. I told her no thanks, but she wouldn't let it go until I was covered in the stuff, then as soon as she left we wiped it all off.

Sal kept telling me to iron my shirt, because she said it looked like a dish rag, and in the end one of the women who works on the show did it for me.

When it was time to go on I had a yarn with the two presenters, Alex Jones and Matt Baker. I always thought he was alright, but that he was a TV wanker. Like all of them, lovely people, but TV wankers. Alex Jones? Lovely, fit, but a TV wanker. Chris Evans? TV wanker. I'm not saying they're bad people. And I'm thinking wanker in a different way to what you probably are. They're not fucking wankers, said with anger. If I call someone that, in an aggressive tone of voice, they're just short of being called a C-word and I usually refrain from using that. So when I say TV wanker, I'm not saying, 'That man's a wanker!' They're just a TV wanker. They're nice people, just not real people. And, at that moment, I was surrounded by them.

Then I got a different impression about Matt Baker. I mentioned something about farming and he said summat like, 'I'm a bit of a sheep farmer.' And I thought, Oh right, TV wanker, I'll soon sort you out. So I asked him, 'Do you know much about far-welted sheep?' Thinking that only boys in the sheep game know that.

A far-welted sheep is one that has rolled onto its back with its feet in the air and can't get back on its feet because of its heavy fleece. I always thought some kind of natural chemical in the sheep's body ran into its brain to kill it, but looking into it more I've learned that it's when the gas in the sheep's stomach becomes trapped and expands one chamber of the stomach so much it constricts the lungs and the sheep suffocates. If you just stand the sheep back up, it'll sometimes fall back over and still die, so you have to stand them up and hold them till their circulation and stomach get back to normal. Matt Baker explained that instead of standing propping up a sheep for ages he straps his sheep to a wooden pallet to keep it upright. That way you have a chance of saving it. He doesn't do it with all his sheep. There isn't a flock of TV presenter's sheep wandering around with pallets gaffa-taped to them; he only does it to a sheep at death's door from lying on its back. You would have to say it was a design fault in the sheep. Back to the drawing board, Big Man.

So that impressed me, but neither of the presenters seemed to understand that buying Snap-On tools are a way of life for me, and that I'm proud of my spanner collection. That's when I think 'TV wanker' again. If you can't understand that a man is proud of the tools of his trade, you're not a real person. When I'm in London on a day like that, everyone is professionally friendly, but I do wonder if they'd be as friendly if I was just a truck fitter from Grimsby.

Sal thought it was all great, though. She does loads for me, posting out woolly hats and stuff, so it was nice for her to come down and see behind the scenes of a different world. And she fancies Matt Baker. Nick Hewer, who I'm told is from Alan Sugar's programme *The Apprentice*, was also on that night, and he said he had a collection of tractors, so we had a talk about them too.

In the end I agreed to a spacehopper race with a schoolgirl that was shown just as the programme finished, and she kicked my arse. *The One Show* is the closest I ever get to feeling like I'm a performing monkey. I don't mind doing the radio interviews, but I'm not keen on doing that show and as soon as we left, me and Spellman said to each other, 'We're not doing that again!' But it's really important to the TV people and sometimes I have to play the game, so never say never ...

CHAPTER 4

65 storeys up, looking the shitehawks in the eye

I was at the truck yard last year when Andy Spellman called me to say North One wanted to do another telly thing before the end of 2014. He said Channel 4 had spent a fortune on a ten-part costume drama starring Julie Walters about the last decades of the British rule in India – it turns out it was called *Indian Summers* – and Channel 4 wanted some other programmes to make an India season out of it or summat. North One got wind of it and had the idea of me doing two one-hour programmes on the 'real' India from my point of view, me being in the role of Judith Chalmers, who I used to watch on *Wish You Were Here ... ?* with my mum and brother and sisters.

North One originally said I'd need to be in India for a month, but I told them I'd struggle being away from work for that long in one go, so they came back with three weeks in November, and that was OK. A while later they cut it further so I'd be away for just two weeks, and that was mint. I could work around that.

The plan for the trip wasn't told to me. Or if it was I wasn't listening. All I knew was I was going to see the good and bad of India, riding around on a motorbike I'd buy out there. I wasn't going to do the usual touristy things; instead I would have a few oddball experiences, buy a motorbike, do a train trip and see what I reckoned to the country.

I was interviewed on camera before we left and asked what I was expecting from the journey. I think the director was expecting something deep, but he didn't get it because I had hardly any preconceptions. I was just getting on the plane and seeing what I found when I got off at the other end. I had the attitude that it'll be what it'll be. I knew it was going to be hot and I'd eat a lot of curries. I wasn't going hoping to be shocked, but I wanted to be educated. I wanted my eyes opening.

In the weeks before the trip I needed to go for three lots of jabs: hepatitis, rabies and malaria, but that was the end of my preparation. It was when I turned up at Heathrow that I really learned the plan. I hadn't tried to find out before because I wasn't bothered. Not in a bad way – I wasn't saying, 'I'm not bothered' – but whatever they chucked in my path I would deal with.

We flew out at 9.30 at night on Sunday 9 November. We were in business class because the trip had been shrunk down to two weeks from four, so we didn't have one rest day during the two weeks. I know what you're thinking, and I would be the same – the TV job is hardly digging foundations or coal-mining, but it can still be graft, especially for the camera crew.

We arrived at Indira Gandhi Airport, New Delhi on Monday morning, after an eight-and-a-half-hour flight. We met our 'fixer', Tony, at the airport. In the TV world a fixer is the person who knows the ins and outs of the local situation and lie of the land. He knows what to say and to who if something needs sorting, arranging or, I suppose, fixing, in a hurry. Tony was from Birmingham originally, but I used to entertain myself by repeating his name in my best impression of a New Jersey gangster accent. He didn't get it, though. He was with us for the whole trip, with other local fixers joining us in particular cities. So there were 12 of us altogether and there was a hell of a lot of gear – boxes and boxes of tripods, lighting, cameras, batteries …

The first things that really caught my attention outside the airport were the billboards everywhere advertising all the western stuff from Volvo to Vodaphone, so my initial impression wasn't good. It just seemed like anywhere else. Then we got in people carriers and were taken to our hotel, The Park, in the centre of New Delhi. On that first journey my eyes were opened. I saw a bloke laid in the street with his kecks down, just shitting. I don't know if he was dying or what, but no one was bothered. Life just went on around him. I'd never seen that before. Not even after closing time in Grimsby.

The idea was to get checked in to the hotel, unpack, then meet an hour later to go and suss a few things out. We didn't film that first afternoon, but we met in the reception and then I went off by myself. The crew are all sound lads and lasses, but with such a big group it was a bit like herding sheep, so I went for a mooch through the market near the hotel on my own. I bought a necklace for Sharon for about 150 rupees, something like £1.50.

While I was wandering around, I stopped and stood for half an hour watching a gang of Indian lads working. They were, I imagined, the equivalent of council workers, and trying to lift a manhole cover. There was about half a dozen of them. One bloke was telling these lads, the labourers, what to do and where to hit the cover with a sledgehammer. It was just a standard manhole cover. I don't know if the labourers were doing it just to wind up the foreman and really could get a grip.

While I was in India I was told about the word *jugaad*, which translates as something like 'make do and mend'. India is built on jugaad. It makes some people a lot of money, but even the president now says, 'Too much jugaad.' You only had to scratch the surface in our fancy Delhi hotel to see self-tapper screws shoved in at any angle.

From what I can tell, jugaad was originally a name for a vehicle made from scrap and powered by a generator, totally Heath Robinson, and not in a good way, but I suppose ingenious for people without a lot of resources. A jugaad vehicle is proper make do and mend and just about better than the alternative, a hoss and cart. Now jugaad is a description applied to anything someone has lashed together saying, 'That'll do.'

On Tuesday morning we all went to a place called Karol Bagh, India's biggest motorcycle market. I thought it would be like a big warehouse, where there would be bikes being sold everywhere, but it's a network of back streets with a load of oddball motorbike shops dotted in it.

The loose idea for the day was to buy a bike and, in the afternoon, go to Old Delhi. Other than that, they left it with me. It hadn't all been researched, so it wasn't a case of 'We are buying a bike from this man, at this time.' I just set about finding a bike and got stuck straight in, but not rushing the job. It took half a day to find a bike I was happy with. Because of the links with Britain and the history of the bike, I wanted a Royal Enfield.

Originally a British company dating back to 1891, Royal Enfield started making four-wheeled, powered 'quadricycles' in 1898 and motorbikes a few years later. Royal Enfields have been made in purpose-built factories in India since 1956. Now, they're bigger than they've ever been and have a new factory as modern as any motorcycle manufacturer in the world. They export to loads of different countries, but sell the massive majority in India. They can't make them fast enough.

If you've got a Royal Enfield in India, it's like owning the Rolls-Royce of motorbikes. There are motorbikes everywhere, a million motorbikes are sold per month in India, but most of them are a means to an end – cheap, commuter-style bikes. Royal Enfields are something else and out of the price range of most riders. The boys that have them take pride in them. Imported bikes are as rare as hen's teeth, so anyone who is riding anything else is just pretty much using it as basic transport, something to go to work on, though that is changing because KTM are making trick-looking little Dukes there and Harley-Davidson have a new factory in India too.

Karol Bagh was the rarest place and it was the first time we'd ever filmed like that. Usually everything is set out – talk to him, talk to her, try to get this bit of information – but this was all off-the-cuff and I was happier. I'm a lot more at ease being filmed now, and I've learned a lot since I first had to walk up to a stranger and start talking on camera, like I did in the first *The Boat That Guy Built* programme. I have also got used to six people stood around filming or recording me while dozens of local people stand around wondering what's going on.

While I was hunting for a bike in the back streets I found some right interesting folk. There was a fella with a great eff-off iron with a furnace in the bottom of it that he was using to press clothes, right there on the street. He put hot coals out of the fire in his iron and he was the area ironer, so folk would bring their clothes to him. I got yarning to him, though he didn't speak English, and he ironed my jeans and shirt for the first time in their lives, while I stood there in my pants. I also met a mad young lass dancing in the street as a busker.

I went round loads of shops and worked out a price for a CG125 kind of a thing, a Hero Honda – a Honda built in India – but I was never going to buy one of them, I was just trying to get my eye in. There were some Royal Enfields for

70, 80 and 90 thousand rupees. They were a bit ratty, with 20,000 km on them.

As part of the filming I had met a bike club from Delhi, the Free Soul Riders, and they knew a bike dealer called Lalli Singh, and told me he was a bit of a legend in the motorbike world.

Lalli Singh is a Sikh, old as the hills, and I went to see him at his shop. He had a 500 cc Enfield, with panniers on it, not even a year old. It was mint and he said it had just been serviced. He explained he would give insurance and all the bits and bobs, but he was asking 130,000 rupees (about £1,300). It was the most expensive one I'd seen, but it came with everything: spare tubes; all the spanners; spare coil; spark plugs; regulator; brake pads; panniers; and it had an electric start. His workshop was tidy and that gave me faith in him. He explained he sold bikes to people doing trips around India, and the TV lot were paying, so I said this is the bike we want, and we did a deal.

When I got the cash in my hand I felt like a gangster, there were so many notes. Lalli shifted a bit on the price and he chucked some petrol in, but Indian petrol is rubbish. You can tell the quality is terrible, because even the 125 cc Hero Hondas are running three spark plugs and the only reason I can think they're designed to do that is so the engine can cope with really poor quality petrol.

Whenever I asked my Enfield for a lot, pushing it a bit harder than it might want, I could hear it start 'knocking' or 'pinking'. They're both words for detonation. As the piston is coming up it is compressing the charge, squashing the air and fuel mixture together, but because there's that much pressure, poor quality fuel explodes before the plug has had a chance to light it, then the spark plug lights it again. This causes very high combustion chamber temperatures and it melts the piston and/or burns the valves out.

The definition of the octane rating, by which petrol is graded, is the ability to withstand compression before auto-ignition. So if you're dealing with poor, low-octane fuel you have to light the charge, with the spark plug, before it explodes under pressure. The problem is, if the bike's ignition is set for the spark plug to light the charge early, you're not making all the power the engine can. If you have two or three spark plugs you can still light it early and get complete combustion, a full burn across the top of the piston, by having them spark at slightly different times.

Early fancy Suzuki four-stroke race bikes, the XR69s, had twin-plug heads, so riders could have the user-friendliness of retarding the ignition but still burn all the air and fuel charge in the combustion chamber.

In the mid-1990s, when Honda swapped the spark plugs around to make the big-bang NSR500 Grand Prix bike, the one that Doohan raced and won three of his 500 GP championships on, Yamaha and Suzuki engineers took oscilloscopes to the trackside and watched the soundwaves to try and work out what they'd done. That's just how a knock sensor works on a modern bike or car with one fitted. The firing order of an inline four is normally 1-3-4-2. The knock sensor sees the soundwave and is expecting that firing order at regular intervals, but if you get detonation (or knocking or pinking, whatever you want to call it), the sensor detects a spike in the soundwave, and adjusts the ignition timing to deal with it. That technology is a bit out of the price range of a Hero Honda or my Royal Enfield, though, so they use multi-plug heads to get around it.

The petrol that was poured into the Enfield had a red tinge to it. Indian petrol smells a bit like petrol but not much. It's properly shit.

Once I bought my bike, that was me set. Panniers on, wing mirrors adjusted, we were ready to go. It had been a long time since I rode any kind of distance on a road that wasn't racetrack, and I chose to make my comeback in Delhi! The place is a disaster. I never had a dodgy moment, but the driving is bloody terrible. My tactic was to drive how they drive. Forget mirror, signal, manoeuvre – if you want to be over there, just go over there. Don't give a damn about anybody else; don't look in your mirrors; just go and get on your horn. I got quite into it.

Indian road surfaces are terrible too. Their roads don't have potholes, their potholes have a bit of road. But it's not just that. You can have a road that is mega for a mile, a dual carriageway the Germans would be happy with, and then, without warning, it turns into a goat track and goes through someone's garden and squeezes between two houses. I couldn't work it out.

On the first day I rode back to the hotel and then out again to meet up with the Free Soul Riders, the biker club I had met earlier, and had a yarn with them. I was 5,000 miles from home, but all of them knew who I was. I couldn't believe it, but it was because every one of them had a smartphone. They knew all the races I'd done and they wanted to know about that, but I didn't really want to talk about motorbike racing and TTs, because it wasn't supposed to be about me. Still, it was good to meet them, nice lads and lasses. I'd been given a garland of flowers necklace and I gave it to one of the lasses in the club as a thank you for their friendliness and giving up their time to come out and meet me, but it got an unexpected reaction. The club started laughing – it meant I'd just got engaged to her.

After that we went back to the hotel and, later on, back out to Old Delhi, a place that is a bit of a shithole to be honest. By then I'd already worn the horn out on the Royal Enfield, but I found a bloke working at the side of the road whose whole job was repairing motorcycle horns and tuning them up with the little screw on the back. I was fascinated and stood watching him for a good while.

Wherever I was in Delhi, it seemed I wasn't far from the smell of human dung. I haven't got the best sense of smell, since getting knocked out during a night out as a teenager in Lincoln, but even I could smell it. One fact I learned was that in India diarrhoea alone causes more than 1,600 deaths every day. Health organisations explain that's the same as if eight, full jumbo-jets were crashing to the ground each day and it makes a total of 600,000 people per year. So, the supply of clean water and toilet hygiene is a massive problem.

In the area of Old Delhi we visited was one of the biggest mosques in India, the Jama Mosque. It was a proper fancy place, famous throughout India. It dates back to 1656, but bolted on the side of it was a lean-to that sold nothing but front suspension struts for cars. Old Delhi went from one extreme to the next: a massive, beautiful mosque, then this scruffy little stall. And it was this stuff, the extremes that you wouldn't see in Europe, that caught my interest the most. You would never have a corrugated iron shack, flogging bits of old Ford Mondeos, stuck like a barnacle on one of the walls of York Minster or Lincoln Cathedral.

It me took over an hour to cover the ten miles from the hotel to Old Delhi, and the same back again, because I had to wait for the TV lot in the people carrier. I only had to do that for the first couple of days. When we got out of Delhi I was free to ride ahead at my, and the Royal Enfield's, own pace.

The next day I rode out to a truck yard to see what happens there, and make comparisons to how I work at home in England. Their stuff was aeons behind European stuff. The trucks at this yard were all Ashok Leyland. Foreign companies can't set up a factory in India, they have to partner up with an Indian company, like Honda and Hero did. So you couldn't do what Nissan or Toyota have done in the UK, move in and set up a solely Japanese-owned car plant, you have to be in business with the Indians. I think it's quite a clever move on the surface. Leyland set up in India in 1948, earlier than Royal Enfield, but in the same city of Chennai, which used to be known as Madras.

The technology and design of the Ashok Leylands they're making in India predates me. It's all eight-wheel rigids, twin-steering, double-drive; no articulated trucks like I spend my days working on. They're kind of the same, because they're turbo diesels with air brakes, but they're just not. Most of the cabs on the trucks in this yard were coach-built, by hand, not pressed in tooling and welded in a mass-produced, production line way.

Nearly every business you could think of that the truck job needed to support it was in the massive yard I visited. So there was a bloke reconditioning engines and another fella reconditioning gearboxes. There were no workshops, they were just doing them on the side of the street. There were no pneumatic windy guns either, everything was shifted using muscle. And no one was rushing; the pace of life was slow. Nothing's getting done in a hurry, but it's getting done. Meanwhile there were cows walking through and a herd of pigs, covered in oil, just mooching about.

No one has a welding mask to wear, so they just arc up the tip of the welder on the job, close their eyes and put a weld on as best they can, blindly. I spotted a fella cutting valve seats in a cylinder head and he was making a proper job of it. Everything else was jugaad, but what he was doing wasn't. He was still as slow as treacle, but doing a good job. He could see I was interested, so he let me have a go.

There was also a 50-year-old woman tyre-fitter that I interviewed through an interpreter. All the trucks still use split rims and inner tubes in India. It's a kind of wheel that is illegal in Europe and has been since the 1970s. With a truck's split rim you have a huge circlip holding the outer rim of the tyre on. It's not a hard job to fit tyres on this type of wheel, but the circlips are prone to jump out when you inflate the tyre, and they've killed loads of blokes, so you're supposed to blow them up in a cage. Fork-lift trucks still use them so I fitted a few myself as an apprentice, and I didn't have a cage either. When I had to do it I would connect the air hose to the valve, put the wheel in a cupboard or a room, close the door and pump the tyre up from the other side of the door. This woman didn't have a cage and she didn't put the wheels on the other side of a door either, she just blew them up. It's not a job that needs a lot of muscle, but it's lethal when it goes wrong. She earned decent money out of it. She was switched on.

One thing I learned at the truck yard was Indian rule number one: don't mess with the cows. Hindus see the cow as holy, that's well known, but she also provides milk, she pulls the ploughs, she looks after you. I've never thought of myself as much of a cow-messer, but if I hadn't had it hammered home in India, perhaps I could have turned into one, because they're so cocky. They know no one is going to mess with them, so they stand in the middle of the motorway looking at you as if to say, 'Yeah? What? Eff off!' They're arrogant, and I don't need an arrogant cow. I don't think any of us do.

I was told if you kill a cow you cancel its next move in the reincarnation stakes, and it comes back as a cow, but they eat beef in India, so I don't know how they get around that. Perhaps they wait until it dies of old age and put up with it being as tough as old boots.

It was a good day at the truck yard, but the fact we were all going back to stay in a fancy hotel wasn't sitting well with me. I didn't want to stay in the four-star hotel in the first place – it wasn't proper India, I didn't think – so I decided to reset the balance. I knew you shouldn't eat fruit or uncooked veg or salad, but I wanted to be pissing out of my arse on the first days to make up for staying in a posh hotel. So, when we went out that night, I broke all the rules given to tourists and I ended up suffering, but I felt it was more authentic. No word of a lie, I went for 15 shits in one night.

The next day we went to the train station to start the next part of our journey through India, and in terms of the stench of human waste it was even worse than Old Delhi. There was a wall dedicated for people to piss up against, more or less in the middle of the train station. I'd been up all night on the bog, and needed the toilet when I was at the train station. Next to the pissing wall was a flashing sign that translated to something like Deluxe Toilet, so I went in there, thinking deluxe was well worth 10 rupees (10p). Instead it was a long drop shithouse, just a hole in the ground, with shit sprayed up the wall and nothing to wipe my backside with. In most places in India there's just a jug of water, and I never worked out how you were supposed to deal with that. Maybe they think we're mad smearing it round our arse with paper, but until someone invents something better, I'll stick with that. I turned round and walked out without even unbuckling my belt.

I went through it in my head. I'd had about 15 dumps the night before, and I was trying to work out the length of my intestine and came up with: 'It's quite long.' I wondered how much I could back up before I could taste poo.

Back on the platform, we had to package the bike to protect it and get it loaded on the train. Local fellas were on hand to help. For a few rupees they'd get rubbish and old sacks, like potato and post sacks, and sew protection around the bike.

Then we realised, at the last minute, we were at the wrong end of the platform to where the goods wagons were, so we had a mad rush to push it right through the crowd to try and get it on the train. It was a bit of a job, but we managed.

I had told the TV lot that I wanted to travel in the regular sleeper carriage, not the air-conditioned first-class one. It was important to experience the roughest part of the journey like a local worker would, and when we finally got on the train, people were packed like sardines in the carriage I was in. Most of the TV lot went in first class, but two stayed with me: Nat the cameraman and James the director.

Our part of the train was rammed with people and luggage. We had bunks to lie in, but as basic as it comes. There were rats running up and down the carriage and the temperature was in the high thirties. I ignored the rats – no one else was panicking, so why should I? And I was still getting over food poisoning, so I didn't have a lot of urgency. We were next to the shithouse, another bog that was just a hole in the ground, this time out of the bottom of the train. It was minging. Every half an hour someone would come through selling chai. It's tea, but too sweet for me, and spiced. I thought it was bloody horrible and it nearly put me off drinking tea forever.

After a seven-hour journey we got off at Kalka in the far north of India, at dawn, unloaded the bike and all the camera gear, then took the Enfield out of its protective packaging and found it had survived the journey.

I'd had to drain the bike of fuel before I could load it on the train, but there was just enough to get to the first petrol station. I filled up the tank and the empty Castrol GTX oil cans I had in the panniers to make sure I didn't get stranded, then rode into the village of Kalka for some grub.

I ate at a roadside place on my own. I'd slept alright on the train and had a biryani and some rice for breakfast. The café was clean and tidy, and it felt quite western, with a telly showing the cricket in the background. Dogs milled about. There was gun shop over the road, a few cows moseyed around, trucks drove by belching smoke. Still, it was totally different to the shithole of Old Delhi where every sense was being assaulted. Kalka was still hot and a bit dirty, but it was another world and nowhere near as hectic.

Then it was time to set off on the 150-mile ride, on goat tracks, towards Palampur in the foothills of the Himalayas. The ride was through what I imagined to be proper India. No McDonald's, no obvious outside influences. There were random chai stalls for truck drivers along the way. The owner of one café I stopped at went out and cut some fresh ginger out of his garden to put in the tea.

When the sun was up it was hot and dusty, but I was still riding at nine that night. The crew were stopping and starting, so they were a bit behind me. I didn't have my gloves with me, and when it got cold I had to ride along with one hand at a time on the engine barrel to keep them warm. When I got to Palampur, I didn't know where the hotel was so I sat and waited for them, but that was all part of it.

I was bloody freezing by the time I got to the Taragarh Palace Hotel, the old colonial hotel we were staying in. It was still sort of posh, but it had a certain patina about it and was a beautiful place.

The whole idea of heading up here was to visit the Bundla Tea Estate, where I met the owner of the plantation, a man called Danesh and his son, Gokul. The son was 25 and had just come back from America where he'd been studying for eight years. He had returned to run his dad's tea plantation. Gokul was a really clever bloke and it wouldn't surprise me if he were a future president of India.

Because the family could see we were right into it – the place, the business and them as a family – they put on a barbecue and built a fire and even had a bit of a sing-song. It genuinely wasn't TV bollocks, it just happened and it was brilliant. Danesh's mate James was there too. James was in his late fifties and it sounded like he was an ex-drug user, and had tried all the pills and potions. He got his guitar out and went mental. It was mint.

The next day I went paragliding. I was strapped to another bloke who wore a massive parachute on his back. We ran off the side of a mountain and flew on the thermals. Not really my thing, but it was alright. Although I was hundreds of feet up, there's no speed, so it seemed a bit gentle. I ended up nodding off. The most interesting thing was seeing the women working in the fields as we came in to land. In Britain we have power harrows, fixed to the back of tractors, to break up the clods of muck after ploughing, but here the women were manually threshing them to break the clods up.

My bike was put on a train to Mumbai for the next leg of the journey, and it did the 1,000 miles on its own while we flew and did a couple of days' filming without it.

I saw the two extremes of the city. There were more skyscrapers being built in Mumbai than any other city in the world, but from the top of them you can see the massive slums.

We went up the tallest skyscrapers, called the Imperial Towers. They're twin towers, residential and 60 storeys tall, so not big by New York or Dubai standards, but when we were there they were the tallest completed buildings in the whole country.

There was lots of talk of the property prices going up, showing the strength of the economy in Mumbai, but the top floors of the Imperial Towers, the penthouses, had been empty for five years. It was arranged for me go right up to the lightning conductor at the top of the tallest building, 210 metres up. Later that day we met the architect of many of India's skyscrapers, Hafeez Contractor. His name comes from the family business, and his name is genuinely Mr Contractor. He's a superstar in India, so we were honoured to meet him, but I don't think the interview ever made it onto TV.

I went up another skyscraper that was being built. This one was 65 storeys tall, and I gave the brickies a hand. I'm not much of a bricklayer, but I've done a bit of labouring. Again, there was no rush. These lads were building the internal walls, and told me they lay 100 bricks, or blocks, a day. It didn't sound much to me, so I rang my old mate Jonty Maw, a builder who lives near me, and asked him what he'd lay. He said on a good day, when everything is going right, he can lay 1,000 bricks in a day, but he'd have to be hanging his balls out to do that many. That shows the difference in pace. But the India lads got paid something like 500 rupees or £5 a day.

There was bugger all health and safety – 65 storeys up and I could walk right to the end of the floor and look over. One more step and that was it. I was looking the shitehawks in the eye, the buzzard-like birds soaring on the thermals. It was mad to look these birds in the eye, knowing how high we both were.

We spent the next day in a slum. We went to a temple to be told about one of the countless Hindu gods they worshipped in this particular slum. I went to a school and had a lesson with the kids and tried to teach them some daft stuff about engines.

It was a slum, but the people and their homes were clean. We had a cup of tea in the home of a bloke called Mr Saraswal. He'd lived there 30 years with his missus and everything was set out immaculately. He used to work for the council, but now he was a pastor. I asked him what would make him happier, and he said he didn't want anything, he was happy with what he had. We could all learn from someone like him. I'm moving house because I want a bigger shed. I should just be happy with what I've got. I didn't think I was a keeping-up-with-the-Joneses kind of man, but maybe I am. I have got a lot of stuff.

While I was in India I read a book about Buddhism. One part that stuck in my mind was the idea of Nirvana. I'd always thought that Nirvana (no, not Kurt Cobain's band) was a state of happiness, but it's not about being happy, because if you're happy, you can be worried that you're not always going to be happy or you want to be happier. And if you're sad you're worried you're always going to be sad and you want to be happy. Nirvana is when you don't want anything, you don't want more or less, you're not happy or unhappy. The Dalai

Lama is always trying to reach this state, but you have to meditate to find true Nirvana. I found it fascinating.

Back in Mumbai, it didn't matter which slum you went in, loads of them had a satellite dish outside and if I stuck my head in the door they were like PC World, they all seemed to have computers. I couldn't believe it. But they only get water for something like three hours of the day.

Mr Saraswal explained that, in very basic terms, he thought he would be better off under the British Raj, because there was a chance of his caste, or class of person, being able to better themselves. I was a bit surprised to hear this.

Since 1947, when India became independent, the caste system has been very rigid. It means, Mr Saraswal told me, that if you were born into a family of road sweepers, you are going to stay a road sweeper, you're never going to get above your station. The British are always accused of being obsessed by whatever class a person is, working class, middle class or whatever, but this pastor in the slums of Mumbai was telling me that under British rule even the poorest person thought they had a chance of bettering themselves. I was really enjoying seeing all these different sides of the country.

My bike turned up just before we were due to leave for the longest riding leg of the journey – two days on the bike heading south to Goa. I left the TV crew in Mumbai and met them in Mahad, 100 miles away in the direction of Goa, for an overnight stop. It was a bit of a frustrating ride. I couldn't get going because of all the traffic and towns. I had hours on the Enfield, plugging away on what is supposed to be the most dangerous road in India. It's not dangerous because of geography – it's not going over treacherous mountain passes or anything, it's just because of the clueless knobheads on the road.

On this stretch I learnt that there aren't many things faster on Indian roads than a 500 Enfield. You go up hills in Lincolnshire and think the truck you're stuck behind is going slow if it's only doing 42 mph, but over there they're crawling at a steady walking pace. When I overtook them on the bike I'd get a blast furnace belt of heat because they were working so hard just to keep moving. The most power you see out of them is 180 horsepower, like what trucks in Britain were making in the 1960s. Trucks in Europe are now making 600 and 700 horsepower.

When I finally got to Mahad, I stopped and watch some lads playing cricket. It's the national sport and Indians play it anywhere. They don't worry about grass; any old patch of dirt will do.

The next day was a fair slog, though I don't think the TV programme showed it how it happened. It was only 250 miles, but on those roads that takes some time to cover. I got up at first light and set off on my own, on this, the last real leg of the Indian road trip. When I arrived in Anjuna, on the top side of Goa, where we were staying, I could see the place was full of people 'finding themselves', something I thought of as a bit of a downside of the whole trip. As well as the whole area being Westernised or modernised or however you'd put it, it was full of people who looked like they all felt they had to dress in a particular uniform because they were in Goa. I don't know what triggers that thinking. It was all rainbow-coloured pyjamas and braids in the hair, and wearing woolly hats even in 30-degree heat. You've got no top on, but you're wearing a woolly hat ... What's happening? And yoga on the beach!

The reason for going to Goa was to attend the Royal Enfield owners' event, Rider Mania, with 3,000 mad Indians. You can turn up on any bike, but if you want to compete you've got to be on an Enfield.

It's a three-day rally and on Friday they do a slow bike race, have a big piss-up and watch a load of bands. I had a go at the slow race, but I was rubbish at it. The next day there was a dirt track race, and I was entered into it.

Before Rider Mania we had a bit of TV bullshit to sort out. It was decided to put the Royal Enfield on a trawler, after taking it out to sea in a little dinghy, because even though I'd ridden down to Goa from Mumbai, the idea was to show me arriving in Goa like the East India Company did in the 1600s, when they first landed in India. This trading company ended up running the country, and had an army 200,000 strong. Eventually they started asking the locals to do some things they weren't willing to, like using cartridges greased with animal fat, and there was a rebellion. It was the start of India being ruled by the Crown, the empire, not a company. The imperial rule, that became known as The Raj – which just means rule – began in 1858 and lasted until India's independence in 1947.

Once we wrestled the motorbike onto the trawler we were on it for four hours, but if they reckon it makes the programme better I'm happy to do it. They know what works. The good thing was, once the bike was on the boat and we'd done our bit of filming, we were stuck on it for a while. I hadn't had a chance to breathe and it was mega to have some tea and a few beers. Being on the boat is a stand-out memory. I had time to think that I was doing a race the next day, then I was going home. Getting the Enfield back off again and into the dinghy was a proper carry-on, though.

When we first bought the Enfield, in the market in Delhi, I knew I was going to race it, so I chose a 500 rather than the more common 350. They weigh the same, so the power-to-weight of the bigger capacity bike is obviously going to be better and that makes it quicker.

On the journey from Mahad, as I got closer to Goa, I had started seeing bikes on trailers heading to the Rider Mania race. They were taking it quite seriously and I thought there's no way I'm going to win against custom-built racers on this standard bike I'd ridden there on. So then I wanted to leave my bike as standard as possible like it had been for the whole trip, with the panniers still fitted and everything, to make a point of it being the bike I toured around on. But when we got to scrutineering, where they check the bike is safe to compete on, we were told to take the panniers and mirrors off. We left everything else exactly as it was – full mudguards, side panels, the sari guard, road tyres, the lot. I just lowered the tyre pressures a bit.

Before the racing started the TV lot were putting the pressure on me. James the director said, 'Right, go out and win, but make it look a bit of a race.' I thought, Bloody hell, there's some proper kit here, it's not going to be easy.

The track was marked out on a field that had a surface of rock-hard dirt with loose gravel on top in places. It was dead simple, but didn't need to be fancy. There were hairpin lefts and rights, but the track was so hard and dry it wouldn't rut up, so there was no benefit from running knobbly tyres designed to grip soft or wet dirt. I spent most of my time riding with one foot down, like a dirt tracker, because the front would wash out and I could use my foot to keep the bike up.

I had two heats with results going towards a qualifying position for the final. I finished first in my first heat, second in the second one, with those two results good enough to get me in the final.

In the last race of the day I was running second and when I overtook the leader he crashed. I wasn't sure if the other competitors really knew how to race those conditions, even though some of them race there every year. You couldn't even look at the front brake or the front wheel would lock, skid and wash out, but the other racers kept yanking on the brakes and losing the front. Instead, you just had to get in on the back brake and get your foot down. Anyway, the TV lot were pleased when I won, and the crowd seemed happy enough too.

The whole trip was good, because even though it was filming it didn't feel like proper work and my body needed the break. I would never lie on a beach for a fortnight, and my mind can never rest, but my body needed to be sat on a motorbike all day for a few days at a time. I didn't do any cycling for two weeks and I didn't have any spare brain space to plan anything for when I got home. When I was on the Enfield I just had to concentrate on the roads to make sure I got where I was going.

It was the first time I'd ridden for pleasure since I was a kid on the Yamaha TY80 trials bike that I was supposed to share with my big sister, Sal. Every other time I'd been on a bike, even on my Kawasaki AR50 (with an 80 cc kit) back when I was an apprentice, it was always about going faster. In India I was riding just for the sake of riding and it was nice. I liked it that I wasn't worrying about being a tenth off the pace here or there. I could see the attraction.

I left the bike in a shed in Goa, at Tony the fixer's place. I'm going to fly out and ride it home one day. It's not because I'd especially bonded with the Enfield, I just think it will be an adventure. It'll properly finish the trip off. I'm 100 per cent, definitely going to do it. Oman, Yemen, Egypt ...

At the end of the two weeks I was asked what I'd miss about India, and I said I'd miss nothing about the place. But it would be the same answer about most places. The only thing I missed about England when I was away was my dog. I like the experiences I had, and having my eyes opened. I'd been and done it, and that was it. It wasn't to say I didn't like it, because I enjoyed the experiences, good and bad.

I wouldn't miss people pipping their horns and flashing their lights when everyone's sat in a traffic jam with nowhere to go. What are you pipping your horn at me for? It's not going to part like the Red Sea. Don't be rude. So that annoyed me. And people spitting in the street. I didn't like that either.

I don't watch the TV shows I'm in now, but I'm sure, when I get older, I'll be able to sit and watch these films from India and enjoy the memories.

I got back to England at ten o'clock on a Monday night, and got straight back into it. I fixed a puncture on my single-speed bike, unpacked my gear, cut the tube of toothpaste in half to get the dregs out (something my mum would always do and I can't get out of the habit of), and I was up at five the next day to bike to work. Back in the routine.

CHAPTER 5

Brian the Chimp

All through this book I'll refer to my inner chimp. I have to deal with him on a weekly basis, more in the racing season, and think about him so much I've even given him a name – Brian. Brian the Chimp.

Everyone has an inner chimp whether they know it yet or not. I learned about the idea of the inner chimp from the book written by Dr Steve Peters, *The Chimp Paradox: The Mind Management Programme for Confidence, Success and Happiness*. I know, it doesn't sound much like a book I'd normally pick up. I suppose it is a self-help book and, if you pushed me, I would never have said I'd read anything that could be lumped in with those kinds of books.

I read *The Chimp Paradox* when it first came out, mainly because I knew of Dr Peters's involvement with Team Sky.

Sky are the team Bradley Wiggins was with when he became the first British rider ever to win the Tour de France; it's the team Mark Cavendish was with when he was winning loads of stages and that Chris Froome rode for when he came second to Wiggins in 2012, then won the Tour himself in 2013 and 2015.

My copy even has this quote on the front from multiple Olympic track cycling champion Sir Chris Hoy: 'The mind programme that helped me win my Olympic golds'. So I thought it would be full of cycling mind games and advice, but it's nothing to do with biking at all. Which is good, it made it even more of an interesting read.

The basic principle of the whole book – and I'm cutting 300-odd pages down to a few paragraphs – is that humans have three main parts that make up their brain. There are more, but for that book, and definitely this one, three is enough to get the gist. These three are Chimp, Human and Computer. Each person has a chimp in them, but they react in different ways. Some people are very good at keeping their chimps quiet, in a box; others aren't. Understanding the brain and how it works helps you keep the chimp on a lead, and that's a good thing, because the chimp's actions are rarely the best choices, or ones you think are a good idea when you look back at them.

The chimp brain is, as you might guess, related right back to our furry ancestors. A male chimp brain is different to a female chimp brain, but both male and female chimps make decisions from initial feelings and impressions, then behave in an emotional and irrational way. The inner chimp acts on animal instincts and often behaves like it would in the jungle. In the most basic language it is driven to protect itself and its troop and to continue the species. That means it's aggressive when it feels a threat; when it wants to have sex; when it wants to be a parent; when it needs to eat, have shelter and security, feel power over others. It makes child-like decisions and has a simple view of the world. The chimp doesn't have a conscience, like a human. Think of one of David Attenborough's programmes on the telly when one troop of chimpanzees gets close to the border of another troop's territory and you can see all these behaviours. The chimps attack to defend their territory, their mates, their young and their food and shelter. They don't get around a tree stump and try and talk it through, it's an instant flare-up.

So you need the human part of the brain to be in charge. The human brain thinks about things and takes evidence and other factors into the decision-making process. Putting it simply, the human is more grown-up about things. It only takes a split second longer for the human brain to react, but if your chimp isn't under control, the human struggles to get a look-in.

The problem, Steve Peters explains, is the chimp part of the brain has a stronger flow of blood, so it gets to make every decision first, if it's allowed to. People who aren't in control of their chimp react immediately, before the human brain has chance to say, Woah, Nelly, wait a minute, he didn't mean that. Or, Does it really matter? Or, Could there be another explanation?

Road rage is all chimp-related. Someone cuts up another driver. They start driving up the arse of each other, slamming on the brakes and speeding up and it all gets messy. If someone else is in the car, they are often thinking with their human brain. The passenger doesn't feel that they've been 'insulted' by the other driver so their chimp didn't react, and they try to calm the situation. But often the driver's thought process is still overpowered by the chimp and won't listen. Their chimp is well out of its box, and won't allow the human part of their brain to tell them it is pointless to get wound up like this. Once everything calms down, the driver who was cut up and reacted angrily regrets acting like a dickhead, and wonders why they get so wound up about stuff that hardly matters. They don't know it's all down to their inner chimp.

I reckon all these Twitter arguments you hear about are chimp-related as well. One chimp says something about a photo or summat, and the other person's chimp feels insulted. Because they have their phone in their hand they can reply immediately – really it's the chimp replying – and it escalates. The human brain knows to just step back and ignore it, but can't get control of the situation. The book reckons the chimp is five times more powerful than the human brain, so you have to learn how to keep it under control. That's where the computer part of the brain helps, but you'll have to read the book to find out about all that. All you need to know, for now, is I have an inner chimp, and so do you. Mine is called Brian and he looks like a scrawny, angry ape version of Don Logan, Ben Kingsley's character in the film *Sexy Beast*.

I have conversations with Brian all the time. He's my alter ego. The best way to keep Brian happy and quiet is to ride my pushbikes, go flat tracking or fix some trucks. Working on trucks is the equivalent of feeding him bananas, and he can't overpower my drive and love of mountain biking. He likes the shed, but not too much of the shed, because he associates the shed with motorbikes – he doesn't like all motorbikes. He liked building the Martek for Pikes Peak, but he doesn't like the TT, where he knows he is going to get screamed at. There's more to life than motorbike racing, is what the chimp tells me. The chimp wants to retire from motorcycle racing. He doesn't like what it's brought. The chimp loves going flat tracking, though. The simplicity, the lack of bullshit, just riding the bike. And it gets me away from crowds.

Some people think I like mountain biking more than motorcycles, but I still love motorbikes, the actual machines. I had the TV bods around the other day and I was telling them all about a Rob North Triumph I'm going to build for my mate Gary Hewitt. It's a custom-built, lightweight racing frame, like my dad used to have, with a 1970s Triumph triple engine. I'm as into the idea of building that bike as I've ever been into anything. I was the same with the Martek and all the preparation for the Pikes Peak race I did in Colorado.

Pikes Peak really brought it home to me that I started racing motorbikes because I love building motorbikes. It goes right back to the AR50 I had when I was 16. I only went racing because I started crashing on the road. Then I got ravelled up in all the bullshit of racing. It has taken me over ten years to realise this, and come to understand that what I really love is building bikes. I have returned to my default setting. Deep down, I do enjoy the racing. Sometimes you've got to dig a long way, because there's just that much massed bullshit, but I do love it. This might be my human and chimp brains' reaction to racing. Brian gets annoyed, while the human brain takes that while longer to weigh up the positives and what I get out of it.

Brian reacts badly to the bullshit and, sometimes, worse still to the loveliest, good-natured people, who come up to me when I'm supposed to be concentrating on racing and say, 'I know you don't like people bothering you but …'

I don't want to be rude, and some people have fascinating things to say, but most people have nothing to say – but they want to tell me it anyway. I'm not being ungrateful, because I never asked for whatever it is I'm getting. One thing has led to another, but because I've been on TV, does that mean I have to stand about for people to come up to me and say stuff and I have to be delighted when they do? I can't do it.

The main reason I started doing solo mountain bike races was so I could do something where no one could get to me. I was on the bike for 24 hours. That was it. Now people are recognising me there, so I need to find the next thing. Again, it might sound ungrateful, but I'm not. I'm just me. At one 24-hour race in the middle of winter in Scotland, a young lad brought me a box of Fudges and a cup with 'I Love Tea' printed on it, so I went in my kit bag and gave him some Hope Orange socks. He was dead happy, I was dead happy – it was after the race, so it was alright. There's a time and a place.

Put Brian in a Transit, with some good music on the stereo, me driving, road tripping to a dirt track race in Spain with a mate or two, kipping in the van, getting up when it's minus three degrees to practise on a deserted dirt oval – and he loves it. He's happy to stay in his box. But put him in a situation where he has to go to a press launch and straight away it is 'What the hell is this shit? We don't have to put up with this shit any more.'

Everyone is different, but at a race I try to sit in the van and read a magazine or a book, stay out of the way. Sometimes my dad will bring someone in: 'This is so-and-so from such-and-such and he would just like something signing.' I'll be dead polite and sign it, but later I'll say to my dad, 'You just don't get it. I'm struggling with all this and you keep making it worse.' Can you just, can you just …

As I've said plenty of times before, my dad is the man as far as I'm concerned, but the chimp isn't mad about him. Everything he does annoys the chimp. Smacking his lips, sucking his teeth, the clunking of the cup, talking with his gob full of food … The chimp's screaming, I'm going to kill him!

I've got the coolest life. All the trick stuff, but these feelings were getting stronger. I've realised the answer is not to put the chimp in those positions if I can help it. He'll end up cutting someone to bits with sidecutters. It's alright me telling friends this and them laughing about it, but when I'm stood in front of the judge saying, 'I told people this was going to happen,' the judge isn't going to say, 'Why didn't you say? Let's just forget about it all.' That's not going to happen.

Brian isn't me, he's his own man. Steve Peters spells it out in the book time and time again: 'You are not responsible for the nature of your chimp, but you are responsible for managing it.' The judge isn't going to understand that if I ever stab someone. But it's not schizophrenia. Brian screams his head off, but I take myself away, so he doesn't come to the front. I'd be locked up by now if I did what the chimp wanted me to, but I have control of him. Sort of. I have to get out of, or not be put in, certain situations to calm him down.

Even though he loves the trucks Brian can make himself known at the truck yard too. When a gearbox won't go in, and I'M GOING TO CHUCK A SPANNER THROUGH THE WINDSCREEN AND NIIIIIEEEE! I haven't done that for a while now, though. The older I get the better I get, but only because I know it's Brian. He still tries to bluff me, but I'm getting good now at recognising when he's doing the talking, better at managing my chimp, as Peters would say. Instead of losing my temper I walk down to the office and have a cup of tea. I haven't had a spanner-chucking moment for two or three years now. My boss, Mick Moody, knows when Brian is close to exploding. Moody helps me to fit gearboxes. The gearbox will be on the forks of the fork-lift truck and Moody will be jiggling up, down, up, down, left a bit, right a bit, as I tell him. If I go quiet, Moody goes away and I go away. We don't say anything, we just walk away. He has a fag, I have a brew, then we come back and, usually, the gearbox goes straight in.

Brian doesn't gain any strength from crowds, he just gets louder and louder. At this point in my life, he's never been louder than in places like the TT.

I was supposed to attend a big motorbike show in Verona with Dainese. In the end, the flight they booked me was delayed, so I missed the connection and ended up staying the night in Frankfurt. The next morning I got back on the plane to try to get to Italy, but because of the snow, we sat on the runway for three hours and then turned back to the gate. I ended up just going home, but if I'd gone to the show I know the chimp wouldn't have been happy. I took Dainese's money for sponsorship, and they look after me, so it was something I felt I had to do. I don't think it would've been as bad as it gets at Cadwell or the TT, because not all the Italians can speak English, so it would've been mainly photos, less small talk.

Being interviewed is different. I don't know what it is, but it keeps Brian quiet. It's like taking my dog Nige out for a run; being interviewed is letting Brian out for a run.

A big moment in my understanding of Brian was when I took the Martek to Cadwell for their anniversary celebrations. The boys who work at Cadwell are brilliant with me. When they have an MSV trackday on they let me ride what I want there. They're dead accommodating when I'm trying to get a race bike ready or whatever I'm doing. All they asked was that I'd come to the anniversary with the Pikes Peak bike, my Martek.

Unfortunately, that event was the straw that broke the camel's back. When I got there things quickly got Brian riled. The bike wasn't running right, I was sat in my van trying to stay out of the way and people were opening the doors to start talking to me. People were being rude, then someone wrote on the back of my van. It was dirty and someone wrote 'So-and-so Woz Ere' or summat in the dirt. That annoyed me. The rules are simple: don't mess with the Transit. That day was probably the beginning of the end of motorbike racing. I don't know when the end will be yet, but that was the beginning of it.

Jason Miles had driven over with his missus and his mate Lee, and was going to cycle back to Mansfield, so I got my bicycle out of the van and rode the 30 miles back to mine with him, just to get out of the way. That put the chimp to bed. And I needed to. Inside I was screaming. That was as bad as I've ever been. My inner self is warning me that I'm going to start stabbing someone.

That made me realise I had to work something out. The only way to deal with those situations is not to put myself in those situations. There's nothing I can do, nothing I can say, in that situation but get out of it and escape.

The first time to test the theory was coming up. Scarborough is where my road racing started, and I remember going there as a nipper when my dad raced there, but I realised I couldn't go to race at the Gold Cup, because I couldn't put myself in the position of being surrounded there. I'd read an advert announcing that spectators could pay an extra £5 to get into the pits to meet me. What? I'm there to race bikes, not to have people queued up to meet me, so I decided not to do Scarborough.

I expected to feel regret at not being at Oliver's Mount racing my bike when I went to work at the truck yard on the Saturday. It was quiet because there aren't any drivers hanging around. I listened to the radio, then I went home and did a few bits in the shed. On the Sunday I went out on my pushbike in the morning, then over to my mate Tim's farm in the afternoon and rode on his dirt track. And I didn't miss Oliver's Mount one little bit.

The whole Cadwell experience got me thinking about packing in racing, and the further I've got down the line, the more I've thought, Hell, I've got a reason to retire. Not racing at the Scarborough Gold Cup made me realise I can do without it. And I'm not missing anything. And it's better for my mental state. And I'm still riding motorbikes, just not at big races. I enjoyed the dirt riding every bit as much.

Really, it's only since the middle of 2014 that I've worked out why I'm getting riled up at all these stupid things. Even the Cadwell thing. I knew I shouldn't put myself in those situations, but it wasn't till I looked back later that I realised it was the chimp screaming.

When Brian has done something wrong, he knows. I don't need to say anything to him. Like when we crashed the go-kart on Mont Ventoux. That was all Brian. The human brain knew from the second the go-kart locked its brakes and skidded out of shape on the very first corner of the run that the sensible thing to do was gently coast down the mountain, adjust the braking or remove some weight and have another go, but Brian hijacked the situation and decided to go flat-out. Then, when we're upside-down, go-kart demolished, my favourite AGV helmet chamfered down by French tarmac, he denied all knowledge.

Is Brian just a scapegoat for my bad behaviour? Yes, possibly. And with all this talk of Brian I'm expecting a knock at the door any day. Hello. Yes, just get into this straitjacket. You're going to a safe place, a kind place, a nice place ... We'll look after Nigel, don't worry ...

CHAPTER 6

No one cares who I am.
I loved that

With the real road race season finished back in August, as fas as I was concerned, I was keeping my hand in with a bit of dirt tracking. I did my first dirt track race, on a borrowed CCM450, at Mildenhall speedway track back in 2009. I did another one at Scunthorpe on another borrowed bike a while later, but I didn't get the attraction of this style of racing when I first started and wasn't in a rush to go back. That all changed when I started riding with local lads on tracks they'd made on their farms. The more I did it, the more I liked it, and now I bloody love it. There are a few reasons. I can just go and ride my bike with no one watching. No one needs a squillion pounds for a bike, because you can dirt track on a

100 cc Honda, have fun and learn a lot. I don't need to wait for a track day at Cadwell or wherever, I just go to a farm five minutes up the road, oil my chain, check the oil and that's it.

On paper, dirt track, also known as flat track, is as simple as bike sport gets. It's raced on an oval, anything from a couple of hundred yards to a mile-and-a-bit long. You set off and go anti-clockwise till the flag comes out. The reason it doesn't get boring is because the track conditions change during the meeting, and also from one part of the track to the other. You can have so much grip that you're scraping the footpeg, then on the next lap you can be on a slightly different line and have such a lack of traction the bike is sliding and spinning up like mad. One part can be like concrete, while a foot to the left it's like trying to ride on marbles. And dirt track bikes don't have a front brake, so you're braking with the rear, losing traction, then turning with the throttle to slide around the corner. Trying to master that and get on the throttle earlier is what keeps me interested.

I don't get a massive buzz from dirt track, but then I only get that from road racing when something goes pear-shaped. It's just good riding. Now all the bullshit associated with me going road racing is outweighing the pleasure of that anyway. Most of the time that I'm dirt tracking, I'm not racing, but just doing laps on my own or with a couple of lads on Tim Coles's farm. But saying I don't get a buzz doesn't mean I'm not enjoying it. It's different and I can get the same satisfaction and the same love of bikes from dirt tracking in a mate's field as I can from an international road race.

When I want to go riding I give Tim Coles a ring to see if his track is dry enough and go by myself. Sometimes there are lads already there, sometimes they come later, and other times I'm there on my own. Tim's nephews, Tim and Tom Neave, live locally and have taught me loads. They are two of the top dirt trackers in England, so I'm not as good as them. When I started they were another league to me, but now I can ride with them, keeping them in sight as they edge away. Soon I'll have my own track.

Tim and Tom are in their late teens now, but you wouldn't say they were more than 16, because they grew up in an even smaller village than I did and they're not streetwise or trying to be cool – they are grafters. They're regularly up at daft o'clock harvesting or feeding the cows on their dad's farm.

I've never got involved with up-and-coming riders, because I've been doing my own stuff, but I help these two out. They're all ears for what's going on and I buy their race tyres for them and rebuild engines now and then. It's nice to put something back in the sport, but I'm doing it because I like them.

A lot of the grand prix riders now ride dirt track to practise between races. Marc Márquez has been doing it since he was a kid, and Valentino Rossi's taken it up in the last few years, building his own track at what he calls his ranch on the outskirts of his hometown, Tavullia. And because the top GP men do it, a load of the other racers are doing it.

Dirt track, as we know it now, is originally an American sport, but the Brits and Australians have been racing dirt track for nearly a century. European grand prix riders' and fans' interest in dirt track really started in the mid 70s when Kenny Roberts Sr came from racing on the dirt in America and was immediately competitive in Sheene-era grand prix racing.

Roberts had road raced in America too, but he educated everyone in a new way to race a motorcycle. Back then, when Roberts and boys like Freddie Spencer came into GPs, these young Americans were almost crashing on every corner, but getting away with it. It was controllable crashing. That came from dirt track, because these riders were used to both wheels sliding at high speed. They'd chuck their heavy dirt track bikes into the corners at 100 mph, both wheels sliding, front wheel turned on the opposite lock, foot on the floor, back wheel spinning. And they'd been doing it since they were 14 years old or even younger.

Whoever was following them in the race must have been thinking they were going to crash, because they'd never seen anything like it, but they'd save the crash and go faster because they were riding beyond the limit of the tyres. The Americans that dominated road racing in the 1980s and early 1990s – Kenny Roberts, Freddie Spencer, Randy Mamola, Eddie Lawson, Kevin Schwantz and Wayne Rainey – were all dirt track racers before they went road racing. The same with Nicky Hayden more recently, and the Australian, Casey Stoner, was a dirt tracker too.

But over the years bikes and tyres evolved in a certain way, and kids started road racing earlier and earlier, and that meant the European way, being inch-perfect and looking very controlled and precise, came back as the way to go fast, with everyone trying to use that style. Five years ago this European way of racing was the way to race a grand prix motorcycle. It was the style used by Jorge Lorenzo, Rossi and Pedrosa and was this inch-perfect, wheels in line, scratching their bollocks off way of lapping, but not a wild style that would make you raise your eyebrows if you saw it on telly.

That style looked set until Marc Márquez came into MotoGP in 2013, and started riding the big bikes really aggressively and winning from the off. You just have to look at the way he rides. He's wild, and it's the same style of two wheel drifts and controllable crashing, learned on dirt tracks, as the Americans brought over in the 1970s and 1980s. It is Márquez's influence that has caused the whole thing to go full circle. But that's not the reason I got into dirt track. As I said, I like it for what it is, just riding bikes.

I built my first dirt track bike in October 2013. It was a 2010 Honda CRF450, but I sold it when I ended up with a Suzuki RMZ450. The Suzuki was the bike I used when trying to break the record for riding on water in the first series of *Speed*. During the filming Suzuki promised to give me the bike. I never asked for it, but they could hardly sell it after what I'd done to it. After we finished the filming I asked if I was alright to take it and they said no, they needed it for something. Then, in the next breath, they asked me to do two press days at the NEC for them. This wasn't anything to do with the TAS team I race for on the roads, it was Suzuki GB, but it made me think, You promised me something that I didn't even ask for, then you say I can't have it, but I need to do press for you, when I don't even work for you? I never worked for Suzuki, I was always contracted to TAS directly. Anyway, I ended up doing a bit for them and got the bike that had been to the bottom of a Welsh lake a few times. I turned that motocrosser into a dirt tracker by lowering the suspension and swapping the wheels. I rode it for the first time at King's Lynn in the Dirt Track Riders Association championship and won the Restricted class (for riders that hadn't been in a UK final). I thought that it was the tool for the job and sold the Honda to my mate, and British Superbike racer, Matt Layt.

The highest profile dirt track race in the world is the Superprestigio in Spain. Even though the only place professional dirt track races take place is in the USA, the Superprestigio gets more attention than American races because it was Marc Márquez's idea and he put his weight behind promoting it and attracting some big names.

The idea is to invite top racers from the three grand prix classes and other riders from all sorts of different bike sports and for them all to race dirt track on an indoor circuit in Barcelona. It happens in the close season so the GP riders (and their team bosses) are less worried about getting spannered. Apparently the original Superprestigios happened years ago, but the first one of the new, Márquez era was in January 2014.

No one wins any money or is paid to race at the Superprestigio, it's a big thing just to get an invite to be involved. The Neaves and some other British lads went out to race the first one. When it was announced in July that another was being held in December 2014, I wanted to be included.

To be invited was a big deal and it was Gary Inman, a journalist who I've known a long time, who helped me get an invite. He's been an amateur dirt track racer in the UK and runs a magazine called *Sideburn* that does loads on dirt track. He had been out to report on the first Superprestigio and got the event loads of coverage when not many other journalists went, and he asked the organisers if there was a place for me. I was really honoured when they said yes.

Me and Matt Layt were riding together at a practice day. I had the chance to get back on my old Honda and it felt miles better than the newer Suzuki I was riding. It felt so much tighter and more precise. I asked to buy it back, but Matt wouldn't sell me the bike, so I sold the Suzuki and bought a brand-new 2015 Honda CRF450 and started converting it.

Pikes Peak had brought home to me how much more enjoyable it all is if I actually build the bike I'm going to ride, and preparing for the Superprestigio gave me the same feeling, though the Honda dirt tracker didn't take a fraction of the work it took to prepare the Martek. I only sold the Suzuki and bought the new Honda because I was going out to this big race.

I made an adjustable suspension linkage; James Wood, who used to work for Honda, lowered some old oil forks; I fitted a Suter slipper clutch, bought 19-inch wheels for dirt track tyres, from Talon, and took the front mudguard off. You shouldn't have a front mudguard on a dirt tracker, they don't look right. I paid for it all, instead of trying to get deals, because I didn't want to end up owing anyone any favours for this bike.

The Superprestigio takes place in Barcelona and there are a few days of free practice on an outdoor track an hour from the city centre, before the night race on Saturday 13 December. I could have probably have flown down and got one of the other lads to take my bike, but I wanted to drive to Spain, and Tim Coles and Peter Boast came with me in the Transit.

Boastie is Mr UK Dirt Track. It might be a bold statement, but you could say that the Superprestigio wouldn't be

Machining the block of the Martek's engine to take the 85 mm big-bore cylinder to make it 1277 cc.

These are the parts of the GSX-R dry clutch that I bought from Goose at York Suzuki to go in the Martek. I had to adapt them to fit. Nothing was straightforward with this bike.

The finished Martek just before it went in the crate to be flown to America for Pikes Peak. Even now I get excited looking at this bike.

And this is it just out of the crate, in New Mexico, ready to be loaded for the road trip to Colorado. The truck wasn't a patch on a Transit, but it didn't let us down.

Cameron Whitworth at the top of Pikes Peak. Top man and the only bloke for that job.

Me and Cammy at Devil's Playground on the first day of Pikes Peak practice. It's summat like half-three in the morning. I'm in shorts and it didn't feel that cold, but we tested the road temperature and it was 2°C, stupidly cold.

This was the café five miles from the Pikes Peak start line that we went to for breakfast after practice. I had biscuits and gravy, an American breakfast of scones swimming in a white sauce. When in Rome …

Pikes Peak race day. Jimmy from Vermont, who races a Suzuki RM250, gave me that licence plate. All the racers at Pikes Peak were proper boys.

A Japanese man taking a photo of my bike. Later, me and Cammy joked that's where the inspiration for the Kawasaki H2 came from.

This is the Freightliner racing truck that crashed off the side of the mountain I took this because I liked the way the big turbo feeds the small turbo. Turbo compounding, but using the gases, not linked mechanically. Fascinating.

A British team took a Ford RS200 out to race up the mountain. It's a limited edition Group B rally car from the mid-1980s and people got them making stupid horsepower. This one was 1,000 horsepower. Trick as they come, but the gearbox shit itself every day of practice and in the race too.

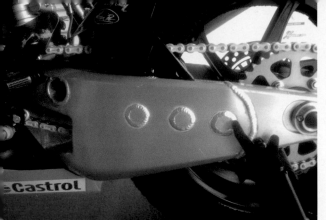

The swingarm of the TAS Suzuki Superbike I raced in 2014. I only used this swingarm at the Ulster, and it allows us to alter the density of the material bolted inside the swinging arm, and that affected the flex. And it did work.

(*Above*) Nige when he was a baby, sat on my knee in the van.

(*Below*) At home with Nige. I'm like a proud father with him and he's the man. I'm convinced Nige and Henry the hoover run the show.

I was loaned a £135,000 Aston Martin to write about for the *Sunday Times*, so that's me, in my mountain bike gear, and Nigel the dog. Good car, but I got in a bit of bother because I said I was doing a squillion miles an hour on the Isle of Man. Even though there's no speed limit where I was doing it, it turned into 'He said, she said', and then went in the papers. Anyway, it came to nothing in the end.

The very top of Mont Ventoux, the day before the best shit in the world.

These are the three real good lasses from Hallam University: Christina, Alice and Heather. They were a big part of the go-kart record we broke.

The Transit we borrowed from Ford to go to Mont Ventoux. The go-kart was too big to fit in my van. My Trannie isn't a proper Transit. It's a Transit Custom, the boy racer one. I want a proper Transit now.

The aftermath of the go-kart crash. Brian the Chimp not pictured. You can see how close I was to the corner.

My beautiful Britten helmet, that Paddy painted for me, scuffed during the go-kart crash.

(*Above*) In London for press stuff and paying £5 for an ice cream. Bloody southerners. It was worth it, though, and this lad was into it.

(*Above right*) Libby Purves and her guests for Radio 4. What a girl she is, and I'm a big Radio 4 listener so it was right up my street. Fascinating folk.

Me and Spellman in London on a rickshaw, a rare photo of us together. He's looked out for me for six years now, and nothing would have happened on the TV without him. He's always up front with me, even if it's not always what I want to hear, and I like that.

At *The One Show*. I told the lass I'm from Grimsby and we don't wear make-up, but she wouldn't have it. Two minutes after this me, Sal and Spellman scrubbed it off with my T-shirt.

happening if it weren't for him. Boastie would never say that himself, though. He wasn't the first to bring the idea of dirt track from America to England, but when he did, in 2006, his enthusiasm for the sport, and determination to make sure it wasn't just a flash in the pan, meant it really caught on in Britain for the first time and then in Europe. Dirt track is left field now, but it was even more of a minority sport then. There had been a race series in Italy in the early 1990s, but it had faded away, so when he started his dirt track series in the UK, using the speedway tracks we have plenty of in England, a handful of hardcore racers would come from Italy and Switzerland. After a while they got their own scene in Italy, and one of the racers who used to come to Boastie's British championship, an Italian called Marco Belli, helped Rossi get his ranch up and running, so it's all linked. Boastie decided to travel to the Superprestigio to act as a bit of a team manager and spare pair of hands for the British riders.

I have known him for years because my dad would MOT his truck, but he's a legend around Lincolnshire thanks to his motorbike racing career. He's done everything. He is Lincolnshire through and through, he speaks the lingo, he's a real yakker and he is into the rarest stuff. He had his motorcycle Top Trump cards with him and we had a few games while we were waiting to drive onto the train at the Channel Tunnel. Boastie is the man, as far as I'm concerned.

Tim was already used to how I do road trips, but Boastie wasn't. I get the idea Boastie would prefer to stop every couple of hours for a bloody café latte. The rules on my road trips are: don't drink, don't piss, because we're only stopping for diesel.

On a trip like this I'm licking on, doing about 90 mph through France and Spain, so the Transit does 500 miles to a tank. We have to slow down for the tolls, so it's about six hours between stops. That's how we drove down to Barcelona, three of us across the front of my Transit.

We had three days of practice at a track called Rancho Canudas, an hour away from Barcelona. It was made to be an exact replica, in size, shape and diameter of corners, of the track that we'd race indoors at the Superprestigio. They prepared it like that so riders could gear their bike, choosing the right sprockets and set-up, and get their eye in. All the top men were there, except Márquez; he was at his own track. I got talking to the American 2013 and 2014 dirt track champions, Brad Baker and Jared Mees, a pair of really nice blokes. They were faster than me, of course, but the difference wasn't night and day. Every time they came past I'd try to follow them and learn a bit. The biggest thing I learned was how they were getting on the throttle. They'd go into the corner, knock the back brake to get the bike a bit sideways, and then be on the throttle while it was still sideways, whereas I'd let it line up a bit before getting back on the throttle. They had so much feel and their body position was different. They were doing just lots of little things differently to me.

I had three days of riding, before going back to our hotel in Barcelona every night. Me, Tim and Boastie would go out for something to eat, and it is a bloody nice city. Then, on the Friday night, all the riders had five minutes of practice before qualifying started on the Saturday morning for the Saturday night race.

The race is held in a municipal stadium, the Palau Sant Jordi, that was built for the 1990 Barcelona Olympics. It's at the top of the hill in Montjuïc Park. Until about 40 years ago the looping road up and down the hill was used as a car and motorcycle road racing track, and it hosted a famous motorcycle endurance race. Laverda even named a motorcycle after the place.

There were a total of 48 riders entered into two classes, 24 in each. The Superprestigio class is for GP riders from MotoGP, Moto2 and Moto3 and other short circuit racers. The current three world champions were all racing: Marc Márquez, his brother Alex, who was the 2014 Moto3 champion, and their mate, Tito Rabat, the Moto2 champion. Scott Redding and Bradley Smith were in that class. Scott Redding came up to me at the practice track and said he'd watched the telly programmes and liked them, which was a nice thing to hear. He'd borrowed a bike off a mate and just come and raced it. I got the impression he thought the race was more laid back than it actually is. Márquez was taking it bloody seriously.

I didn't speak to Bradley Smith. I'm not the kind of person to go up and introduce myself and he might not be either. I don't know him, but seeing him driving around in a van with a number plate that reads GO BRAD said a lot to me. What made it even worse was it was on a Volkswagen Transporter and I tar all Transporter drivers with the same brush. I know I had one, but that was before they were the emperor's new clothes.

In the race I was in the Open class with the dirt track specialists and off-road champions. There were three Americans: Jared Mees, Brad Baker and Shayna Texter, a young woman racer who has won big races in the support class out in the USA. There were a load of fast Spanish and Italian lads; top enduro man Taddy Blazusiak; long track champion Joonas Kylmäkorpi; supermoto champion Thomas Chareyre and the best British lads: Tim and Tom Neave, Ollie Brindley, Alan Birtwistle and Aidan Collins – but Collins spannered himself at the practice track and was too injured to race. These were riders who were at the top of their game in enduro, supermoto and dirt track. I'm not the top of any sport, so I don't really know why I was invited. It meant I was going into it with no expectations. I was just going to ride and, hopefully, enjoy myself.

For this indoor motorcycle race the pits were underneath the stands. And the riders were jammed in like battery hens. Opposite me was the world supermoto champion Thomas Chareyre, a bit further down was Bradley Smith. Ten yards further on was Márquez and his brother. On the same side as me was the American Mees. All the European dirt trackers and some of the Moto2 and Moto3 riders were in another pit just next door.

Right next to me was a British rider I was pleased to meet, Christian Iddon. He's a legend, in my eyes, because of what he can do with a supermoto … He's four or five years younger than me, but packed in supermoto racing when he was at the top and went into short circuit road racing. He has won some supersport races, but not consistently. So I had Christian

Iddon on one side of me and the Australian, Troy Bayliss, on the other. Bayliss is a three-time World Superbike champion and had won a MotoGP race for Ducati. He was a car painter and became a professional bike racer later in life, off his own bat. He's proper. He was there with his own bike, that he pointed out he'd bought with his own money, and had shipped over from Australia. He made sure I knew that, but I appreciate that dedication. He shaves his armpits, though. I didn't get that.

There were a couple of short practice sessions on the Saturday morning, then it was straight into the two timed qualifying sessions.

Brad Baker set the fastest lap, but he was pushing hard, crashed and broke his shoulder, putting himself out of the race he had flown from America to compete in. He was the favourite for the win, having won the first one in January. The fastest qualifier behind him was Tim Neave, one of the twins from near me in Lincolnshire. Then it was 2014 American dirt track champion Jared Mees ahead of Marc Márquez, with Tim's brother Tom just behind Márquez. It was brilliant qualifying by a couple of Lincolnshire lads.

I didn't have expectations, but I did shit. I'd learned loads riding for three days at the track in Spain, but as soon as I went to the stadium I forgot it all, and went back to how I was riding before. I felt the pressure of riding in that place. Not the crowd, because they didn't know or care who I was, just the company.

I don't get nervous before a road race, but I was nervous here. Someone was sticking a camera right in my face, and

I hit his lens with my arm when the motocross-style starting gate dropped and the first race started.

There was no game plan for the races – you couldn't plan, the racing was so hard and close – so I just went out as fast as I could go. I slid off a couple of times in practice, but not in the races. I didn't want to look stupid. I was slow, but I wasn't a million miles off.

I might not have been the fastest, but I reckon I looked the part. I was riding my own Honda CRF450 and Dainese made me some special leathers that looked like old Freddie Spencer Honda ones. I love the whole look of dirt track and had seen photos from Peoria in the 1980s, where Honda riders like Bubba Shobert and Ricky Graham raced. I loved the look of their old-school leathers, with the number on the back. I was going to have Honda on the front, but Spellman pointed out that would cause trouble with TAS and BMW, so Dainese ended up putting GUY on the front, that I'm not keen about. Gary Inman pointed out it should have said KIRMO, but in Honda writing, as a reference to Kirmington, the centre of the universe.

I didn't make it into the finals, but I still loved the experience. Of the British dirt trackers, Ollie Brindley and Alan Birtwistle made it into the Open final, with Ollie coming fourth to go into the grand final. Bradley Smith qualified for his final and through into the grand final too, riding really well.

I stood and watched the final next to Bayliss, Boastie and Tim. That was another great thing about the event: when I'm in Barcelona at a bike race with three Spanish world champions, no one gives a fuck who I am. I loved that.

Before the event, I wanted Brad Baker to win the grand final, but he'd spannered himself. So then I wanted Jared Mees to be Superprestigio champion. It's a dirt track race, so you should have a dirt track racer win it, but Márquez won. It's not right to have a MotoGP rider beating a dirt tracker, but he rode hard and deserved it.

Márquez is special and he had a trick HRC engine in his bike, I could tell just looking at it and noticing things like the hydraulic clutch.

Oliver Brindley was the top British rider, coming sixth in the grand final, an impressive result considering he'd broken his shoulder in a qualifying race, when he crashed into Boastie's bike after he'd been taken out. That was only a few weeks before and Brindley is only 16. Tim and Tom gave so much promise, qualified brilliantly, but then it all turned to shit. Perhaps they were like me, feeling the pressure.

I thought it was a brilliant event for the whole of motorcycling, but dirt track especially. I can't think of a ball sport equivalent – for which you could take a top footballer, top tennis player, top rugby player, put them all together and make them compete in something where they would all be so evenly matched as we were and for it to be a proper event worth paying to watch. The motorbikers were all from different disciplines, but all chucked into this one oddball event, and they were all there or thereabouts.

The race finished at 10pm, and we got the van loaded up and were on the road for 11pm. Because we didn't stop for anything but diesel, we were at Calais at ten the next morning. Boastie had to drive the last stretch in France from Paris to

Calais. I couldn't stay awake any longer, so I climbed in the back and had a couple of hours' kip. Then I was alright to drive from Kent to Lincolnshire.

Boastie only realised when we got back to England why I do road trips this way. As soon as you start stopping, the average speed drops massively. All the other lads stayed in Barcelona and by the time they'd got up in the morning, got to the airport, and had to drive home from the airport, we were already home. We were home at two on Sunday afternoon.

I cut the lawn thinking, What a week off. If I had to make a choice between the Superprestigio and the TT, I'd go to Spain. It was a cool thing to be involved in.

CHAPTER 7

You can afford it

The road trip out to Spain for the Superprestigio in the middle of December would normally be the last motorcycle competition of my year, but I'd had an invite out to race in New Zealand on Boxing Day.

There are only a handful of places in the world where motorbike races are still held on public roads. Ireland and the Isle of Man have the most, and they are the biggest and most famous, but there are also real road races in Belgium, Germany, Pikes Peak in America, the odd one in Spain or Portugal, Macau, and one or two in New Zealand.

I first raced at Wanganui in 2005, when the Kiwi racer Shaun Harris asked me to go over. Shaun had raced over here and at the TT a load of times and we talked at races, so I must have stuck in his mind as someone up for the craic.

I didn't race at Wanganui after that first time until 2013, when I was invited back by the organisers. Julie and Alan, also known as Flea – who is a former New Zealand 125 champion – are the couple who do the lion's share of the organising of the Tri-Series, a three-meeting series that takes place in New Zealand. The New Zealand national series, the equivalent of British Superbikes, is only four rounds and the Tri-Series runs before it, but it seems bigger than the national series in terms of interest, because the Tri-Series has the Wanganui race, the biggest and most famous race in New Zealand.

The three meetings of the Tri-Series are held at Hampton Down, Manfeild and Wanganui. The first two are short circuits, purpose-built circuits like Brands Hatch or somewhere, while the Cemetery Circuit at Wanganui is a road circuit through the town. Wanganui is the only race meeting I compete in, and I race both on modern superbikes and classics.

I don't get any start or appearance money, but I get flights covered for me and my dad. In 2013 Julie and Flea gave me some expenses, even though I didn't ask for or expect any, but for 2014 I said not to give me any money, but get us better seats on the plane if they could. You're sat on a plane for over 50 hours in the space of ten days and my dad, though he's as strong as an ox, is getting on. He was 67 when we took this trip. We ended up flying premium economy with Air New Zealand. That way we had a bit more leg room, a bit more elbow room and a proper metal knife and fork. Terrorists don't fly in premium economy, obviously.

For the 2014 race we flew out on 17 December. When we got to Heathrow airport I drove to the long stay car park and my dad piped up, 'Why don't you go in the short stay?' I told him because it would cost a bloody fortune. And he replied, 'You can afford it.' I won't forget that, but I wrote it down anyway. Bugger me! I went to work at half-five this morning to work for £12 an hour – I'm not going to waste it on short stay parking. And we had all the time in the world, anyway. Ten days in the short stay? That would've cost a grand! I always park in the cheapest place if I can. I don't know what he thinks I think, but I noted it for future reference.

One reason I like going out to this race is because I get to see Benny, one of my real good mates from growing up. He emigrated out there earlier in 2014. Another reason is that I don't see much of my dad any more and he's right into the trip out there, so we go together. I did wonder if my mum would be bothered about him being away for a lot of the holidays, but Big Rita seems all for hoiking him off for Christmas.

Because of the length of the flight and the time differences, we set off on Wednesday the 17th and landed in Auckland at 8am on Friday morning, after a four-hour stop for refuelling in Los Angeles. Once we landed in Auckland, we caught another one-hour flight down to Wanganui.

Wanganui is on an estuary, on the west coast of the North Island. It's a pretty small place of about 40,000 people, but has a fair bit of tourism going on. I get the feeling it's a bit of a retirement spot. There's not a lot going on there.

I could have organised things a bit better, because the next day we drove 250 miles back to Auckland, where we had flown in to, to see Benny. On the way, because I was out there with me dad, I thought we had to go see summat a bit touristy, so we visited Waitomo Caves. They're famous because they have glow-worms in them. The glow-worm is tiny, the size of a larva or a maggot, and the snot that comes out of its arse is what glows. Not my cup of tea, to be honest, but we both like a bit of culture and Dad likes to see the touristy side of things now and then.

Benny is an old mate, but not one of the Kirmington lot. If he was Kirmington he'd have never left, obviously. He went to the rival secondary school. I went to the Vale of Ancholme, in Brigg; he went to the Nelthorpe. I had a Kawasaki AR50 (with an 80 cc kit ...) and he had a really trick Fizzer, a Yamaha FS-1E. He knew about my legendary AR and I knew about his legendary Fizzer, but we never actually raced each other. We never worked together either, but we met because we did our apprenticeships at the same time and I got to know him well at college where we both did our day-release. I was working for John Hebb's Volvo truck yard and Benny was at Gallows Wood Recovery, where I had done my work experience when I was still at school.

When there's a real bad car crash and it's obvious the people in the car are dead, the emergency services don't cut the dead bodies out at the scene of the accident, they transport the car, with the victims still inside, to a garage. Gallows Wood, where Benny worked, was one of these depots. It sounds grim, but the cars could be there, stored in the workshop, for a couple of days until the recovery crew could come and cut the bodies out, with Benny and his workmates spannering next to the crashed cars. They'd be under a tarpaulin, but still ... Once the remains have been removed, the cars are moved out to the yard. When I did my work experience there I had to walk past all these smashed-up cars to get to the tea room. Sometimes there would be gizzards and stuff left in the cars and in summer it could get a bit ripe. Later, when I left John Hebb Volvo to go work for my dad, Benny went to Hebby's. So that's Benny introduced.

Four million people live in New Zealand, half of them in Auckland where Benny is, and I don't think he's totally sold on the place. The grass is always greener, isn't it?

The first night we had a barbecue, then the next day I went to Rotorua with me, myself and I for some mountain biking on the trails they have down there. Dad stayed back at Benny's, sunbathing and reading his book about the V-Bombers, the Vulcan, Victor and Valiant.

I hadn't done any research, but I knew Rotorua was well-known as being a good place to mountain bike. In 2006 it hosted a mountain bike world championship, so I thought there'd be a decent mountain bike shop, and I knew most bike shops in areas like this have a rental desk. It turned out I was right, so I hired a bike, a Giant, a trick thing, but not as good as my Orange.

Rotorua is about 140 miles from the centre of Auckland. It's a big spot for tourists because there's lots of geo-thermal goings-on, like geysers and bubbling mud pools. The sulphur that comes out of the ground smells of rotten eggs.

Riding around Rotorua reminded me why I like riding my mountain bike. It purged the system. My dad's the man, but he does annoy me. I respect him, and I feel an idiot for being wound up by him, but I still can't help it sometimes. It's things like the way he stirs his coffee. He has to stir it for 30 seconds and clank the spoon on the side of the cup as many times as is humanly possible. There is absolutely no reason to do that. I've told him it is impossible to make more noise than he does with a spoon and a mug. Just stir it! That's all you need to do. When I worked with him I couldn't say that because I knew it would turn into a raging argument. And the way he eats a yoghurt and scratches every last molecule of yoghurt out of the pot! It. Drives. Me. Fucking. Crackers! The thing is, on this trip he told me he does it because he knows it annoys me. That makes it even worse!

We didn't have a cross word in New Zealand, because I could get on the bike and escape for a while. He's me dad, we don't need to fall out, but for him to say he did these things because he knew they annoyed me took some swallowing.

Between visiting Benny and the Boxing Day race at Wanganui, I had a trackday at the Manfeild circuit to get used to the bike I was racing, and I was also going to tick something off my Do Before I Die list: ride my favourite bike of all time, a Britten.

Before that though, I got to know the Manfeild track on the bike that had been arranged for me to race, the spare Suzuki GSX-R1000 of a local racer called Sloan Frost. The bike was superstock spec, not a full superbike, but you don't need any more than that for the Cemetery Circuit. It's only a 40-second lap and only needing second and third gears. You only change gear twice per lap. I had a few sessions on the Suzuki, just to get into it, and then it was a big moment in my life: my chance to climb on the Britten.

John Britten built this bike from scratch and did things that were totally different to every race bike manufacturer at the time. But it wasn't just different for difference's sake, it worked. It won races.

I like everything about it. I like how it was built, how it looks. Lots of people think the whole story begins and ends with John Britten, a man in his shed who built this amazing bike, but the more I learn about the bike and the story behind it, the more I realise it wasn't just him, though he was the man who had the drive to make it happen. He had the vision, but not the complete vision. He stoked the fire for all these local people to channel their energy into one motorbike, whether it was the man doing the casting, the cam design, the fuel injection system, the carbon fibre, the suspension. John Britten was the driving force, and a bloody legend, but he also had help from a lot of clever people.

There's a British ex-pat, called Steve Roberts, who is part of the story. He had a bike that raced at the TT in '82 or '83 with a Kiwi rider on board. It was called the Plastic Fantastic, and it was a monocoque bike. By monocoque I mean the bodywork also forms the rigid frame of the bike. The vast majority of motorcycles have a frame that the engine is bolted into and the front and rear suspension fastens to. On to the chassis goes the petrol tank and any bodywork or fairing, but monocoque designs are different. Roberts's Plastic Fantastic wasn't the first or most successful. Peter Williams, a total legend, built and raced a Norton Monocoque that won the 1973 Isle of Man Formula 750 TT.

Steve Roberts moved out to New Zealand when he was in his twenties and he must be 60-odd now. I met him and saw the Plastic Fantastic and I could see right from the off that Britten took a lot of inspiration for his bike from this one, but Steve was so humble he wouldn't take any credit. The Britten was only inspired in part by the Plastic Fantastic, but the way Britten put the rear shock in a different place and made the monocoque chassis, using the engine as a stressed member, was similar. I'm not taking anything away from John Britten. What a feat to build a bike like he did.

I've virtually worshipped the Britten since I first read about it in *Performance Bikes*, but the first time I had seen one in the flesh was at the Ulster Grand Prix in 2013. Kevin Grant is the Kiwi who owns this one, one of only ten in the world, and had brought it over for the TT, the Classic TT, the Ulster Grand Prix and the Goodwood Festival of Speed. He was doing a bit of a tour with it, and that was the right thing to do, I reckon. There's ten in the world and Kevin is the only owner who lets his out to be ridden as it should be. All the others are sat in museums doing nothing.

I had a sniff of buying one a couple of years ago, but I had to pass on it and that was the sensible thing to do. The bike was a hell of a lot of money and it ended up going to America, unfortunately. The Yanks keep buying them. I don't regret not buying it, but I do wonder when another *is* going to come up.

When it came time to ride the Britten, Kevin, the owner, let me warm it up on its stand. Before it had even moved an inch I was amazed by the feel of the throttle. This thing was so sharp. There's no weight to anything in the engine and the throttle response was incredible. It sounded like a Formula One car.

I'd learned the track in the morning on the Suzuki I was going to race at Wanganui. Manfeild is only a short track, but there's a heavy camber on everything, so you could really pile into corners. The surface was a bit rough, with potholes and gouges from car crashes in it, but nothing to worry about.

Before I went out Kevin had said, 'You're running it in.' It had been rebuilt after it had been in Europe the year before. He has to have the pistons specially made for it in England. Kevin made his money from making carbon-fibre wings for planes and obviously had a few quid, but he didn't shout about it.

I was really nervous. You would be – this is a £300,000 bike. You can't get bits for them if anything goes wrong. I did five laps, and took it steady because of the fresh engine.

When I came in, Kevin said, 'You didn't rev it very hard.' I told him I wasn't going to, explaining I was showing it some respect. He looked at me and said, 'Lick her on, mate, you're alright.' I didn't need telling twice.

The Britten would rev to 11,000, but they set the rev limiter to 9,500. So I went out the second time and let it have it. I revved it out all the way. It was the strangest feeling. Once it got above 7–8,000 rpm the bike felt like it had a supercharger on it. I could feel the harmonics of the airbox under my legs, the pulsing of the airbox, and it seemed to leap forward. The faster I went, the faster it went. Really, the power should've been tailing off, but it just kept pulling. It was the strangest feeling.

I wasn't *going* for it, going for it, but I was pressing on a bit. It would do anything I wanted. I could brake later. I could let off the brakes sooner. It was egging me on, but I only wanted to go so far. This ride wasn't about lap times, but I was more impressed than I thought I would be. I was totally prepared to be disappointed, but it was quite usable. It would tick over like a road bike and you didn't have to rev the nuts off it to get it to move from a standstill. It went so much better than I thought it would for a 20-year-old bike.

I'd been on the track in the morning on a current Suzuki GSX-R1000, the make of bike I had raced at the TT and everywhere else for the previous three seasons. The Suzuki, in superstock form, weighs about 190 kg and makes 170-odd horsepower, while the Britten had 165 hp and weighed 135 kg. The 2014 Suzuki had the potential of 20 years of difference, so it should have felt day and night better, but it didn't. The biggest difference was the feel of the front end, because the Britten has girder forks and doesn't dive on the brakes. You need to recalibrate the brain to get the most out of it. They reckon that this is a better design of front suspension for a motorbike, because you've got constant geometry, but hardly anyone uses it.

Virtually every bike, except for some BMWs and a few oddball contraptions, have telescopic front forks. It doesn't matter if it's a 125 commuter bike, a Royal Enfield or Marc Márquez's HRC Honda grand prix bike, they all have telescopic forks, so it's what everyone gets used to. As soon as you pull the front brake lever on a bike with traditional telescopic forks the weight is thrown forward, making the forks compress and changing the geometry of the bike. It's what every racer is used to but it's not ideal. The Britten just stayed flat, not diving onto its nose when I got on the brake. There is a little bit of transition, but hardly any.

My mate, the tuner and engine builder Chris Mehew, worked on the Elf grand prix project in the 1980s. The oil company poured millions into building grand prix bikes that tried to do things differently to every other bike out there. They experimented with unusual front suspension designs, like hub-centre steering. It was more radical than Britten's girder design, but it shared the same lack of dive on the brakes. Mehew told me once that you need someone who has never ridden anything but girder-style forks to really exploit the handling of a bike like this. Get them young, so they don't ride anything else, and they will be world champion. The science of it proves it's a better design, but it's just getting your head into it after years of being used to telescopic forks and the weight transfer you get from that set-up.

After ten laps on the Britten I could understand what Mehew was saying. It is such an alien feeling, because compared to what I'm used to, there is no feeling because nothing dives. It made me think, If there's ever a reason for having a kid ... I'd build flat trackers and mountain bikes with girder forks. But a normal motorbike? You're not going on it.

I love that Kevin allows his Britten to be ridden, and I thought that before I even got a chance to sit on it. These bikes need to be on the track so people talk about it like I'm talking about it. It was a proper dream come true.

After the test I drove back to Wanganui and got done for speeding. Writing this reminds me I forgot to pay the fine. I'll have to get onto that.

By 23 December, we were back at our hotel in Wanganui. We had a suite-type family room with separate bedrooms and then a room to sit and watch TV in or read. Last time me and my dad came out to Wanganui we had a twin room and I ended up sleeping in the corridor for a week because my dad snores so loudly. Perhaps that's why my mum is happy for him to clear off. He thinks it's funny, but he snores like hell. I think he's going to inhale the curtains.

On the morning of Christmas Eve, we watched a documentary on the Arabic TV channel Al Jazeera. I don't have a TV at home, so when I'm in a hotel I watch quite a bit of telly if I've got the time. I got into Al Jazeera when I was in India. This documentary was about al-Megrahi, the Lockerbie bomber, and it was fascinating because it painted a wholly different picture to what you'd see or hear on UK media. I'd heard a radio show on BBC Radio 4 about the Lockerbie bomber, and their conclusion was totally different.

My dad is brainwashed by the BBC and he wasn't keen on watching Al Jazeera at first, but I told him it was just a different point of view to what he's used to. The only news any of us get to see is what they, the broadcasters and the governments, want us to see. It's all versions of propaganda. In the end he was converted.

My view on the news and media has been changed by Orwell's *1984*. How I see it now, the whole idea behind cheap beer, football and *The X Factor* is to channel the energy of the masses. By getting us to vent our energy into getting excited about who is going to win *X Factor* or the Premier League is what the powers that be want. If we didn't have these trivial things to get excited about, the proles, us, the masses, would have enough energy for a mass revolution. I don't know what to do with this new view on the world I have. As I tell people, I'm not clever enough to deal with the ideas these books are filling my head with, but I do see things a different way since reading that book. It has changed my life.

Back to the motorbikes ... The Wanganui race is always on Boxing Day, so Christmas Day is more like a normal day. Sandra and Stu are another two of the race organisers and they invited me and Dad to go to their relatives' house for Christmas dinner. It was a dead laid-back barbecue. Sandra's brother was just getting into endurance cycling and he was telling me about a race around Lake Taupo that sounded like ideal preparation for a big race like the Tour Divide – which I'll be coming back to.

That afternoon I went to scrutineering, where I bumped into Billy Redmayne. I had met him before at the Isle of Man. He won the 2014 Manx Grand Prix Newcomers. He's a real nice Manx lad and was there with his mates, who were all Paras and sound lads. I took Billy for a few laps round on pushbikes, because I'd been before. Then we went to the pub and talked about conspiracy theories. They had a few, like how they reckoned the Twin Towers wouldn't have collapsed like that because of the burning temperature of steel compared to aviation fuel and the towers were actually brought down by a controlled explosion. It was a brilliant way to spend Christmas Day afternoon.

You have to pay to get into the Wanganui race. In Ireland and the Isle of Man, all the races are free to spectate, unless you want to go in the grandstands, but in Wanganui they put shipping containers across all the roads leading to the part of the town with the track, so there is no way in without paying. On Boxing Day morning I got lost trying to reach the pits. We were driving around in the little Suzuki Swift we'd been loaned and I didn't know which one was the pit entrance and I couldn't get in at first, but everyone was dead helpful.

The race is a mass-start of 35 or so riders. The crowd is really close to the track in the start line area, behind a barbed wire fence. Last time I was there I was on the start line, not exactly trying to psych myself up, but seeing what's happening and getting in the right frame of mind, when a bloke in the crowd, pint in his hand, called over, 'Are you alright, mate? Have a good Christmas?' I looked at him and said, 'Spot on, thanks.' And then the flag dropped. It was a bit odd.

The name Cemetery Circuit sounds a bit masochistic, but it doesn't bother me in the slightest. It's called that because there's a boneyard on the left and right-hand sides of the track.

This is what a lap is like. I don't remember any of the corner names, because they're named after local sponsors, so you have the Mars Petcare Turn and the brilliantly named Hookers Transport Straight, though one is named after racer Robert Holden, who was born in England but emigrated out to New Zealand with his family when he was a teenager.

The track starts on a steep downhill section that leads into a tight right, with a real steep camber up to the centre of the track. This bend has storm drains in the gutters that stop you going right to the kerb. Because of the crown in the road, you end up jumping out of the corner like a bloody supercross berm. Then you're on a real short straight that you don't need to be changing gear on. You're in second gear, going into the

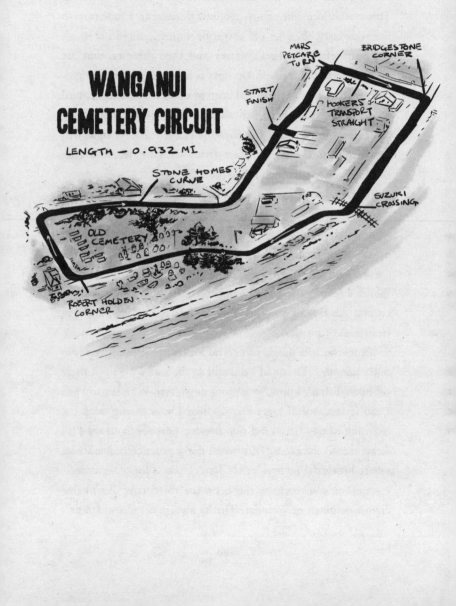

WANGANUI
CEMETERY CIRCUIT

LENGTH — 0.932 MI

MARS
PETCARE
TURN

BRIDGESTONE
CORNER

START
FINISH

HOOKERS
TRANSPORT
STRAIGHT

STONE HOMES
CURVE

SUZUKI
CROSSING

OLD
CEMETERY

ROBERT HOLDEN
CORNER

next tight right-hander. It's another road-end junction, with a steep camber so you don't want to apex tightly. You end up jumping out of this one too and exit onto a longer straight. This one is long enough to get into third gear. I brake up to the tramlines, then let off to go over them, thread through the right-left; past the Cemetery and then the pits, that are on your left at that point. Up next is another 90-degree right-hander, that is a flat, normal sort of corner. I'm still in third gear, braking into another 90-degree right-hander, then a long right-hander. I go back to second gear for the next tight left, that leads back onto the start–finish straight, where I grab third on the Suzuki on a flying lap.

All the overtaking is done on the brakes. You have to fire it up the inside, screwing up both yourself and the person in front. If you're coming up the inside, to make what they call on the telly 'a block pass', you're on the wrong line for the corner, but the rider on the better line can't turn in because there's a bike in the way. It's not the quickest line through the corner, but there's no other way to pass unless the person in front makes a mistake.

Wanganui is a tough race. The locals are bloody fast. No one's hanging about and I did shit in the races. I go out there on bikes I don't know, so it's not easy. Two years ago, when I did it last, I didn't get on the bike I was racing until the morning of the race. I did two five-lap practices and then it's straight into the races. This time I got a practice at Manfeild, where I rode the Britten, but it didn't make a lot of difference.

I qualified seventh or eight, on the third row. And came eighth or ninth or summat. The locals are on it and I didn't feel comfortable on the bike I was borrowing. They'd fitted Pirellis, because that's what I'm used to (Pirelli and Metzeler are the same company, but which name is on the side of the tyres just depends on which brand is getting a marketing push that year). But just because it's a Pirelli doesn't mean I'm going to get on with it. I hated the feeling of the control tyres they make for the British Superbike series. It just collapses on the brakes. I couldn't deal with it or ride around it. They make the tyres so they collapse like that, so you have a relatively large footprint of rubber on the track, but I find it hard to turn in. Pirelli Metzeler ended up making a special tyre for the roads that was a stiffer construction, with a cross-belt, which is like twice the plies and it gives a real firm feeling in the front. A lot of the road racers don't like it, but I love it. I couldn't get that tyre out in New Zealand, and I missed it. Instead, I had to hold onto the brake to get it around the corner. My style over here is let go of the brake and just keep turning the front in. I wasn't willing to hang my balls out. Sounds sad, doesn't it? But tomorrow's another day. Perhaps the organisers are fed up that I'm not battling at the front, but I tried as hard as I could. I didn't ride like a fanny, I was pressing on.

I also raced a classic and won both races. I raced a Manx Norton too. One built by UK specialist Andy Molnar. I was going to race one of his Manx Nortons at the Classic TT of 2013, but I was excluded from the meeting because I missed the first practice. I'd told the clerk of the course I couldn't make the first practice, and was told it didn't matter, as long as I got along for the next one, but when I turned up at the

Isle of Man I was informed I wasn't allowed to race. I think the TT were trying to teach me a lesson, but I had discussed it with the clerk of the course, the man who runs the meeting, and he said it was alright. I didn't make a fuss. Maybe they thought I was disrespecting the competition by missing the first practice, but that wasn't my intention. Surely it was me who was missing out by not practising. I was hardly going to be a danger to anyone else because I hadn't done one session. I've raced classic more than a lot of those boys and I know my way around the place. I wonder if they'd have let Valentino Rossi race if he could only make it over for the second session of practice (not that I'm comparing myself to him).

At Wanganui I did better on the classic than I did in the Superbike race, beating the local champion, who was racing a 650 Manx, when I was riding John Marsh's 500 Manx. John Marsh owns a car garage and had this classic race bike he lets people race for him. Flea had come to me asking if I was interested in racing it, and I was up for it.

I was going hard enough in the race that I lost the front a couple of times, but the old bike, at slower speeds, was giving the confidence to push that hard and stay on. When I'm not getting the confidence I won't push. It was the bike owner's 70th birthday. John said it was the best 70th birthday he'd ever had. It was only a while later that it clicked: it was the only 70th birthday he'd ever had.

That night was an awards evening in a function room at the Wanganui Jockey Club, the local horse racing track. I handed a few trophies out, and then another member of the club that organises the race turned up in a 1940s Chevy truck that was on airbag suspension, so I had a good look around that.

The Paras I'd been talking to the day before were there and said they were going to the Red Lion. I'm not much of a boozer, but my dad was up for it. I went back to the hotel and read up on the CNC programming system for my milling machine. I've no idea what time he came in, but we were both up in time for the flight back to England after what had been another memorable trip to New Zealand.

CHAPTER 8

My farts could be one of your five a day

After getting back from New Zealand I was straight onto the mountain bike for the last bit of preparation for my fourth Strathpuffer 24-hour mountain bike race, and my third as a solo. I mentioned this race in the autobiography, and talked about the attractions it has for me – attractions that aren't obvious to other people – and since writing that book the draw of 24-hour solo mountain races has got even stronger. I love them.

I had thought that once I got on the podium in a solo 24-hour bicycle race, that would be me done with them, because I thought I'd have to dedicate my whole life to training and it would be so miserable I'd never want to put myself through it again, but I came third in my first year and I've come second in the last two years.

The 2015 race took place on 17–18 January, in Strathpeffer, north of Inverness in the Scottish Highlands. It's a 450-mile drive from my house in north Lincolnshire, and plenty travel further than that for the race. This was the tenth year of the Strathpuffer and it's thought of as the toughest 24-hour race, because it happens in the middle of a Scottish winter. That also means a lot of the training takes places in autumn and winter, so you have to be dedicated to put the miles in.

I always try to keep my base fitness at a decent level, by biking to work and back, 19 miles each way, but the ideal way to be properly prepared for a solo 24-hour race would be to train like hell for 12 weeks leading up to it. You should structure your training with three increasingly hard weeks and an easy week. The third of the hard weeks is always the toughest, but that distance becomes the start of the next set of three weeks. It's all about hours on the bike. People say you really don't want to be doing anything for seven days before the race, but I do, because I can't stay off my bike. I do short intense stuff so it doesn't burn off any glycogen from the muscles, it just helps with capillary structure in the muscles.

In the final week I get up early, and batter myself for one 15-minute intense session a day on a turbo trainer. A turbo trainer turns a regular bike into a static exercise bike. You take the front wheel out, bolt the forks into a frame that sits on the floor, and the rear wheel runs on a roller.

I do it before breakfast, pedalling until I'm coughing up a lung. If I did it after I'd eaten I'd be throwing up. I do five minutes' warm-up, five minutes' killing myself, then five minutes' slow-down. In that last week before the race, I bike in to work one day and get a lift home with Belty, the fella who valets the trucks at Moody's. I don't do anything on the Friday, the day we drive up to Scotland.

I'd been drinking plenty of beetroot juice. It's like a legal form of cheating, because it slightly increases the haemoglobin in the blood, and that means the blood carries more oxygen to the muscles. That's exactly what Lance Armstrong and all the Tour de France dopers were trying to do with the EPO drug and blood doping. With blood doping they'd train at high altitude, in a very specific way, in the mountains, in winter, before the season started. Training like that naturally increases the red blood cells, so the blood carries more oxygen to the muscles, and the muscles can be worked harder. When the riders had reached a certain red blood cell count, a doctor, employed by the team or by an individual rider, would drain an amount of the rider's blood. I don't know how many times they'd do this, but the winter training blood would be kept until the Tour de France or another big race came along. Then, when the rider was knackered, after a week of the race or summat, and they were heading into the Alps, where so many races had been won and lost, the blood would be taken out of storage and transfused back into the rider.

There were no drugs involved, so no one could tell at first. The anti-doping tests were looking for EPO and testosterone. This was just blood, the rider's own blood. Armstrong was so blatant about cheating, he's now admitted him and his team would be doing this blood doping on the bus, with the press and TV lot all stood outside waiting for interviews. Eventually, the anti-doping folk got an inkling about blood doping and then they started testing for that too at various times during the season and the race.

But I wasn't doing any of that, I was just drinking beetroot juice. It's bloody dear, £3 a litre, and it tastes horrible, like eating a handful of dirt. I can see why Lance Armstrong didn't bother. And it turns your pee pink.

Still, even with drinking that stuff, I thought my preparation for this year's race had been crap. I had been doing so much travelling I hadn't been able to get the miles in. First I was in India, then Barcelona for the Superprestigio, then New Zealand. Even though I rented bikes in New Zealand, I still wasn't doing as much as I normally would.

And all this came after the disappointment of the World Cup 24-hour race, at Fort William on 11 October. I reckon the World Cup was the biggest race of my life up until that point. I was drinking beetroot juice like mad before that, and got down to 67 kg, but I blew the race. It went to shit, I finished 15th or summat in the Elite class. A lack of sleep the night before didn't help. My dad was snoring so much that I had to get out of bed in the middle of the night and sleep in my van. And he thought it was funny.

Tim Coles was with me during that race too, and part way through it I stopped and was sat in the footwell of my van behind our pit, mentally broken. It was three in the morning and Tim and my dad were talking to me, but I couldn't suss out what they were saying. I was gone. Eventually, Lee Eaton, a triathlete and endurance racer who was helping Jason Miles, came over. Perhaps it was because Lee had done tough races that he knew what to say, or that I was listening to him because I knew he'd been in similar situations, but whatever it was got me back on the bike for another six or seven hours of racing.

Even after all that, on the way home, I had to wake myself up and drive because I couldn't stand my dad driving my van any more. He's too hard on the brakes. I was trying to sleep, but I could feel him braking for roundabouts, as most people would. I was slipping off the seat and I couldn't stop thinking about my 100,000-mile brake pads. I try to drive looking so far ahead that I hardly ever have to brake. I want to get 100,000 miles out of my Transit's brake pads before I change them. My dad is the man, but I had to drive.

My first 24-hour mountain bike race was as a team of four with a few mates from Tealby. I did it just because I liked riding. When you race in a team of four, you take it in turns like a relay team, so in a team like that you're only riding one lap in every four, if everything goes to plan, and each rider will do about six hours' pedalling in 24 hours. Next I did a couple of races in a pair, with Forbes Dungait. We finished second in the pairs at the Strathpuffer, then third in the Relentless.

Forbes is Francis's younger brother. You'll be introduced to Francis in a few chapters' time. Forbes is a painter and decorator for the Queen, at Balmoral. The brothers have very similar characters, very matter-of-fact – this is how it's happening. Forbes is in his fifties, but, if anything, he's even fitter than Francis and that's saying something. He's tall and so thin you'd think a good shit would kill him. They're from that far north they're nearly Norwegian and have soft Scottish accents.

After those races competing as a pair went well it seemed a natural progression to then do it as a solo. You might wonder where's the enjoyment in a 24-hour race? But summat clicked and I thought, I'll have a go at that, and once I committed to the idea of competing as a solo, I wanted to find the hardest 24-hour race anywhere in the world and that's the Strathpuffer. It has that reputation because of when and where it's held: the middle of winter, right in the north of Scotland. There are 17 hours of darkness. Even getting there is a pain in the arse.

For this year's race I met Tim and left at 11 in the morning for the drive up north. We try to stick to the road trip rules, only stopping when the van needs fuel, but I'm drinking so much, about four litres a day, to try get fully hydrated, that I have to stop and run behind a bush every now and then.

I reckon I had a bit of a cold coming on too, so I was drinking even more. I'd been training like hell when I could fit it in, but as soon as I backed off it gave my body the chance to get a cold, I reckon. The germs thought they detected a sign of weakness and were in.

We rented a house, instead of staying in a hotel or B&B, so I didn't have a disturbed night's sleep, and I had two pints of Guinness on the Friday night before the race. I think it set me up just right.

The race starts at ten on Saturday morning. I like this morning start because you can get home on Sunday night ready for work the next day. The Le Mans 24-Hour motorcycle race starts at four in the afternoon, so you've been up for hours that day, before you even get on the bike, and it makes it a bugger to get back home in good time after the finish.

You don't have a race face on at the start of a bike race like this, because all you're doing is playing the part. The race was won or lost three months before. October, November, December, January is the worst time of the year to be riding a bike in Britain, and that's when you have to do your preparation for the race, sat on your bike for 15 hours a week, every week. It's pretty grim. I know, for the eight or nine hours I'm driving up there, that I'm not going to enjoy it.

The Strathpuffer loop is about seven miles long and takes 50 minutes or thereabouts for me to do a lap. It's a forest track, the same every year, or at least it has been since I've been doing it. Half the Strathpuffer course is very technical, but just after the pits it's a fire road through the forest so I can eat or drink going up that bit. A fire road is a path cut through the woodland to contain a forest fire spreading from tree to tree and also to allow forestry traffic to move through. It's made of hard-packed shale on mud.

When I say the course is technical I mean it's single track, covered in rocks in some sections. When Forbes raced he would jump off his bike, put it on his back and run through these sections, but I stay on the bike. He's as good at running as he is cycling, but I'm not much of a runner.

The gradients are steep enough that I'm choosing the lowest gear to keep climbing and there is 1,500 feet of ascent per lap. A normal pub-on-a-Friday-night bloke would struggle to do one lap.

If I come up behind slower riders, I just say 'On your left' or 'On your right' and people let you through. Later in the race I'm just spouting gibberish: 'Nnnee. Bu.' Anything to

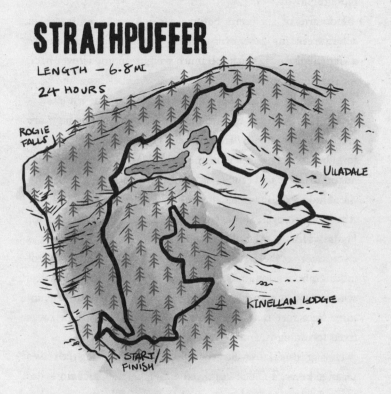

STRATHPUFFER

LENGTH — 6.8 MI

24 HOURS

ROGIE FALLS

ULLADALE

KINELLAN LODGE

START/FINISH

let them know you're there. It's the same for riders passing me. You respect each racer and they respect you. There's a fella, he must be 70, who does it solo. He's done it every year I have. I'm lapping him within a few hours, but he keeps plugging away.

I do five or six hours before I stop. I get given water, in a bottle for my cage, every time I pass the pits. I don't use a CamelBak because it's too much weight on your lower back for that length of time.

It might be me on the bike for 24 hours, but the race is such a team effort. Boys are getting the bikes ready, boys are getting the food ready. Tim, Francis, Forbes and Alan all come to help, and my dad has in the past. Alan is the person who introduced me to Francis and Forbes, who then got me into the whole 24-hour thing. I'd been asked to be a guest at the Alford Motorcycle show, years ago when I was still riding for Hydrex Honda. Alan picked me up from the airport. He was a scrutineer at the TT and builds sidecars from scratch. We got talking about mountain biking and he mentioned his mates, who turned out to be the Dungaits. Forbes needed a team-mate for a race that was coming up and asked me how I was fixed for doing it, and it grew from there.

During this latest Strathpuffer I swapped between two Orange bikes, a Clockwork and a Gyro. The Clockwork has front suspension and a hardtail frame, while the Gyro has suspension front and rear. They both have 29-inch wheels. I need two bikes, so one can be serviced while I'm out on the other. The gears are cleaned and the tyres are changed. In the middle of the night the bikes need spiked tyres, because the fire roads turn to solid ice, like glass. I run road tyres with tungsten tips in them. Hope, the parts company, gave me them. I've had the same ones for years because they don't wear out.

The temperature is never above freezing, but I only notice the cold when I stop and my sweat cools. My feet are cold, but I don't want to wear more or heavier socks because it's too much weight. Think of how many times you're lifting those socks over 24 hours ... It would add up. But I got the start of frostbite in my toes this year and it has made my toenails do funny things.

During the 24 hours there was snow, sleet, a double-hard frost and bright sunshine while it was still stupid cold.

Tim tries to stay awake for the full race. The first time he came to a 24-hour race with me, both him and my dad fell asleep. I came knocking on the van, saying, 'What the hell are you doing?' Fair play to them, they haven't dozed off since.

Tim doesn't give me any words of encouragement or talk any shit. He just keeps his gob shut and feeds me. That's all I need. He makes his own recipe of broth that is my rocket fuel. We're on the fourth evolution. Tim makes it with turkey, sweet potato, broccoli, carrots, spinach, quinoa, lentils: the best proteins and carbohydrates, he reckons. He's done his research. We used it for the world 24-hour tandem record that I did with Jason Miles for the *Speed* TV programme, too.

The temperature of the broth is important. It has to be tepid, just right, like Goldilocks would have it. If it's too hot, I'm wasting time waiting for it to cool. Is it's too cool, my body needs to use energy to heat it before digesting it. If you put cold food in your body, it sends blood to your stomach to digest it, rather than to your muscles.

Tim makes loads of this broth, because you're better looking at it than for it. I probably get through about the equivalent of five soup tins in the 24 hours. I have a bit of ravioli, some rice pudding and a coffee every now and then, as well. There comes a time when I just can't face food, but Tim seems to know when and he manages to get me going. Even if he just gives me some plain water for a lap.

We raid petrol stations on the way up for takeaway coffee cups, so I can drink the broth or coffee on the bike and chuck the cup away. The route is cleared up later.

I wear Five Tens, proper biking shoes that look like trainers, with overshoes on top, and Sealskinz waterproof socks, but my feet still get bloody cold. I wear shorts over leggings and, on top, a tight base layer, and a cycling top I bought from Lidl or Aldi. If it chucks it down I usually have a waterproof jacket, but I forgot it this year. I went to buy one from an outdoor shop on the way up, but they wanted £50, and I wasn't going to pay that, so I did without.

The race doesn't really start till two or three in the morning, 14 hours in. You have to be there or thereabouts till then, but that's when it sorts the men from the boys. At that time of the morning you start noticing riders having longer pit-stops. Tim and Alan will be checking the lap times of the other riders too. There's a timing screen, but it's a half-an-hour walk to it from where we pit.

No one even tells me where I am in the race till three in the morning. Part of me wants to know, but I have to ride my own race and not be influenced by anyone else. If I found out my position earlier it would be easy to push on to try and make up places, but that risks changing the whole rhythm of my race and might mean I would burn up energy I need to conserve for the end of the race. Finally learning my position in the race after 15 hours of pedalling can either be a little boost or a kick in the bollocks, depending where I am.

I found out Keith Forsyth was leading and I was second, then Jason Miles came past me. There are riders all over, but you don't know who you're racing, because there are teams of four and pairs and even teams of ten this year, but I'm only competing against the other solos. And the teams should be much quicker than us. If you look closely enough you can see the solo boys because they have a dibber thing, for lap-scoring, around their wrist, not around their neck like the teams. Otherwise they're just another figure in the darkness.

I've been soloing for a few years now and I know that what I used to think was hurting, isn't actually hurting. My body might be screaming at me, but I can ignore it and still put the power out. It's a state of mind. My back, arms, chest, neck, knees and feet are all hurting, but I'm mentally strong enough to get past it. That's how I was able to unlap myself from Jason Miles at 20 hours and unlap myself from Keith Forsyth a bit later. He was still ahead of me, but we were on the same lap. I was going through the pain, but I could deal with it. But those two looked broken. Forsyth was riding at a snail's pace, but I was still strong. I like getting into that state of mind, and this was the best I've ever been at dealing with the pain.

Some people say three or four in the morning is the worst for them, but it's always the last hour that is the worst for me. If there's any chance of winning I'd do whatever it takes to keep going, but otherwise you're just sustaining where you are. That was the position I was in this year.

In hour 23-and-a-half I was on the same lap as Keith Forsyth, but I'd taken longer to cover the same distance. It looked like if I set off on another lap – lap 28 – I would win. I started mentally trying to psych myself up to get back on the bike, even though I thought I'd done my last lap. I was absolutely and completely knackered, but I was prepared to go again. Then Tim learned he had missed Forsyth going again. Fuck, shit, bastard! I was in second place, out of 92 solos, and nothing I could do about it.

I had pushed hard, but I didn't win. Another hour and I think I would have, because I was going much quicker than the winner was. He had had it.

It was at the end of this race that a young lad brought me the box of Fudges and an I Love Tea cup, and I gave him some socks and we were both happy. Another fella came up at the end and gave me some lights off the bottom of a Lancaster's wing. They had belonged to his dad, who'd passed away, and the son gave them to me because he knew I'd appreciate them. And I do.

I pull on a pair of jeans, without having a shower, then brush my teeth. That helps me feel a bit better, because my teeth feel like sandpaper after all the salts and electrolytes in the energy gels I've swallowed. I don't feel properly recovered for two weeks after, though.

The prize-giving is in a tent, with a few hundred people, but to me it could be the MotoGP podium. The organisers save the awards for the solos till the end, and make a bit of a fuss of us.

The feeling of satisfaction on the drive home from the Strathpuffer can't be beaten. I don't need to say anything and no one needs to say anything to me. We're in the van by 12 or one and stop at Perth for Sunday dinner and a pint of Guinness with a drop of blackcurrant in it. We take it in turns to drive and we're back before midnight.

This year it was just me and Tim in my Transit and I felt sorry for him. He says I was like an old ewe on turnips. I don't have the best sense of smell, but I could tell it wasn't good. You could have my farts as one of your five a day.

The main reason I started doing solo mountain bike races was so I could just do some racing and push myself without getting mithered. I am on the bike for 24 hours and that was it. Now people are recognising me there, so I might need to find the next thing. It might sound ungrateful, but I'm not; the people who came up to me at the end of the race were lovely folk, but I do enjoy doing stuff as just a face in the crowd.

There's a race in North America called the Tour Divide, from Banff in Canada to New Mexico. It's the longest mountain bike race in the world, over 2,000 miles, 200,000 ft of climbing, in 14 days, or however long it takes. There are no stages, no designated overnight stops, the riders choose their own schedule and sleep when they want for as long as they want. First man to the finish wins. People are riding for 20 hours a day for two weeks. You can't eat enough to keep going, so your own body is eating itself. In a situation like that it's about keeping your head, while everything is trying to break you. And I like the sound of it.

CHAPTER 9

I had the confidence that my brain was cleverer than I was

I've done a lot of interesting stuff in the process of filming the *Speed* TV shows, but some of it has been a bit dangerous. Cycling blind at 112 mph on a beach, in the slipstream of a racing truck, got the heart pumping. Flipping that racing hovercraft could have been messy. Nosediving a Suzuki 450 cc motocrosser into a Welsh lake knocked the stuffing out of me. I crashed the sledge at 80-odd miles an hour, and you've already read how Brian had a hand in demolishing the beautiful carbon-fibre, downhill go-kart on Mont Ventoux in France. But it all sounds a bit 'So what?' compared to the next challenge. The idea is to set the highest speed ever recorded on a Wall of Death.

This popular fairground attraction dates back to the early teens of the 20th century. Motorbikes had hardly even proved themselves on the dirt roads of the day before folk were building huge wooden barrels to ride around, defying death on the vertical sides of the walls, stuck by centrifugal force. The Wall of Death looked amazing then and it still does today, a century later.

There used to be dozens of them in America and Britain, some set up permanently at seaside resorts, while others would travel to shows. The different walls would try to out-do each other with dafter ideas until one show had an adult male lion in a sidecar. Not many walls remain now, just a handful in Europe and America, but showmen in India have started building them again. From what I've seen, though, they're a bit jugaad.

Probably the most famous show still working is the Ken Fox Wall of Death, and I'd seen it at the Spalding bike show a few years back. The show lasts about 15 minutes, costs a couple of quid to get in, and the family have been touring since 1995. The crowd stand around the top of the wall, under a Big Top type tent, looking down on the wall and the riders below. It's mega when they have the race, with three riders on the wall, all zig-zagging up and down at 30-odd mph, nearly touching the wire at the top, right under the noses of the crowd. The whole thing is a good show, but even while I was watching it there was a little bit of me that was saying, in a squeaky little voice, *I could do that, I could do that.* It's not screaming, not drawing attention, just quietly stating it.

When I saw the show I never thought I'd get a chance to

see if I could, but that's the TV job for you. The original idea was to attempt 100 mph on a Wall of Death, over three times as fast as anyone reaches on the world's remaining walls, but when the researchers looked into it they reckoned that would be impossible because I would have to be pulling 10 g to do that. 10 g is ten times the force of gravity. Under 10 g a bloke who has a mass of 11 stone, about what I am, weighs 110 stone. That's because mass is constant, but weight is relative to gravity. If you were on the moon, where the gravity is about one-sixth of what it is on Earth, you could pick up something that you could never shift on earth, but its mass is exactly the same. A human head, that makes up about 8 per cent of the mass of an adult, in my case would weigh about 12 lb, or 5 kg, if you chopped it off and put it on a kitchen scale (but just take my word for it). At 10 g my neck muscles would be trying to hold up 8.5 stone (55 kg) of head, plus the 15 kg or more of helmet. But that's not the main problem; it's the fact that the g-force is too much for the human body's circulation system and the heart isn't strong enough to pump enough blood to the brain. The blood congregates in the lower half of the body and that causes black-outs and a g-LOC – a gravity-induced Loss Of Consciousness.

It was decided – I can't remember who by – that I could probably cope with 8 g, at the very most, and that equates to a speed of about 80 mph. Still, the chances of blacking out and losing consciousness are high. And to even attempt that speed we need to build the biggest Wall of Death ever made.

Hugh Hunt, an Aussie professor at Cambridge University, worked out the ideal diameter to be 120 ft (36.5 metres). Ken

Fox's Wall of Death, the one I saw at the bike show, is 32 ft (9.7 m) across. I always weigh up the length of things by how they compare to a truck's trailer. The biggest trailer you get on a British road is a 40 ft fridge box, so the diameter of Ken Fox's wall is less than the length of one of those. The wall that will be built for my record attempt is three times as big. It's so big that it makes me think, How am I ever going to stick on the wall?

But that's all well down the line. When I said I'd do the TV programme and attempt the record, all I knew about the Wall of Death was what I'd seen with the rest of the crowd. The TV lot approached Ken Fox to be involved in the programme, to be the expert and teach me how to do it. He agreed, and on 10 February I went to visit him and his family at the yard they're based in, near Ely in Cambridgeshire.

Ken Fox is the third generation of his family to be the owner of, and rider on, the Wall of Death. It's a family business that involves his wife, two sons, Luke and Alex, and his daughters-in-law, Luke's missus Kerri and Alex's other half Abbi, plus Jamie, a young woman rider, and other riders and crew like Danny Danger and Ken Wolfe. The Fox family have two walls; one dates back to 1928, and Ken built the other one himself, from Oregon pine, in 1994–5. They're loaded onto the back of trucks and driven around Britain all season. The walls take a good day to assemble, but only three or four hours to break down. They ride antique Indian Scouts, one of them over 90 years old, 1970s Honda CB200s and a motorised go-kart.

It was arranged that I'd spend two days with them, learning the basics, and I turned up knowing nothing. I didn't make out I knew what I was on about or even had the first clue, so anything Ken and the family told me, I listened. Right at the start Ken said I would be better off not even knowing how to ride a motorbike, and being a completely blank canvas.

To put the shits up me, before I even started to be taught how to ride, I sat on the handlebars of his Indian while Ken set off and rode the wall. He was dressed in his jeans and trainers, like he was off to walk the dog, and so was I. As we were riding round and round he was pointing at the camera and telling me where to look and saying all the things he could see, but everything was a total blur to me and then I started to feel sick. Ken told me to wave, but because of the g-force I couldn't lift my hand up, I was just glued in place. But in the show I'd seen Kerri and Jamie, two slim women – eight stone soaking wet, I reckon – doing what they can do, none-handed, lying on the bike, riding side-saddle none-handed, and it's amazing.

Then it was my turn. Lesson number one was me sitting on the bike being pushed around on the flat base inside the wall, with the engine running but in neutral, so I got used to the noise of the bike. Even that made me dizzy. Next I rode around the bottom, completely on the flat, and after that I was so dizzy the boys had to hold me up when I stopped.

I'd sit down for five minutes and try again, but I was getting dizzy really quickly after every break. I still hadn't reset the system in each five minutes off while I sat on the floor, so Ken said the best thing to do was half an hour in the wall, then go out and have a cup of tea, before going back in for another half an hour. That 10 or 15 minutes having a cup of tea and reading the *Daily Sport* in my van was enough to reset the system and get back on it. When we climbed back into the wall we'd start where we left off, but up another gear on the bike so I was going quicker, or a bit higher up the track. The track is what the Foxes call the 45-degree banked section that forms the transition between the flat and the vertical wall.

During a riding session we'd break halfway through and spend five minutes talking about what I'd done and what I was expected to do next, while we stood in the centre of the wall. Then I'd do a bit more riding before going outside for another reset.

At this stage, when I was still on the track, I was riding in my woolly hat. None of the Fox riders ever wear a helmet and I was all for doing it like they do, but then Ewan, the director, said, 'Look, you're going to have to wear a helmet when you do the attempt, so you better get used to riding with a helmet on.' Fair enough, I thought. It made sense, so I wore my black and yellow road race AGV helmet. It's not part of the Fox family's show to wear a helmet, but for what I was planning to do they understood.

No one mentioned if the girls or Alex, the youngest son, had ever had any crashes, but Luke had a big one in Germany when he was younger. He put his wheel over the top of the wall, and there's only one outcome when you do that. He was thrown 18 foot to the ground and skinned his chest. He finished the show before going to hospital, though. They say you've got to get back on straight away, if you're physically able to.

Even Ken had crashed the year before I joined them for lessons. He was stood on the side of his Indian, so both feet on one of the old-fashioned footplates that were fitted back then instead of footpegs; his arms straight out, crucifix-style, looking up at the crowd stood around the top – it's one of the most impressive stunts they do on the Indians. Then one of the brackets holding the footplate to the frame broke and he came off. As I said, the Wall of Death riders don't wear helmets, they look more like they're off to ride a horse than a motorbike, so when Ken hit the floor he didn't have any protection. He bashed his head and did this, did that, and nearly ripped his ear clean off. It was hanging on by a thread, Luke says, and it had to be glued back on at the hospital. As Ken was in the ambulance the police turned up at the wall and wanted to impound everything, but Luke, the eldest son, wasn't having any of it. He got onto his dad (who must have had the phone to his good ear) and Ken was all for pulling his boots back on and discharging himself to sort it out; but Luke rang the Health and Safety bloke who inspects the wall and he told Luke the police had no right to take the bikes because no one else was injured. Eventually they left them to it.

So although people might think they could ride the Wall of Death, even the professional riders, who've been doing it for half their lives or more, are pushing their luck and when it goes wrong it hurts. The problem is, they make it look too easy.

I wasn't trusted with the Indians, I was doing all my riding on an old Honda CB200, from the late 70s, early 80s. If I saw it on the street I'd think, what a heap of shit, but it's a Wall of Death machine. Big respect.

By the end of the first day I'd only got halfway up the track, the 45-degree slope. I didn't know if that was good or not, compared to other learners. It didn't feel too good.

Normally when we're filming, the cameramen, the soundmen, the directors and I are all as thick as thieves and stick together, usually going out to eat together, but I was invited to eat a homemade curry with the Foxes that night and I was happy to. Right from the off, me and Ken were on the same wavelength. Ken is really straight-talking to the point of being rude. Very Mick Moody-ish in that way. And like with my boss, you know where you stand. Ken is a Scania man too. And you can tell he enjoys going on the wall every time he rides it. He wouldn't tell me his age, probably in his mid fifties, and you wouldn't mess with him.

Even after spending all day there, I was sat round their table talking with the whole family for five hours. In winter the family live in static caravans in their yard, and when I first met them, in February, they were itching to get out to the shows. They're out from before Easter to October and I think that's great. I love the whole idea of it. Ken runs one wall, while Luke runs the other one, so they can cover twice as many events.

Luke, the eldest son, was 28 when we started the filming, and had a baby due any day, with Kerri. She got the job of a Wall of Death rider after seeing it advertised in the local job centre. At the time she applied she thought it was something to do with horses, and had never ridden or had any interest in motorbikes. She was 19 when she landed the job and joined the Ken Fox Troupe, and Luke must have thought all his Christmases had come at once, because she's not hard to look at.

While he is younger than me, Luke sees a lot of things the way I do. He loves his job, but he wants to try different things as well as the Wall of Death. He's just put a 1000 cc Yamaha R1 engine in a Mini, mucking about to get a Subaru back axle to fit. Luke and his brother Alex started riding the wall when they were 11 years old, and Ken's dad and granddad were Wall of Death men too.

They explained they class their show as family entertainment, not a motorcycle show. Their biggest event is the Glastonbury Festival, another big one is Bestival, the music festival on the Isle of Wight, and they do other music festivals. They also do country shows, steam festivals and bike shows, but they say they get better crowds, who appreciate them more, at music festivals than at bike shows, because at bike events the 'Power Rangers' – the kind of sportsbike riders in bright leathers who think they're it – rock up and they all think they can do it so they don't get into it the same way.

I've met some sound people, during filming: Jason Rourke, who built the top speed record bicycle; Dave Jenkins, the racing truck driver; David from Hallam University – and the Foxes are right in there, though I'm not classing one better than the other. These people are the soundest I've ever met, but this filming job was different, because it's probably the first time that I've really entered someone else's world. Normally they're brought in to help me.

Late that night I drove back to the hotel and sat on the bed thinking things through. I had arrived at the Foxes' yard in the morning believing, I can do this. Then after riding on Ken's handlebars all I could think was, Bloody hell … When

I started going round in tight circles, even at walking pace, I was so dizzy that I felt the chances of me riding on the wall were even worse. I couldn't even ride on the track at the bottom. These two days were dead important, because if I didn't get a grip of riding on the wall then the whole thing that had been planned would be off. With everything I'd done before, all the speed attempt records, I just thought I had to put the effort in and we had a good chance, but this time I had my doubts. After sitting on the little Honda and being pushed around by Ken that morning, I honestly thought, This isn't happening, but after a cup of tea stuff would slowly improve. The familiarity helped things fall into place. As I sat on my bed I was fascinated by how the human body was working. I'd felt so dizzy I couldn't stand, but then the brain started working out the maths of the situation and decided, Right, we need to do this, this and this. I don't know what was happening, but my brain was working out how to deal with it.

At the start of the second day, I had the confidence that my brain was cleverer than I was and it was working out how to deal with the job in hand. It was working it out subconsciously, saying, We need to alter this chemical balance here and we've got a bad earth there.

We started the second day where we ended the first day. I'd do a run of five laps, stop, sit and talk about it, run again, then go outside: fresh air; cup of tea; *Daily Sport*. Then back in again and aim to go a bit faster and a bit higher for another five laps. With the speed I was going at, the centrifugal force was trying to sling me out to the side of the track and onto the transition of the banked track and the vertical wall. Ken explained that it was good that I could keep control of the bike and I had enough confidence to turn it in and keep the bike on the track when nature's forces wanted to send me and the bike onto the wall, but I still wasn't going quite fast enough to stick to the wall. I had to fight to keep it on the track to build up enough speed to make it stick to the wall.

I did that for a while and then Ken said, 'Right, you're up to the right speed and you're not too dizzy, you can get up on the wall now.' But getting my head into making the transition from the track onto the vertical wall took some doing. By now it was really hard to stay on the track because the centrifugal force was pushing me off it.

Ken was a brilliant instructor. He's taught a load of people to ride the wall, and the way he splits the lessons makes it not seem such a big deal to be riding around a vertical wall, only a day-and-a-bit after I was dizzy just being pushed around on the flat at walking pace. He went about it the right way. I'd ride at one part of the track, then we'd go out and have a cup of tea, then I'd ride a little bit higher.

Ken would say, 'Look at the wall, look at the front wheel, look at the wall, look at the front wheel.' He repeated it until it got boring, but he was right. He had me on the wall in less than two days and I did 40 laps solo. The problem is, when I did make it onto the wall I didn't know up from down or left from right. I was totally disorientated.

The right speed for Ken Fox's Wall of Death is about 25–30 mph. It feels fast in a 32 ft wooden drum, but it's bugger-all compared to the speed I'm going to attempt. Ken and Luke said they can get to 40 mph on their wall, but at that speed they are at the point of blacking out from the g-force starving their brain of blood.

Because of their experience they know what happens just before they black out, and that when their vision goes they need to tense their whole bodies and back off the throttle slightly until their vision returns and they can go again. Tensing the body tightens the blood vessels to stop the body's blood sinking to their legs. They know where that crucial point is: the rider's vision goes grey; then they get tunnel vision, where you lose peripheral vision; then you lose vision totally, that's the black-out; finally you lose consciousness. It can happen quickly and I've got to learn where the point is. I need to learn what it feels like to very nearly black out and come back again. If I do black out, it can go one way or the other. I can collapse on the handlebars, let off the throttle and crash into the bottom. Then it's a case of straightening everything out, dusting myself down and going again. But the other way is I pass out, keep hold of the throttle, got out of the top at over 80 mph, and go into the rafters. Which is likely to kill me. I don't need to be doing that. I need to learn, Right, I'm blacking out. Tense up, back off.

With a much bigger wall, you need to be going faster to stick to the wall, but because it's a bigger diameter the g-force is lower than it would be for the same speed in a smaller diameter wall. Still, I'm trying to go twice as fast as blacking-out speed on the Foxes' wall. I was told most people black out at 6–7 g. And I'm trying to withstand 10–12 g. There was talk of me wearing a g-suit, like fighter pilots wear. These compress the body to help deal with slightly higher g-forces for longer. It's not a magic bullet and at the time of writing it's been decided there isn't a lot of point in using it, so I've got some serious acclimatising to do.

Plus, I don't just want to be the fastest ever rider on the Wall of Death, I want to do it on a bike I've built myself. The default would be to use a modern 450 motocross bike, something that would only need a few modifications and then be ready to go, but I explained to Ken that I wanted to do it my way, like I did with the Pikes Peak race. That isn't always the easy way, and I'll admit it isn't always the right way, but it's in my DNA. Ken had seen the TV programmes, so he knew about the Pikes Peak Martek. The bike I plan to do the Wall of Death attempt on is an old Triumph Triple engine, from the 1970s, in a Rob North replica racing frame. It's a bike like my dad owns. Ken liked the idea and his lads came to see the bike at my house. Well, it was still a bare frame when they came, but they reckoned it would work because the centre of gravity looked like it would be in the right place, nice and low. Then it's a case of getting the handlebars in the right place.

It's more important for me to build this bike for the Wall of Death than for me to spend time preparing a bike for the TT or anything like that, because I really believe nothing else I've done in life can compare to this attempt.

I can't even imagine what the wall is going to look like. It will be built for two weeks and the TV show is going out live, with, I'm told, Davina McCall presenting it. What's it going to be like stood in the middle of this 120 ft diameter, 20 ft tall wooden Wall of Death? It was originally going to be built in my garden, but because the TV show is going to be broadcast live – or that's the plan – the TV bods don't want the weather to be an issue. So it will be built in a warehouse and have shipping containers positioned around it to stop it from flexing.

Even after the speeds I've been at the TT and the Ulster Grand Prix, and now with the little bit of experience I've had actually riding a Wall of Death, I still can't imagine what it's going to be like. And I have the added problem of trying to fit in the training that Ken says I have to do, plus build a one-off bike, in what is turning out to be the busiest year of my life.

CHAPTER 10

I don't want any regrets when I finally do stop racing

I had been thinking about packing in road racing on and off since the 2014 TT. Probably even before that. If I'm on the ferry home from the Isle of Man and having to ask myself the question, 'Did I enjoy that?' – no matter what the answer is, if I'm even having to ask myself that question, is it really the right thing to carry on doing? And when the answer to the question is, 'No, I'm not enjoying it', then something has got to change. But then I'd go to three of my favourite races, the Southern 100, Armoy and the Ulster Grand Prix, and I'd be back into it again, which would make me feel positive about racing into the next year, and at the Ulster meeting I'd normally sign up with Philip Neill, the TAS team manager, for another season.

I wasn't thinking about stopping racing completely, just trying to work out if I could miss the TT and the North West. But then I'd wonder which serious team would want a road racer who isn't going to compete in the biggest meetings of the road racing year? So perhaps it would be the end.

When an interview in *The Times*, in February 2015, reported that I was packing in racing, stopping filming anything for TV and all this, that and the other, everyone started saying I was retiring, but I hadn't put it like that at the time. I was only ever talking about the TT and giving TV a rest for a bit after a busy year of filming in 2014. The interview took place after I'd signed for TAS, but if I really had had enough I wouldn't go to the TT, contract or no contract. If I backed out, it wouldn't be in a cowardly way or to join another team, it would be because I realised enough was enough. I've always said when it stops being fun I'll stop doing it. It's not my bread and butter, so I don't have to do it. But I suppose it made a better headline if it sounded like I was going to jack it all in.

Even if I did stop entering road races, I had it in my head that I'd still race other bikes in other types of events. I still love the Southern 100, but only when I'm competitive, and to be on the pace you have to be racing regularly on the roads. If the only road race I did every year was the Southern 100, I wouldn't be quick enough. I like the idea of a season of World Endurance Racing. I've done Le Mans and the Bol d'Or 24-hour races, and I like the whole team effort involved in a race like that. I'd like to race the Suzuka 8-Hour in Japan, and that's part of the World Endurance series. I'd do Pikes Peak again, too. I'd still race dirt track. I want to be good enough to race the Peoria TT in the USA. That's a big goal of mine. What the Americans call a TT and what those of us who have been brought up with the Isle of Man think when we hear TT is totally different. Peoria is part of the American Grand National dirt track championship. It's a dirt track race with one jump.

When I try to weigh up whether or not I want to race the Isle of Man TT, I think about the last one I really enjoyed and that was the first year with the TAS team in 2011. A bit of that enjoyment might have come from me proving that I still had it after the 2010 crash. I knew my head was alright, but it was still good to have a fast lap of the TT under my belt, be on the pace and not be scared, apprehensive or distracted by what happened at Ballagarey the year before. The final hour of the 2014 TT was the other side of the whole TT experience. I was trying to load up my van, leave the pits and catch the ferry, and it was just hard work. I had just finished third in the Senior, I'd had an alright TT results-wise and should have been pleased with what the team and I had achieved, but any gloss there was from a job well done was taken off sharpish by people being rude when I was trying catch a ferry and get home after a long two weeks. Before the 2015 season started I already had a feeling I wasn't going to enjoy the TT. Even so, it's like a 24-hour mountain bike race: during it I'm not enjoying it, but after it I know I put all that effort in and got something out of it.

I still want to win a TT, but after the 2014 TT I felt I'd gone as far as I could with the Suzuki I was riding for TAS. The GSX-Rs were fast and well sorted, just not fast enough.

I was always the first home on a Suzuki superbike in the races I finished, and beat every team-mate I've had at the TT on the big bikes, either the superbikes or superstockers, again in the races I finished. William Dunlop beat me on the GSX-R600 in 2014, though.

The financial crisis hit the Japanese sportsbike market hard and all their development slowed. There was no word of a new or radically improved GSXR-1000 coming any time soon, so the basis of the bikes I was racing was getting left further behind. I want to go to the Isle of Man thinking I can win. I don't want to spend two weeks of my life over there just making up the numbers.

Something had to change, and it did when TAS's team manager Philip Neill told me they were splitting with Suzuki, who they'd been with since 2000, to run BMWs instead. Up until I got the phone call it had all been 'he said, she said'. Would Paul Bird or Buildbase or TAS become the official BMW-supported team? But in early December Philip confirmed that TAS had been chosen. The challenge of riding the BMW gave me the reason to continue for another year at least.

If TAS had have stayed with Suzuki for another season, then it's pretty likely 2014 would have been my last Isle of Man. I didn't want to race for any team other than the Northern Irish lot, and I felt I couldn't do anything more than I had already with the Suzukis as they were. It didn't leave me many options.

In the road bike world the BMW has kicked the arse of the Japanese since it was launched in 2009–10. Not on the racetrack, because the Kawasaki had been very successful too, but in all the magazine tests and also in terms of sales.

I had only ever had a short ride on a BMW S1000RR, when it first came out, but the standard road bike, that anyone could buy out of a showroom for £12,000 or summat at the time, felt quicker than my tuned, mega-money TT superbike. Then Michael Dunlop got on the BMW for the 2014 season, with BMW backing, and won a TT the first time out. (He'd won on other makes too. Never a Suzuki, though.) I beat him at other races that season, and the BMW seemed to struggle at some tracks, but it went well around the Isle of Man.

I don't know what happened between BMW, Michael Dunlop and the Hawk team, who did such a good job at the 2014 TT, but they split. That left a gap for TAS to move in. Michael signed to race for Shaun Muir's Yamaha team, and William Dunlop and I would be on the BMWs.

The news of the BMW deal changed everything. I don't want any regrets when I finally do stop racing. I know that if I didn't race a TT with the TAS team and BMW, I would grow old a miserable bastard thinking 'What if? What if?' – so I decided to do one more. That way I shouldn't have any regrets. I've got everything set out in my head. I know why I'm going to retire. I know why I'm not going to enter a particular race or why I am going to race another. Nothing is spur of the moment; even though some rare thoughts go through my mind, everything is calculated before I go ahead and act on them. It is hardly rocket science, though. It's just considered.

In the area of motorbike sport I'm involved with, all the road racing team announcements usually happen a good while after the MotoGP and World Superbike teams finalise their team line-ups. I don't know why, because TAS are hardly waiting to see if Marc Márquez is available before deciding to stick with me for another year. It's just the way it is and it's no skin off my nose. It always gets sorted out.

A few weeks before the TAS and BMW news broke, there was an announcement that Ryan Farquhar was returning to race superbikes at the TT. He had retired after his uncle, Trevor Ferguson, died racing at the Manx Grand Prix in 2012. Farquhar made the decision to pack in just after the fatal accident and it was totally understandable. He was even quoted as saying, 'I'm finished with racing. I've been racing a long time and I've lost a lot of friends in that time, but it's different when it comes to your own doorstep.'

The quote continued, referring to the accident: 'What I have witnessed in the past 24 hours I've never seen before. It's the people who are left behind who suffer the most. Trevor probably didn't know anything about the crash, but the people left behind are hit the hardest.

'His wife and girls are in pieces. I don't ever want Karen and my two girls to ever have to go through something like that. This is a sport I love, but I can't risk putting my family through something like that any more – I have to think of them.'

Ryan had been racing a long time and has two daughters. After he stopped racing in 2012 he continued to run his own KMR team and had some high-profile success, but a while later he announced he was making a comeback and would ride the smaller bikes, the Kawasaki 650 twins he had developed and had won a lot of races on. Then came the news he was coming back to race the superbikes at the 2015 TT. He added, 'I'm not going out there to waste tyres and fuel.'

When I found out about his decision it made me think, Spread your wings, boy. Farquhar is a clever bloke, a good bike builder; I just hoped he'd get out of it. It seems he's been blinkered, indoctrinated into the motorbike world. Like he can't see past his nose end. He had got out alive. I'm not trying to make road racing sound like someone signing up for their tenth tour of Afghanistan, but quit while you're ahead. And it looked like he had. He'd had a mega career, he won more Irish races than anyone ever has, and probably ever will. But it seems he hasn't found anything to replace the buzz he got from racing. He got massively into clay pigeon shooting, but that obviously hasn't filled the hole. My advice would be, Keep looking for something else.

I look at my fellow racers and think, That is not what I want to turn into. That's another thing that is pushing me away from road racing. By moving on and doing something else, I'll stop falling into that trap. But one more time wouldn't hurt, would it?

Another rider who has been doing it a long time and doesn't seem to be thinking about packing racing in is John McGuinness. The man is a legend, but he went down in my estimation at the 2014 TT. During the Superstock race I pulled up at Parliament Square in Ramsay, when the front wheel spindle nut came off. The person who saw that nut fly off was mega. They not only saw it and knew what it was, but they had to be bloody confident to tell a marshal to black flag me, and ruin my race. Fair play. I'd like to meet him or her. I wouldn't have the bollocks to do what they did. If I was spectating I'd convince myself into thinking it couldn't have been a wheel nut ...

The reason it came loose enough to fall off was because I'd asked for a slightly softer setting on the front forks. When the bike was hitting the bigger bumps the forks were cracking off the bottom of the stroke. That was happening right from the start of the race. The impact of the forks bottoming out twisted the fork slightly and allowed the nut to work loose. I'm not trying to convince myself, so I can trust the team again; I know that is a fact. Anyway, four clamp bolts in the bottom of the fork legs hold the front wheel spindle, so it wouldn't have gone anywhere, but the marshals did exactly the right thing. I could've finished that race, and nobody would have died and no one would've been any the wiser, but I'm pleased whoever noticed it spoke out. Still, without being over-dramatic, I know who tightened up that bolt and I still trust him with my life.

Anyway, in that Superstock race the black flag was waved at me halfway through the third lap. The black flag is to tell a rider to stop straight away, normally because there is something dangerous about them or their bike. It only applies to the racer it is shown to, and usually another marshal holds a chalk board with your number scrawled on it to make sure you know it's you, so you're not left thinking it might be a rider in front or behind you.

I'd had my one and only pit-stop of this four-lap race and I was running second, third, fourth – nip and tuck, nowt in it between three or four of us. After I pulled out of the race

I was having a brew, waiting for the race to finish, so I could get picked up and taken back to the pits, when McGuinness came through on his last lap. He was riding injured, after damaging his hand crashing a dirt bike in the winter, and hadn't been right for the whole of the TT, but he came through waving at the crowd. He was still in the top ten, but I thought, What the fuck are you doing? We come here to race and try our hardest. You don't wave at the crowd unless you're winning by a country mile. You can't blame him for not riding balls-out, because his wrist was in bad shape, but he'd only come for the money and he was trying to soften the blow by waving when he'd made himself look daft.

I still have a massive amount of respect for McGuinness's achievements; the list of TT race wins speaks for itself, and he won the TT Zero race on the Mugen Shinden that week; but I just have a bit less respect than I did have. I would have had more if he hadn't raced at all.

So, for now, I'm still an Isle of Man TT racer. My entry is in and accepted and I'll be running number eight.

One complication about TAS changing from Suzuki to BMW is the fact BMW don't make a Supersport bike. This means at race meetings where I would normally race Superbike, Superstock 1000 and Supersport, I no longer have a default little bike for the Supersport races. If you race for Suzuki you have their 1000 and 600. The same with Kawasaki, Yamaha and Honda.

Ideally Philip Neill would prefer me riding nothing in the Supersport class, but that doesn't appeal to me. At the TT racing the extra class is pretty important to a rider because it gives you more laps during the two weeks you're there. You have more bikes to concentrate on setting up, but the trade-off with the amount of time you spend on track is worth it, I reckon.

Philip Neill's second choice would be for me to ride one of the TAS Suzuki GSX-R600s they already have from 2014. Riding one of last year's 600s wasn't floating my boat either. It's outgunned now. William got on the podium in 2014, but I was sixth and tenth in the races I finished. This might be my last TT, so I wanted the right bikes. That meant I had to start looking for a 600 to ride.

In the background of this was an interesting offer from Metzeler, the tyre company I've used for years. Their idea was for them to organise an opportunity for me to try and break the motorcycle lap record at the Nürburgring. I'd get a crack at trying something I've been interested in for a while, and Metzeler would use the record attempt to promote their tyres.

The Nürburgring was originally built in 1927 as an alternative to racing on the public roads of the area. There's a modern F1 grand prix track there too, but the track I'm talking about is the Nordschleife.

Like the Isle of Man TT course, the Nürburgring Nordschleife is now a public road. It runs through forests. When it was built it probably didn't seem any more dangerous than any other racetracks, but it got a reputation and the Formula One driver Jackie Stewart nicknamed it the Green Hell. Back when driver safety wasn't any kind of priority it wasn't marshalled properly, so if someone had an accident, it took a long time to get to the injured driver. Sometimes cars would crash and the authorities didn't even know until the team realised their car and driver hadn't come through on schedule.

Now it's a toll road and a bit of a do-before-you-die destination for bike riders and car drivers. You can buy a ticket to do a lap of the track and fill your boots. There's no speed limit, but on a public day there are no marshals or ambulances and there's all kinds of vehicles out on track, from Porsche Turbos to tourist buses, all doing massively different speeds and taking different lines.

The more I thought about Metzeler's idea, the more into the whole thing I got. I'd been learning the track for months. I watched an on-board video of the current motorcycle lap record on YouTube in my break. The record is held by an English fella called Andy Carlile. I don't know him well but I've met him and he's a good old boy.

There might have been someone quicker round there, but there's no evidence of it. The fastest recorded motorcycle lap is Andy Carlile's at 7 minutes 10 seconds, set in 2012.

The record was set on a regular public day. Carlile passes five bikes and three cars. I don't know what time of day he did it, but I reckon it's early in the morning. You can never do a full or flying lap of the Nürburgring on a regular day, because you enter the track after going through a car park-style barrier, and then, at the end of the lap, you take a slip road back into the car park. So the lap is recorded from 'bridge to gantry'. It's set from the time you go under a footbridge, just after entering the track, to the time you pass under the gantry where you have to start braking for the car park. You can't pass the car park. The bridge to gantry lap is supposed to be 11.9 miles.

Metzeler had started talking about renting the track. Lots of car companies do that for testing and filming, but I wanted my attempt to be under the same conditions as Andy Carlile's – open to tourists, with the chance of traffic to deal with.

When we told the TV lot at North One about the idea they were dead keen on filming it. Then Andy Spellman got talking to Triumph headquarters at Hinckley about the whole Nürburgring thing and they said they'd do anything they could to help, supply a trick bike, using Metzeler tyres of course, and all this and that. It was suggested they could supply a supersport bike for the TT as well.

I reckon I could get a BMW S1000RR to ride at the Nürburgring pretty easily. TAS would be all over it and BMW too, I would have thought, but I preferred the idea of a British bike and a British rider taking on a German track. I like that the Triumph's triple engine is a bit different too, not the regular superbike four-cylinder. I know the Triumph 675 is fast, but it's not as fast as a BMW S1000RR, so why not get the fastest bike possible? I originally thought that. I was even thinking about building a bike with a supercharger on it. Then I consider using my Pikes Peak bike, the Martek with its turbocharged Suzuki 1271 cc engine, but it's not all about speed around the Nürburgring.

The track flows and is similar to the TT – both are about momentum and rolling through the corners, not braking almost to a stop and accelerating hard out of hairpins. It's about maintaining momentum, the kind of riding I like. There is only one little bit where it's head down, arse up, elbows and knees tucked in, so you're not going to gain much by having a million horsepower. You need good, usable power and nice handling. The record is set on a Yamaha R1, making 150–160 horsepower. A really good Triumph Daytona 675 can make 142 brake horsepower, and weighs less than the R1.

Andy Carlile lives near the track, or he did when I met him, and he'd moved out there in 2007 with the single aim of becoming the fastest man on two wheels around the Nürburgring. That was his sole focus, but the reason I think I can go out a few weekends in the summer, then have a go and beat his record, is because I reckon I'm a better rider than him. Valentino Rossi is a better motorbike racer than me and I'm a better one than Andy Carlile. I see it as a cold, hard fact. I watch the on-board video and see he's not applying the TT mentality to the job. Cadwell Park mentality isn't the best for the Nürburgring. And his technique is closer to Cadwell than Isle of Man. He's having the back end chattering, skipping on the brakes, into the slow corners as he locks the back brake up, when really it's about braking early and carrying the momentum through the corner onto whatever straight follows. He knows the track miles better than me and he'll be miles faster than me to start with, but I will beat him. His lines are good, but his momentum isn't as good as it could be.

I'd watched the video 20 times before I started seeing where I could be quicker. Up till then I thought, He's bloody good. Now I watch it, and while he's still bloody good, I know all his mistakes. Maybe he's already broken his own record and is keeping it quiet until someone breaks his 7 m 10 s lap.

Metzeler had got a fair way down the line with organising everything, when the folk at the Nürburgring shit themselves.

After seeming like they were all for it, they got in touch with the tyre company and said, 'We don't want any motorbike records breaking around here. The track's not designed for motorbikes.' So that immediately put a stop to the TV programme. North One is a proper company and couldn't be involved with something that had been officially blocked, but I still wanted to do it anyway and it might turn out better for me. The TV lot wanted me to attempt the record in April 2015, but I wanted to go for it later in the year, to give myself more chance to drive over there with the bike in the back of the Transit and do practice laps. And the weather is unpredictable in April. Leave it till later in the year and I'd have more luck getting a better day. Doing it to my own timescale would give me the summer to plan, go and do laps to get up to speed and hopefully break the record. If I could fit it all in.

After they heard there wasn't going to be a Channel 4 TV show about the attempt, Triumph seemed to lose a bit of interest unless I was tied into some commercial deal with them, and I wasn't mad keen on that. The whole Nürburgring thing had escalated from the original idea, so it was no bad thing, but it was the middle of February, I was without a supersport bike for the TT and the Nürburgring was all up in the air too. I had to get some irons in the fire.

Back at the 2014 TT, I was in one of the two Supersport 600 races when Gary Johnson passed me on Sulby Straight, one of the fastest parts of the TT circuit. I'm not taking anything away from him, because he was riding well and went on to win the race, but I was tucked in, arse on the back of the seat to be as aerodynamic as possible, not hanging around, and the Triumph came past me so easily I thought, Bloody hell! So when I started thinking seriously about supersport bikes my first call was to the people who built his race bike, Smiths Triumph.

Before I spoke to them I didn't know that much about their set-up, but I knew they were in road haulage. Then I found out they have a load of businesses and one of them is the race team. The team is run by the company founder's daughter, Rebecca Smith. They'd been in business as a race team since 2010. Their first year on the roads was 2014, when they won a TT. I also knew John Trigger builds their engines. I made my first call to them in the middle of February, saying, 'You've got proven bikes. I want to buy one.' They quoted me silly money, £36,000 or summat for a Supersport 600. And it was one of last year's. Ten minutes later they rang me back and asked if I'd race for them. I didn't give them an answer there and then, saying I'd think about it.

The following week I was in work at Moody's on Monday, then filming Tuesday and Wednesday, then back into work Thursday morning. Moody came in at dinnertime and said, 'What are you doing tonight? How are fixed to go to Holland tonight and come back Saturday morning?' He wanted me to go out with him to Holland and pick up some Scanias he was buying over there and selling over here.

Me, Moody and Darren, who owns Kelsa, a company that make all the truck light bars, all went out in the Transit and two of us drove trucks back, with me driving one of the Scanias. It was a two-pedal and beautiful to drive. None of the big V8s have a gear lever, it's all computer-controlled because they have that much torque there's too much chance of abusing the gearbox. The log men, the drivers who transport loads of tree trunks out of the forests, want three-pedal, like a regular manual car, because they need a bit more control when they are on dirt roads and struggling for traction. General haulage and fridge work drivers choose the two-pedal option.

The reason this trip with Moody to Holland is relevant, and thanks for bearing with me, is the boss of the Scania place we were collecting the trucks from. He didn't know I was into motorbikes, but for some reason we got onto the subject and it turns out he knew someone at Ten Kate. A tuning company based in Holland, Ten Kate run a team that has won seven World Supersport world titles and one World Superbike championship, all with Hondas they've tuned and prepared themselves. James Toseland won the 2007 World Superbike championship on one of their Fireblades, and they've had loads of top riders race for them including Leon Haslam and Jonny Rea.

The Dutch Scania bloke said he would have a word with them about a TT bike. A few minutes later he came back and said Ten Kate would build me a Honda CBR600 Supersport but they wanted to meet me face to face and it would cost €35,000. So, at that stage, if the Smiths Triumph thing didn't happen I could go out the following Monday and order a bike from Ten Kate.

Mates have asked why I didn't buy a road bike, tune and build a good Supersport bike myself, and you might be wondering that too, because in the past it was the way I'd try to do things. The reason I wouldn't do that this time is: if I built the bike it would be quick, but my Honda wouldn't be as quick as Ten Kate's and my Triumph 675 wouldn't be as fast as Smiths', because they've been working with those bikes for four seasons or more and they've been right round the houses with them, trying different port shapes and cam profiles ... So there's no way I'm going to get mine as good as either of theirs with the first bite of the cherry.

I had the Smiths and Ten Kate options to consider when another Supersport bike offer came in. And when it did, it made me wonder, in a roundabout way, if it's me getting old. I'm not stuck in my ways, I like to think I never would be, but while I was trying to sort all the 600 job out, Taylor Lindsey got in touch. They are a building company from Lincoln and a big way of going. They also have a motorbike team. The owner of Taylor Lindsey said, 'I heard you're after a 600. Why not ride ours?' My old mate Ivan Lintin, also known as Ivor Biggun, rode for them in 2014. He had a good 600, so I was interested. We got talking about this and that and the Taylor Lindsey man said, 'The best thing to do is come over to Lincoln, have a coffee with us and we'll have a yarn about it.'

As soon as he said that, the deal was over. I knew I wasn't going to ride for him, because he said coffee, not tea. Loveliest bloke in the world, offering me to ride his motorbike, but as soon as he said that sentence it was like a default in my head. You don't meet up to go for a coffee! Not in Lincolnshire. You've been watching too many episodes of *Friends*! Meeting up to go for a coffee? People don't do that in England. Well, I know they do now, but only because they've been watching too many American TV programmes. If he'd have said, 'Come over to Lincoln for a brew,' I might have been riding his motorbike at the TT. It niggled me for days. It wasn't until I had seen beans on toast on the menu of a café in Liverpool that I felt everything was alright again.

A couple of weeks after my call to Smiths Triumph I arranged to go and visit them in Gloucester. I had a £203,000 Aston Martin Vanquish Carbon Edition, that the *Sunday Times* had organised for me to test, but I left it at home and went in the van with my dog. I had arranged to meet Rebecca Smith. She's 25 and seems to know exactly what she wants, and that's to organise a motorbike racing team as efficiently as possible. When I talked to her I knew she was spot on. When her mum walked in, Rebecca said, 'This is my mum. She wants to know about you wanking in the back of your van.' I knew I was on the right footing when she was talking like that. She mentioned that Nigel, the dog, had a hard-on too. She doesn't just manage the racing team, she is involved with all the family businesses and runs a farm with 70 cows and calves on it, with her boyfriend. She's got at least as much going on as I have.

Rebecca's dad, Alan, has 250 wagons. Skip wagons, uplifters, and they do demolitions too. They're not messers. Alan came in wearing an old duffle coat, with ten dogs all following him round. He was driving a 51-reg Hi-Lux, so I was glad I hadn't gone in the Aston Martin. I liked him from the off.

Alan Smith was into his motocross, a national level racer. The family business started sponsoring a local national road racer, Dan Cooper, by buying him tyres. When the team he was riding for starting mucking about, the Smiths ended up running the team for him and another rider, Matt Whitman, whose team had also folded. Alan threw his daughter Rebecca in at the deep end. She was only 19, but she was managing a two-rider team in the British Superbike paddock – one in Supersport, one in Superstock.

They've been at it five years now and they've won two British championships and a TT. They're right people. They're not a team that goes racing every year and every winter they need to go looking for sponsorship. They are a haulage-cum-skip-cum-demolition company that happens to have a racing team. They don't need to attract sponsors, they fund it themselves and they've got good ones through their other businesses. But they're not playing at it. So we did a deal.

When the news got out, it was reported in a paper that Gary Johnson was surprised that Smiths Triumph had decided that they wanted me to race for them rather than him, the man who got them the win in 2014. The newspaper quoted Johnson saying something like if we were team-mates he'd 'mentally destroy' me before the race. I don't know how he'd do that. I don't know how I'd go about mentally destroying someone else. I know that I don't have all my eggs in one basket so I don't have to ask for a squillion quid to race someone's bike, which is the real reason the Smiths didn't do a deal with him. They weren't willing to pay what he was asking.

Racing two bikes with two teams is something I'd never done before, but plenty of boys do. It's the kind of challenge I needed to make me want to go back to the TT, that and the fact these are potentially the most competitive bikes I've ever ridden and I'm saying that before I've even sat on them. That Triumph's proven at the TT and the BMW's not going to be crap. Stewart Johnstone and the whole TAS team will get it to work. They'd get a farm gate to handle. With my input they'll get that BMW to work. Let's get stuck in!

CHAPTER 11

Steam-cleaning muck from under trucks

Work. Work. Work. Work isn't the TV job or motorbike racing, that's all stuff I do away from work. Work is, and most probably always will be, fixing trucks. I've been doing it since I was a nipper. Except for a few months here and there, most recently after I left my dad's place in 2010 and worked as a labourer, I have been a full-time truck fitter since leaving school and going to John Hebb Volvo as an apprentice. Even for some of the time I was living in Ireland me and Johnny, my mate and mechanic, were fixing concrete trucks during the week for one of the team's sponsors. I've had other part-time jobs at the same time as the trucks: glass-collecting; engine-building; driving trucks down the docks; bit of harvesting to help out on the farm, but the constant is trucks. Now I work for Moody International in Grimsby, servicing Scanias, preparing them for MOTs and getting brand-new ones ready for IVA tests. I reckon I'd give up the TV job and racing before I pack in the trucks.

I started working for Mick Moody in early 2011. You may remember, if you read the autobiography, I was handcuffed, arrested and stuck in Scunthorpe nick on the way to the interview. It didn't stop me getting the job and I'm still there, but at times my boss has had to be more flexible than most would be. I cleared off to India for two weeks, then there's all the racing commitments and filming an average of one day a week for most of the year, but I graft when I'm there and leave enough notice for him to get cover if he really needs it.

Moody works in the office on his own. There's probably room for eight people to work in Moody International's four-room, one-storey office, but it's just Mick and whoever he's selling trucks to, or drivers coming in and out. I'm in the shed a hundred yards away. It's a tall, steel truck shed with two roller shutter doors, both tall and wide enough to let a Scania Topline through. When it's windy the doors make a hell of a noise, rattling in their runners. The traffic on the A180 dual-carriageway, right outside the back, rumbles past all day and night too, but I've got used to it now.

If it was empty you could probably squeeze four trucks, without their trailers, into it. In the far corner is a storeroom. A workbench runs down the right-hand side and my black Snap-On work station is butted up to the storeroom. A staircase, the one the Rolls-Royce Merlin propeller half-demolished when I took the restrictor off it, leads up to the top of the storeroom and big parts are held up there. I work, in and out of the pit, on the left half of the shed. Most of the right-hand side of the floorspace is covered in parts of older trucks we're doing up to show standard. These are all Moody's own trucks.

I'm the only employee on the company's books, but Belty is our regular valeter who comes in to clean the trucks and do other jobs as a sub-contractor. I quiz him to death because he's had a life very different to mine. Years ago he used to be a heroin addict and I want to know all about it, but he doesn't like talking about it. He nicked from his family to get his drugs, but he's been off it for 16 years now. I reckon you're only playing at the drug thing till you've done heroin. I think the ultimate test of strength of character would be to have a night on the heroin, then that's it, never touch it again.

Belty has never done porridge, but Moody has. He'll say to me, 'See matey boy there? He's been in the house.' When he says that, it means the bloke he's talking about is not a messer. These aren't fellas who've been inside for violence or thieving, but offences related to 'working too hard' on the trucks: tachograph stuff, mainly. I know things can go badly wrong when tired drivers are behind the wheel, I get all that, but there's still a bit of respect for people who've been 'in the house' – for a bloke in the haulage industry who has done time for getting the job done. Maybe you'd compare it to some kind of honour among thieves.

I never cut corners to get a truck out. A driver could be calling me all the names he can think of to get a truck out so he can catch a ferry, but it's not leaving the yard until I know it's right.

I think about work a lot when I'm not there, but I like that. Often I know I have to get in early to finish a truck, so the driver can leave for Peterhead to go earn his living.

The worst job I have to do is steam-cleaning all the grease and muck from under the trucks. You can't do it and not get blathered. Really it's a job Belty should do while I get on with fixing the trucks, something no one else in the company can do, but whenever we've given Belty a truck to steam-clean he does such a half-arsed job that he doesn't get asked again and I end up doing them. He's like the husband who makes such a balls-up of the washing-up he gets out of it.

Moody's business, and my part in it, took a new turn when the value of the euro went right down compared to the pound. Moody started bringing in a load of trucks from Holland and Hungary to sell. He'd buy rare stuff drivers in the UK wanted, but Scania GB weren't bringing in. He saw a gap in the market and went for it. Scania GB aren't happy with us, because Moody is getting trucks they can't get, the BlueStreams that some people over here want. They're the highest spec you can get, and owner-drivers like them. They're buying the truck for themselves, and they know they're going to be in them for a million miles, so they want the right tool for the job. Trucks like this are not usually bought by a company's transport manager for his drivers. Someone like that thinks about the price, not the specification.

There have been changes to the law since the last time Moody did this kind of business. It used to be that you could MOT a truck to get some UK paperwork, and with that you could get a UK registration for the new truck. It was all a paperwork

How much time I've put into this bloody car, but I love it. This is the Volvo's engine and it's a proper bit of kit, but I've completely rebuilt it twice now, because it shit itself. It's still the fastest, coolest Volvo ever.

The Transit and my dirt track bike, somewhere in Spain. I love a road trip in a van, especially when there's a push-bike or motorbike in the back.

The Honda CRF450 I bought and converted into a flat tracker for the Superprestigio.

This is near Wanganui,
New Zealand, on a day off.
I rented a pushbike and went
out all day riding on my own.

Me and Benny, who used
to work at Gallows Wood,
but now lives in Auckland.

A big moment in
my life, actually getting
to ride the Britten.

I always say if you came to my house you'd never know I raced motorbikes, as I don't collect trophies and pictures of myself racing, but looking at this you'd probably get an idea I do a bit. You can just see the knackered go-kart on the left and the Martek is next to the toilet.

$$a = \frac{V^2}{R} \qquad G = \frac{mph^2}{25\,D}$$

$$1G = 9.81\ m/s/s$$

That is the maths behind the Wall of Death attempt – how fast I'll need to go to stick on the wall. It was worked out by Hugh Hunt, a lecturer at Cambridge University. It's beyond me.

(*Above*) This is Hailwood's bike that won the Daytona 200. I thought it was interesting because it had a four-leading-shoe drum in the front, with a disc brake in the back. An oddball combination.

(*Left*) Dirt tracking at Tim Coles's farm. I probably spend more time doing flat track than road racing. I love it.

In Germany, going to suss out the Nürburgring, on the Autobahn with no speed limits. The Transit's cruise control is limited to 102 mph.

An assortment of five Scania Blue Streams, 6x2s, 4x2s, tags, mids … Moody deals in fancy trucks and this is the ultimate. It's a limited edition Scania, only for mainland Europe, but Moody gets hold of them.

The gearbox of the Scania 143-500 I'm restoring. When you add it up, I've probably spent two weeks on that gearbox alone. All new pipework, all new plugs, vapour blasted the brass couplings …

Hector Neill, legend. His son, Philip, runs the TAS team, but Hector started it and he's the front man. He's always good for a laugh.

My first impression of the TAS BMW race bike. That's a factory exhaust stub that must have been machined on a five-axis mill because it's convex and concave in every direction. Trick.

only take pictures of stuff that jumps out at me. This is from testing with TAS in Spain, when I drove down with Francis (after he smacked the dog). That's a £900 rear master cylinder. I need to get a deal on one of them.

This is another one from Spain. A 3,000-mile round trip for the Transit.

I thought I'd try a skinhead so Jonty's missus Ruth, who's cut my hair for yonks, did the honours. It was genuinely life-changing, for a while at least. I walked into Tesco and no one recognised me, so I could look up and not at the floor.

My kitchen. I swapped that BMX with my mate from Ireland for some leathers. The Martek is now in the hallway, and that's a Scania crank on the floor. It had knocked a big-end out and it looked too good to chuck, so I brought it home to live in the kitchen.

Me and Gary Inman in my back room. He helps with the book and press stuff. I've known him years, he knows his onions and we can jaw all day. Looks like Nige has found something warm.

Life-changing book. Spellman gave me that. Reading it made me very sceptical.

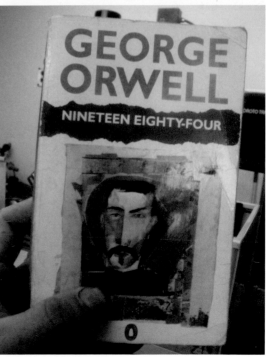

GEORGE ORWELL

NINETEEN EIGHTY-FOUR

One of Racefit's creations, a Harley that Andy Spellman bought.

Some of the TV bods. From left to right: Andy Chorlton the soundman, James Woodroffe the director and Nat Bullen the cameraman. These are some of the boys I've worked with from the very start.

job, and away you went, quite easily. But the authorities have clamped down on it in the name of road safety. A truck that is type-approved for Holland is a slightly different specification to one approved for the UK, so the government agency in charge of road haulage says the truck must go through a special test called an IVA – Independent Vehicle Assessment. The IVA is the equivalent of a very in-depth MOT on the truck and is needed for the truck to be sold legally in the UK. If you look at it too hard it doesn't really make sense, because any foreign-registered trucks can come into the UK and drive wherever they want. If they're safe to drive around without an IVA, why isn't a brand-new truck bought from Holland? Anyway, I've been busy preparing the brand-new trucks Moody buys in Europe to sell to UK drivers.

We get the truck in and I make sure all the boxes are ticked and it will pass the test. Then I drive it the 35 miles to Beverley, North Yorkshire, to the VOSA station. The Vehicle and Operator Services Agency is the organisation that tests trucks for roadworthiness and checks compliance of road haulage vehicles and drivers. I take it to the most local depot that can carry out the IVA test. The tests were booked in for most Mondays while we were selling plenty of trucks and once this caused a bit of a problem.

I got a call from the TV bods at North One in the middle of the week, asking if I wanted a hotel in Chichester for that Sunday night. I waited a second before asking, 'What do I need a hotel on Sunday for?'

They told me it might make sense, as we were filming early on Monday, right in the south of England. But there was nothing in my diary for that day except an IVA test on a Scania in Beverley.

Then I was reminded of a phone call from weeks before, asking me to do three days' filming. I said I couldn't. North One came back saying two days' filming, but I gave them the same answer, so they settled on just one, and I agreed, mainly to get them off the phone.

I didn't write it in the planner in my diary, because I was up to my elbows in a Swedish truck. The shit hit the fan and they got on to Spellman. When I last met up with him he got hold of my diary and wrote stuff in. He wrote this filming day, like a lot of people might, on the page for the relevant week in the middle of my diary. And because he'd put it in my diary he'd felt he had no need to remind me. The problem with that was, he didn't know the rules of the book. The first two pages of the diary, the year planner with all the months shown on the inside front cover, is where I look for what's coming up. The rest of the diary is where I write what I did or where I've been. So I wouldn't see what Spellman had written on the Monday page till I got to end of that day and wrote what I'd been doing or where I'd been. It's simple. What's going to happen in the front, what's happened in the middle. What's going to happen, what's happened. It's not rocket science.

North One had booked a stunt plane and a pilot, who was an aerobatic expert. They had hired all the film crew, soundmen, directors and everyone else, and most of them are freelancers, so need booking well in advance; they'd arranged to film at an airfield; booked the specialist cameras and checked the weather. Conditions were perfect and everything was lined up.

All they needed there was me. I had to make a decision, and there was only one thing to do: I had to tell them I couldn't make it to the airfield, so don't bother booking me a hotel room in Chichester. The truck job won. I couldn't drop Moody in it. There are times when he bends over backwards for me and there are others when he puts his foot down, but I didn't even ask him if I could go filming. It might have been possible to get someone else to drive the truck to Yorkshire for the IVA test. I'm sure North One would have paid, or Spellman could have organised it, just to make it all happen, but it was the principle of the thing. Yes, I'd buggered it up. Obviously it was Spellman's fault for not writing the details in the right place in my diary, but I'm man enough to take some of the blame. I had to make it clear to everyone, including myself, that trucks are still the big picture for me, even in the same week that everyone says I'm the next presenter of *Top Gear*. For me the truck job is it, and even though it was a total ball-ache for the people who had done all the organising, they'd have to do it again. Sorry.

There so much about the job I love. I love calling in at Fleet Factors for parts and having a yarn with Paddy and Dean behind the counter. They're as dry as owt, but funny. Then there's Nige and Rick at Action Truck Parts. I always have a brew when I go there. When I call in for parts at either of these companies I'll ask them, 'What do you know?' And nine times out of ten I'll learn something. Back in the yard, I have the same kind of small talk with the truck drivers – it's the kind of stuff that drives me crackers at race meetings, but the big difference is I'm talking to the drivers and parts men, they're not quizzing me. And it's in the real world. Everyone's real world is different, but mine is the road haulage business.

During the day Moody will call me up and ask if I want a brew, so I walk over to the office and have a passive smoke. He can be a rude bastard. And blunt. Blunt as you like. Everyone knows where everybody stands, but I like that. He's brutally honest about everyone and everything. He's cynical. His whole world revolves around trucks. He's in here on Christmas Day. He's 52, but you'd put 62 on him. He smokes 80 a day and there's more meat on a butcher's pencil. He likes his fancy clothes, too.

Moody wants to know everything about my life. He wants to know the far side of Meg's arse, as my dad would say, but I don't know anything about him other than what I see at the truck yard. I've never asked him because I don't need to know. And that's alright by me.

He doesn't seem to give a damn about human beings, but he loves his dogs. You see a different side of him when he meets my dog, Nigel. He's respected in the trade, because he's a hard-nosed bastard, but he's as daft as a brush with my dog. I don't bring Nige to work much, though, because he's into everything and would end up eating something important.

The yard is surrounded by a big fence and the only way in is through a heavy-duty electric gate. Moody has some CCTV monitors in his office and can see who is pressing the buzzer to get in the gate. Because I mentioned where I work in the previous book, people started turning up at the gate.

A woman arrived, with some fellas, and pressed the buzzer before explaining she had a tattoo of me on her arm and wanted me to autograph underneath it so she could have my signature permanently inked on. I met her at the gate and signed it there. Moody wouldn't want them in the yard. I'm sure they were the loveliest people in the world, but Moody is cautious.

Other times people will come and press the buzzer and tell Moody they're here to say hello to me, but I don't get to hear about it until later, because he simply tells them, 'He's here to work.'

One fella that was let in was Austin Mitchell, the former Labour MP for Grimsby, who'd held the seat for 38 years. He came because Sacha Baron Cohen is making a film called *Grimsby*, due to be released in 2016. From what I've heard Grimsby was chosen as the title town ahead of Scunthorpe, Hull and Newcastle. The actor, who is most famous for his characters Ali G and Borat, plays a football hooligan whose brother is a 'black ops spy'. Locals have been complaining because it portrays the town as a violent dump of a place where mums give cans of beer to their kids to shut them up.

All the Grimsby business community and the local well-to-do want to do something about the town's image. Austin Mitchell, who works for Ingsoc, is in charge of making a ten-minute film that, so I'm told, will be shown in cinemas before the comedy. The idea of it is to show what Grimsby is really like (or bits of it are like). He wanted me to say why I liked the place and why I was proud to come from this shithole.

I like Grimsby because it's home and a real place, but I still think the whole world is mulching into one big thing, kids all talking the same, looking the same, doing the same things. I tried to conform when I was young, but now I do what I can to make sure I don't.

Mitchell is a right intelligent bloke and we got on the subject of George Orwell, and channelling the masses' energy in ways described in *1984*. I told him I got all that and I saw it was happening. He disagreed, using all these big words, but I wasn't clever enough to argue my view on it. I still disagreed, though. The whole of British politics is just trying to baffle the masses. Even I'm clever enough to understand that. It's the whole Eastasia, Eurasia thing from Orwell's book. Football, cheap beer, *Strictly Come Dancing* – it's all nonsense to keep the masses from thinking too hard about things and becoming restless.

That was a far from normal day in the truck yard, but that's the good thing about it: there aren't many normal days. Recently, Moody has said he'll give me this business when he retires. I hope he stands by it.

CHAPTER 12

When Francis smacked the dog

The beginning of every year involves a lot of grafting in miserable conditions, though I get a kind of perverse pleasure from cycling to work in the freezing cold and dark, then working on filthy, dirty trucks in the windy yard before cycling home again in the dark. But I was ready to get on the new BMW race bike and see what it was like.

Pre-season testing for the motorbike job changes from year to year and so does my attitude to it. I've gone into some seasons with an attitude of leaving no stone unturned in the preparation, and it hasn't made much difference. Then, in another season, when all I've done, for whatever reason, was the odd day at Kirkistown, I've had good results. With me there seems no right or wrong way. There are that many variables, I just have to do what feels right at the time and what fits in with the trucks and everything else.

This year, because I'm on the new bike, one I've never raced before, it made sense to go to the south of Spain for a few days' testing with the TAS team in pretty much guaranteed half-decent weather.

Our test started on Monday 9 March and my plan was to work Friday, set off leisurely on Saturday morning for the Monday morning start of testing in Almeria. Then it turned out one of Moody's refrigerated trailers needed an MOT, so I ended up running around like a knob.

I could have set off Saturday morning, but the weather was looking good all weekend in Lincolnshire, so I had a word with Tim the beef farmer, to see what his dirt track was like, and it was right for the first time that year.

My mountain bike mate Francis had driven down from Scotland on Friday and he was coming to Spain with me in the Transit.

There are three mates, all as important and interesting as each other: Francis, Forbes and Alan. Francis is in his mid sixties, a proper sound bloke who lives the top side of Aberdeen. He has spannered for me for a few years at 24-hour mountain bike races. You need the right people looking after you in those races. His main job is for BT, planning fibre-optic systems out to the Scottish islands, but he's a part-time gamekeeper. He makes very special rifle bullets for people too. He's a real interesting bloke.

He has holes in his trainers, but a right collection of limited edition Ducatis. I'd known him a long while before I knew about his bikes. I don't care about any of his Ducatis, but he told me he had a Bimota 500VDue and that got my attention.

Bimota are Italian and have gone out of business a load of times, then come back to life with new owners and investors. From the 1970s to the 1990s they built great-looking superbikes with the best Japanese engines of the time in Bimota's own Italian-made frames and bodywork. It was the best of both worlds – Japanese power and reliability with Italian style, and this was at a time when Ducati were at death's door, so they were the trickest bikes you could buy.

When Bimota built the VDue, the bike Francis had, they made their own engine, a 500 cc V-twin two-stroke with fuel injection. It was ambitious, to say the least, and helped ruin the company, again. The bike had potential and was as exotic as you like, but the little Italian company didn't have the financial clout to persevere and get it right. I went to the NEC motorbike show when I was about 14, when the VDue first came out, and remember thinking, Bloody hell! Those bikes are the bollocks. Well, they weren't, they were rubbish, but that's what made them the bollocks in my eyes.

There were only three in the country that were untouched, still with the fuel injection on them, because all the others were recalled to Italy to have carburettors fitted to them. Francis's was one of those three original models.

He rang me up one day and said, 'That VDue of mine you were right into? Do you want to buy it?' And that was four or five years ago. He'd never ridden it and I bought it. I've ridden it a couple of times, and it is rubbish, but I still like it.

With the weather and Tim's track being dead right, me and Francis rode till about four in the afternoon. I hadn't ridden a motorbike since Boxing Day, in New Zealand, so I felt I needed to do something to get back into it before climbing onto the BMW.

After we finished, we came back to mine, had a wash, then dropped Nigel the dog off at my sister, Sal's house.

Francis has a dog, a cross between a Border Collie and a Burmese summat or other, so it looks like a Collie with a Labrador's head. Francis logs all the miles he's run, and at the last count it was over 100,000 miles, and he reckons his dog has done a quarter of them with him. Twenty-five thousand is a lot of miles for a dog. And it is really well trained.

Nigel, on the other hand, is a bit unruly. He's his own man, and I like that. He scratches at the back door and I let him out to go roaming for an hour. Francis doesn't like that, saying dogs shouldn't do that, but Nigey-boy always comes back. Still, Francis isn't impressed, adding I should be more of a master. I think Nigel is just young and daft and he'll grow out of it.

When we dropped the dog off I booked the midnight crossing for the Eurotunnel on Sal's computer, and while I was doing that Nigel was sticking his head in the bin to see if there was anything worth nicking. Sal told us he keeps doing it. Then, without even thinking, Francis walked up and gave Nigel such a hard smack on the snout. Nigel didn't whimper, but clearly thought, Right ... He walked off, lay under the kitchen table and didn't come out. Sal and I were both shocked and for a moment I thought she was going to lamp Francis.

Nothing more was said about the dog before we left for Kent. On the long drive me and Francis discussed Italian build quality – and my opinion that it's terrible – and stocks and shares, too, with him explaining to me how the global stock exchanges work. He has a good view on *The Archers* too. He had a different opinion about Ruth to me, but I agree with him now. I thought she was a happy-go-lucky, up-for-it Geordie, but it turns out she's very manipulative. He has a good knowledge of World War II and Peenemünde, where the Germans developed the V2 rockets. We disagreed on Walter Kaaden and Wernher von Braun, though, and I still think I'm right.

We covered some ground and listened to everything from AC/DC to Morcheeba. I was reminded of a Stereophonics song, 'A Thousand Trees', that has a great line in it: 'A tree can make a thousand matches, but a match can burn a thousand trees.' I've always thought that's quite clever.

We crossed the Channel and carried on driving, non-stop, to Albacete, between Valencia and Benidorm, but inland. We got there at six or seven on Sunday evening, about 24 hours after leaving Lincolnshire. There is a track at Albacete, but we were testing at Almeria, a bit further south. I was knackered, and we decided to stop.

We had something to eat and a couple of drinks, then found a hotel. I told Francis to wait in the van while I went to reception, because if the room was dear we'd kip in the van. It's good because he's as tight as I am. It was €50 for the pair of us in a twin room, so that was alright. We were in bed no later than eight and up at six in the morning, for two hours' drive on back roads to Almeria. Because it was a BMW-run test, nothing started till 11, so I didn't have to rush about.

It wasn't the normal kind of test that I'd been to in Spain before, it was more like a trackday with BMW-owning riders and only a few racers, and we could only get on the track every now and then. Still, over three days, we had plenty of time.

My team-mate on the roads, William Dunlop, was testing and TAS's short circuit riders were there too. I met Tommy Bridewell for the first time and he seems a nice lad. He's in the British Superbike class with Michael Laverty, who I already knew. Alastair Seeley, who raced for TAS a couple of years ago, is back with the team and in British Superstock. He'll race the North West 200 too. He goes well there.

Most of the team were there: Mark McIvor, the foreman; Philip Neill, the team manager, and his dad Hector, the team owner. Stewart Johnstone, the chassis man, was there too. He was working with Laverty, because he's a rider that's really good at setting up bikes. I was just there to put in some miles and I never saw a lap time. The team got Francis grafting, fuelling all the bikes between sessions.

Mark McCarville is the mechanic I work the closest with and he's an inspiration. This time last year he had a pain in his balls and thought it was a pulled muscle. Then his missus told him a mole on his neck had changed shape and he should get it looked at. While he was at the doctor's he mentioned the pain in his groin. The doctor had a feel and sent him straight to the hospital where they whipped one of his bollocks off within hours.

Once he got out of hospital Mark carried on as normal, worked for the team at the TT and all that, before going back to the hospital for some tests where they told him he still had cancer. That's when he started with two months of chemotherapy. He lost all his hair, and put a load of weight on from taking steroids that he'd been prescribed. The chemo didn't kill the cancer, so, in January of 2015, he had an operation to remove whatever was in his chest and now, a few weeks later, you would not know he'd been through anything. He's 100 per cent. It made me realise you can think you've got stuff on your plate till you hear a story like that.

During the test I did 585 miles in three days – I know because the superstock bike I was riding had zero miles on the clock when I got it. I spent time riding on shagged tyres, with no traction control, to see if the chassis talked to me. I thought the bike was good. I didn't ride it back-to-back with the Suzuki, and it had been six months since I'd ridden my TAS GSX-R1000, so it's hard to say how much better the BMW was, but the noticeable difference was on corner entry.

With the Suzuki, I had to keep the front brake on to make it around corners without running wide. I think the very slight braking pressure kept the tyre distorted in a certain way to give me enough grip to get me around the corner. I would hold the brake right to the apex of the corner, but by doing that I'm increasing the chances of crashing, because I'm carrying a lot of lean angle with the brake on, which you shouldn't do if you can help it. By riding like that, I'm asking a lot of the front tyre, and I'm losing momentum, because I'm braking, so I'd have to put more stress on the tyre and the chassis exiting the corner to make up the time I'd lost from the start of the bend to mid-corner. But I'm still winning races and finishing on the podium doing that.

Metzeler made me a special, stiffer tyre, so I didn't have to stay on the front brake for so long. It was offered to the other Metzeler-supported road racers, but none of them liked it. You might think a softer tyre would distort more and help, but the answer, as far as I was concerned, was actually a cross-ply tyre with a stiffer carcass. It only ever made the best of a bad job, but I must have been doing something right, because none of my team-mates beat me during my time on the big Suzukis.

When I tested a customer Dunlop tyre on that Suzuki I could let go of the brake and hold a line, but I never raced on them. At one point, a few years ago, I offered to buy Dunlops myself, but it came to nothing. Anyway, Metzeler, and their parent company Pirelli, have been good to me and I like the people there.

So the BMW was better in the corners, and I had the ability to let go of the front brake even on a regular, treaded superstock front tyre. The bike did go well, but all those modern 1000s do. I'm not going to start raving about how fast it was, the top bikes are all much of a muchness.

As far as the track goes, Almeria isn't much of a test of a road racing bike. Kirkistown in Northern Ireland is better if you're lucky with the weather. The Irish circuit is fast and flowing with a couple of balls-out corners. And it's bumpy, so much closer to the kind of surfaces we race on. Almeria is quite long for a short circuit, but there's hardly any hills or dips and it's slow. There aren't any really fast corners, but there is a quick straight, so you brake from 180 mph-plus into a 30 mph, first gear right-hander. Other than time on the bike it isn't doing me or William a lot of good for the kind of tracks we specialise in racing. It's a different kettle of fish for the BSB boys, because the stop-start nature of the place is more like the tracks of their championship.

Me and Francis had tea with the team one night, and did our own thing the other nights, before going back to the room we were sharing. Francis then put the BBC World Service on the radio, but he'd have to turn it off, because I was reading a book, and I couldn't concentrate. I'm a slow reader, but I was reading a bloody brilliant book called *Red Notice* by Bill Browder, about Putin, Interpol, Russia, all the oligarchs, and explaining how they got rich after the end of Russian communism.

The author explains part of the Russian mentality using an old fable he's told. The story is a Russian man is walking down the street when he spots a magic fish in a stream. The fish says, 'You can have one wish, whatever you desire, but before you choose, you must realise that your neighbour will get twice what you choose.' Without hesitating the Russian says, 'Take one of my eyes.' I don't know if it is a real Russian fable, but that kind of bloody-mindedness appeals to me in an odd-ball way.

At the track I wasn't learning anything on Wednesday afternoon that I didn't know by the end of Monday, but just having handlebars in my hands and a seat under my arse wasn't doing me any harm. By Wednesday the other riders were doing shorter sessions. It seemed their enthusiasm had gone a bit, or perhaps they'd done everything they felt they needed to do. Every time the green flag came out, I was out till the end of the session, and once I ran out of petrol.

I had early nights in Spain, because I knew as soon as we finished testing on Wednesday I'd drive straight home. We were at the diesel station outside the track at 5pm on Wednesday, then set off. It took 24 hours of solid driving to get to Calais. We stuck to my rule: we only stop for fuel. To do that you have to drink accordingly. I know that when the fuel gauge gets to a quarter I can start drinking from my Camelbak, because we only have an hour to go and I can hold on. Francis gets it now. It's a bit of pain, but you're home in half the time. Really, I should've flown, and it would've been cheaper, but I like being in my van and I like driving.

I didn't have any aches or pains after the test, but I feel I've got to show my body some respect. I never give it a rest. An example of that is the following weekend.

We got back to my house at ten on Thursday night, 26 hours after leaving Spain. I had the superstock bike with me, so we emptied the van, moving the Martek from the bench in the shed to the hallway and put the BMW on the bench. I got into bed at getting on for midnight and was up at six the next morning, Friday, and in work for seven. At dinnertime I drove, 60 miles, to York Railway Museum to meet some Mr Porky's competition winners. Mr Porky's Pork Scratchings had sponsored me the previous season and this was part of the deal. I left York at three; got home at five, had a big tea, then drove to Kirton Lindsey to pick up my mate Dobby, whose house I used to live in, in Caistor, when I moved out of the Lancasters' farm.

for an IVA test at VOSA in Beverley. So don't tell me you've got a lot on till you've had a weekend like that.

And Sal told me Nigel stayed out of the bin for all of two days before he was back in it.

CHAPTER 13

Waiting for a dickhead like me

In early spring, before the roads season has started, I think about doing a national race or two in the British Superbike series to get my eye in. It's not really my thing, though I have raced plenty of BSB and British Supersport races in the past, including a full Superbike season with Hydrex Honda in 2008. Racing at a national round is different to pure testing. It's somewhere to get some laps in and find out where you stand.

We had been struggling to get a test date that suited both me and the Smiths Triumph team, so Rebecca Smith, the team manager, asked if I wanted to enter the first race to get some time on the bike, adding there was no pressure.

Rebecca asked me to race at Donington, the first British Superbike meeting of the year, in the Supersport class. One of their riders, Graham Gowland, had spannered himself in testing and it looked like he was going to be out for most of the season.

I did the official British Superbike test the week before the race, on 26 March. It was a mid-week session, wet and shitty, but Rebecca and the team were brilliant. They're very straight to the point, no messing. What do you want changing? What are we doing with this? What do you want there?

The downside of the official British Superbike test, compared to testing in Spain, from my point of view, was there were too many folk there. People had paid to come and watch the test day, and they all had access to the pits, so a crowd of people were stood around the back of our garage. Rebecca hadn't experienced anything like that. She and the team's mechanics couldn't get between the garage and the truck to get spares, because people wouldn't move out of the way. If this is what it was like on a miserable Thursday test day in March, she wondered, how were they going to deal with it at the TT?

When it came to riding the thing, I struggled with the Triumph, because even though it is fast, it's different to the Suzuki GSX-R600 I had been racing since 2011, when I joined the TAS team. The Smiths Triumph has won a TT and it's a rocketship, but I thought I'd just be able to jump on it and be away and it's not that easy. I had to get my head around it and was trying to adjust to this bike while every man and his dog wanted this or that signing. It seemed to be ten deep – not ten people, *ten deep* every time I walked out of the garage to go to the truck. Going to Donington to test a bike for the first time was like airing my dirty laundry in public and I would have preferred to do it on the quiet, but that's just the way it is.

If you go looking for it, and I don't but I'm told, there's a lot of talk in *Motorcycle News* and on the internet about the amount of people in the pits now road racing is more popular than it's been for a long time. I can't pretend to like having hundreds of people waiting for me. It's not a case of being ungrateful or rude; I'm not cut out for it mentally. Brian starts shaking the bars of his cage.

MCN put something in about the club that organises the Scarborough meetings making a specially designated spot for me at the Spring National race that was coming up, like I had asked to be split off from the rest of the paddock. That was a load of rubbish, but it gave them the chance to talk to other TT racers who said they'd do anything for the fans because 'it is the fans who pay their wages'. But I've heard these same racers refer to fans as 'lickers', meaning window-lickers – even when they're talking about their own supporters, the ones they tell *MCN* they'd walk over broken glass for.

I came away from the Donington test thinking I was going to pack in racing there and then. No British Supersport race at Donington, no new BMW, no Isle of Man TT. The end.

A day later I spoke to Tim, the beef farmer, telling him I wasn't enjoying any of it and I didn't want to race at Donington, explaining the feeling of being hounded. I told him I was left wondering, What's the point? I'm not getting paid to race, but I am sponsored by Dainese and AGV, because I race motorbikes. I don't need to race to keep a roof over my head. Tim told me that I shouldn't race Donington, adding that he didn't know why I was racing there in the first place. What I hadn't told him was if I didn't have the stomach to race Donington then I wouldn't race anywhere and that would be it, retirement. Stopping that suddenly and unexpectedly would piss a lot of people off, but if I don't want to be there, competing at these risky races, I asked myself again, what is the point? I struggled to think of one.

I was still considering it when I told Gary Inman, a journalist who I trust, what I was thinking and he pointed out that I don't enjoy the mountain bike racing when I'm doing it. And he's right, but it's different, because the pain and discomfort of being on a mountain bike for 24 hours non-stop is the actual thing that makes me go back and do it again. It's part of the achievement. Not being able to go from the garage to the race truck to speak to a mechanic or change a visor in a hurry is nothing to do with the job in hand, it's just something I don't enjoy dealing with. Mountain bike discomfort is physical and a means to an end; the mithering at the racetrack doesn't achieve anything. It comes down to two things. One is me not understanding why anyone could be bothered hanging around for me to sign something. I don't get it. I probably never will. If you have paid to watch a motorbike race, why are you stood outside the back of a garage waiting for a dickhead like me? If you're going to a motorbike race, watch the motorbike race.

The other thing is the way it sets Brian off. I've made no secret of the fact the small talk makes my brain short circuit and sets the chimp screaming and thinking oddball thoughts, thoughts someone dealing with the public perhaps shouldn't be thinking. I explained in the autobiography that a psychiatrist said, without beating around the bush, that it isn't a good idea for me to be in those situations. I've got a bad earth or summat. Still, Gary did have a point. The feeling of achievement I get from a race well ridden is there whatever is going on in the paddock.

There was a week between the Donington test and the British Superbike round at the same track, and I didn't say anything to Rebecca or the Smiths team in the meantime. For much of that week I did genuinely think, I don't care who I piss off, that's me done.

The race was to be held over the Easter weekend, so practice wouldn't take place till the following Saturday. It was Thursday, just two days before, when I made my mind up that I would go. Only a handful of people knew that I'd been thinking about packing it all in, and I didn't tell either of my teams, Smiths or TAS.

As normal, the BSB round was a three-day meeting. For this one, practice was on Saturday, qualifying Sunday, and the race on Bank Holiday Monday. I reminded myself that if I wasn't enjoying it I could miss the race.

If anything there were more people around our garage at the race, but I enjoyed the riding, and just got my head down. I learned a load about the bike and felt more comfortable on it and decided that we'll be alright.

The whole Smiths team is sound. John Trigger does the engines and a fella called Jason Jones is the Smiths team's equivalent of TAS's Mark McIvor. Still, returning to BSB made me think nearly everyone in the paddock is brainwashed. All the same people are there from last time I was there, seven years before. There's nothing wrong with that, but I feel like putting my arm around them and saying, 'It's OK, there's other things in life than racing the British Championship.'

The season will finish and they're all worried about the next season. I was the same when I was 20 or 21. My life revolved around the British Championship, but there were people doing it before I started that are still doing it now, 14 years later. I admit I was happy then, in Junior Supersport, because I didn't know any better, but I'm happier now my eyes have been opened. I never thought, even at 21, If this takes off, I won't have to fix trucks for a living.

Giving credit where it's due, the standard of racing is brilliant, everything is really well organised and it is the pinnacle of racing in this country, but those involved are brainwashed into making their whole life revolve around British Superbike. And no, I don't admire that single-mindedness. People will say my attitude proves why I haven't won this or that race, but I know motorcycle racing is not sustainable. It's all chasing, chasing, just so you can spend a bloody fortune on tyres. It's good that they're channelling energy into that one thing, but they're like clowns in a circus paying to perform.

Donington was a Bank Holiday race, so nothing was happening on track till Saturday morning, but all the racers still had to be there for the riders' meeting on Friday afternoon. It's a pain in the arse. It wasn't finished till six, so there was no point in driving home, just to turn around and be back at nine in the morning. Instead, I had a yarn with a couple of lads. They were racers I didn't know, but we were talking about

Transits so that was alright. Then I just went back to my van, read my book and kipped in the back of the Transit.

The next day I ended up qualifying 18th. One of the men to beat in the Supersport class is my Triumph team-mate, Jake Dixon, who qualified third. His dad, Darren Dixon, is a legend, a sidecar champion who then went solo racing and won on them too.

Jake was only 19 at the time, but he won one of the Donington races and came second in the other. I didn't quiz him about set-up, even though he was flying; I just did my own thing. I'm not going quick enough to make changes to the bike to try and improve it. I have to get up to speed with the settings the team recommend before I do that.

I finished 16th in the first race and 17th in the second one – one second off 12th place crossing the line. During the race I was in the battle for tenth place with a load of other riders. I would pass someone, and lads would come past me taking the paint off my fairing and knocking the bars out of my hands. I'm not scared of hard passes, but I wasn't going to hang my balls out for tenth place in a British Supersport race, because it's just not important to the rest of my year. I wasn't exactly saying, 'After you, mate,' but I was there to test, not looking for championship points towards an end of season total. Everyone was in their own race, but I wasn't going to spanner myself at Donington, a few weeks before the TT.

At the end I thanked Rebecca and the team. I don't know what she thought of the results, and I'm sure certain people could look at the results and see me in 17th, with Jake Dixon,

DONINGTON PARK

LENGTH — 2·48 MI
CORNERS — 12

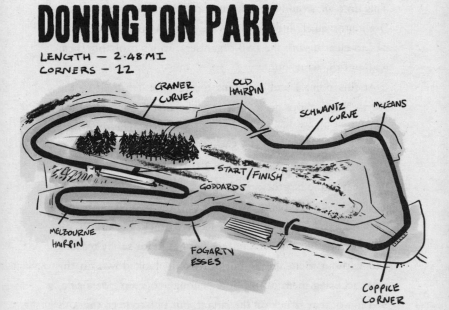

CRANER CURVES

OLD HAIRPIN

SCHWANTZ CURVE

McLEANS

START/FINISH

GODDARDS

MELBOURNE HAIRPIN

FOGARTY ESSES

COPPICE CORNER

in the same team, winning, but I couldn't give a monkey's. I was there to do my own job.

I wanted more riding, so we decided I'd probably race the Triumph again at the Oulton Park BSB round, on 4 May. This time we would try to keep it quiet. I think Rebecca kept Donington quiet, and I only told the people I trust, but Rebecca had to clear it with the BSB organisers, so it's probably them who put the word out.

At this point I had no plans to take the Triumph to the North West, choosing to just race the BMW superbike and superstock there, but there was still a chance. The organiser, Mervyn White, offered the Smiths team twice as much start money to go in 2015 as he had in 2014, which was the Smiths' first year at the Northern Irish race.

Mervyn is a top bloke, straight down the line, lives for that meeting and I like him. I don't like the track, because of all the chicanes, but I understand they're put in for safety reasons and without them the authorities would look down on the race, accusing them of not doing enough to keep riders safe. So I'm not that struck on the circuit, but I go to keep the TAS boys happy. They're a Northern Irish team and it is the biggest race in Ireland, the biggest sporting event in the province full stop, most years.

In 2014, Mervyn asked me to attend a 'meet the riders' signing at Coleraine market place, on the Friday before Saturday's race, but I didn't go, because I was out on my mountain bike. I told Mervyn I'd get there if I could, but don't bank on it. In the end I didn't. Mervyn came back telling me it was in my contract to turn up. I wondered, What are you on about? What have contracts got to do with anything when I haven't had my prize money from the previous year? I wasn't going to push for the prize money or kick up a fuss or ever ask for it, because they had a meeting rained off, and times are hard. But I think it's only fair that the North West don't start revving up with all contract this and contract that when I end up not doing something I hate doing and told them I didn't want to do in the first place.

Even though the Tyco BMW 1000s and the Smiths Triumph are the most competitive pair of bikes I've probably ever been on, the Donington experience felt like another nail in the coffin of me and motorbike racing. It wasn't just not wanting to do the North West and TT any more, it was the whole of racing I was willing to pack it in. This wasn't the chimp making a rash decision. I've had time to think about it. I have pros and cons for both sides of the argument and there are a lot more cons.

I could carry on racing, have something go wrong and screw up the rest of my life, or I could win everything and be the happiest man ever. It would be a big decision, either way. Life-changing, really. I'll have to see how things pan out in the rest of the year.

CHAPTER 14

The Maws are my default setting

I described the Kirmington bubble in the autobiography. The one-pub village I grew up in was the centre of my universe until my late twenties, when I moved out, and it stayed that way even when I was living in Caistor. It's where I grew up; learned to ride a motorbike; learned to spanner in my dad's chicken shed; and where I was taught important life skills, like how to lift heavy things and assemble Black & Decker workbenches, by our legendary headmaster, Mr Acum in the one-room Kirmington Church of England Primary School. But I'm well and truly out of the bubble now.

I have strong links to the place, because my mum and dad still live there, and my sister Sal and her two lads have even moved into their own house in the village. I have plenty of mates from that time that who I see when I can, like Shorty and his wife Hannah, but the strongest friendship, that goes right back to that time growing up, in my late teens and early twenties, is with the Maws.

I didn't meet any of the Maws until I was 18, but I knew of the legendary Dave Maw. He was just leaving the Vale of Ancholme School as I was starting there, and it was a big deal for the school because he was already three times world BMX champion.

I never met him but, but I knew the name – everyone knew the name. Then, halfway through my time at the secondary school, he died after crashing a VW Beetle down Elsham Hill in December 1996. And that was all I knew of the Maws: Dave, this legend who died when he wasn't much more than a teenager. That was until I left school and started going out with Sarah Chadwick, my first proper girlfriend. She was a nurse, real nice lass, and seven years older than me. I was with her three years, but she just wanted to settle down, I think, and it would be a long time before that was going to be in my plans. Anyway, she was dead good mates with Dave Maw's older brother Jonty and Ruth, who he would later marry. So I got to know Jonty and Ruth about 2000.

Jonty was as good on a BMX as his brother, but he wasn't competitive. He was great at styling it up on a bike, though. I became good mates with Jonty, and when me and Sarah split up, I kept in touch with the Maws. Now I see more of them than I do of my mum and dad or brother and little sister.

You should have got the idea by now that I'm either at work or working in the shed as soon as I get home, or at weekends I'm motorbike racing or mountain biking, and in between all that there's the TV job, but I try to keep Monday as a night off, and I go to the Maws for a brew. If I'm training for a race, I'll bike that way home and have my tea at the Maws, or if I'm not I'll go in the van and take the dog, because Nigel likes both their dogs. Maximus, who is a Heinz 57 mongrel and is named after Max Biaggi, isn't mad about my dog. But Roxy is a German Shepherd cross and she likes Nige.

Jonty is married to Ruth and they have two daughters, Georgia and Lucy, and a son, David. I'm godfather to Lucy, so I always try to remember her birthday, but I miss it every now and then. I don't take the role very seriously, but I bought her a little Snap-On ratchet and I engraved a piston out of a Honda CBR600 with her name and date of birth for her christening, back in 2005. I also took Jonty to his wedding in my Saab, when he married Ruth in 2004.

Jonty's a builder by trade, in the family business with his dad, but he's in a digger most of the time because he subcontracts to the YEB, the Yorkshire Electricity Board. He has an auger on the back actor of his digger for drilling holes into the ground and he puts all their electricity poles up.

The Maws don't care where I've been or what I've done, they're just nice people and don't annoy me in any way or ask me for anything, so it's never hard work. I just sit down and watch a bit of telly, have a yarn with the kids, watch Nige try to shag Roxy, or go in Jonty's shed and see the VW Camper he's building. It's not that I don't get on with my mum and dad, I do, but I feel more at ease with the Maws than anyone else. I stay there till 10 or 11 at night, before it's back into the work/shed/biking/filming/racing routine.

It's not surprising that the whole Maw family took the death of Dave really hard, and I don't know if that's affected how Jonty views the world, because I didn't know him before, but he's not overly impressed by anything. That's not to say he's miserable or cynical, though. He's just one of those boys that have no real ups or downs, it's just the Maw. A constant. He loves his toys and hobbies. If I'm ever thinking about buying something and I can't decide to go for it or not, I go to see Jonty and he always talks me into it.

It's not so much that the Maws are a link to another time, but if I go anywhere else I sometimes feel like I'm under scrutiny and I'm getting quizzed about stuff. Monday nights at the Maws is a proper default setting for me, and I think everyone needs that. Jonty and Ruth would be the first to tell me if I was getting above my station, and ask me, What are you doing, dickhead? They did with my mistakes in the past, but they've met Sharon now and they like her and she likes them. Not that I need the Maws' approval, but it does help. Ruth wouldn't say if she didn't like an other half of mine that I introduced them to, but I know when she genuinely does. And Ruth has cut my hair for years, so I manage to kill two birds with one stone.

There still aren't many places I could live except for North Lincolnshire. I like it because I know if there's something I'm struggling to do then there's someone over there who knows someone who can do summat. I've got that web of contacts here, built up over 20 years, since I started working part-time for my dad. You can't be an expert in everything, so you always need to know people you can rely on to do stuff for you. I can get just about anything done round here and I like that.

I think the only other place I could live and feel the same way is Northern Ireland. I've spent enough time over there that I know people in different trades that I could get things done, but I don't have any plans to move away.

I've had a dirt track built on a local field, with the help of Tim Coles, and I needed a tractor to grade the track, keep it smooth and in good condition. At first I thought I'd buy a cheap, shitty old tractor, then I spoke to my mate Dobby, who is in the potato industry, and he told me how much he pays contractors to do tatie leading from September to October.

The tatie leader is like a tatie harvester. You have a tatie lifter, that lifts the potato out of the row, then puts them on a riddler, while someone is driving alongside in a tractor at 20 mph, and there's a conveyor that feeds the spuds into a trailer being towed by the tractor.

They're paying lads £750 a week during potato harvest, and I thought, I could do that. It's an opportunity to get a foot in another door. I've already got plenty of feet in plenty of doors, but another one can't hurt. So it got me thinking that I could buy a shitty old tractor to prepare and maintain my dirt track and that would be alright, but I could buy a decent one and earn a few quid out of it, renting it out with a driver.

I had a word with a few lads: Dobby, Tim Coles, Tim and Tom Neave, and everyone said the Fendt is the most expensive, but it's the best. And the biggest of the Fendts is a 9-series. It's bloody massive. It's overkill for the dirt track, but it'll do it and much, much more. So I had a word with Spellman, asking if he could get me one out of the TV bods at North One as payment for the new round of programmes, instead of pound notes, and he got it sorted out for me. So now I have a brand-new, dark green Fendt 9-series tractor.

It's German, and I'm getting right into German engineering. The BMW I'm racing is impressive; the Metzeler tyre factory I visited to see where they made my racing tyres; the Fendt … Ja, das ist gut.

We're not short of farmland in Lincolnshire and the potato harvest is 12 weeks a year. Before that, in July and August, is wheat and barley harvest. Then there are all these big digester plants being built round here. They produce methane by simulating what a cow's stomach does. Farmers fill their digester plants, that look like a big white domes, with animal shit and silage, then agitate it as it's rotting down. The process creates all this methane that is then purified, taking the corrosive elements out of it, before the methane goes into an internal combustion engine that drives a generator, that then feeds power into the national grid. I used to be dead cynical about 'green' and renewable energy, because it was hardly producing any percentage of Britain's total power output, and I thought nuclear was the solution, but that's changing – more power is coming from renewables – and my views are too.

The by-product of the digester plants is waste that can go on the fields as fertiliser. And there are so many organic digester plants round our way that they need people to spread the shit.

I plan to learn the job inside-out, then probably put Sharon on it, in the Fendt. She sounds like she's up for it, but first I want to know everything about it, so I can comment on it. If I don't know what's going on, I can't say anything about how much diesel the tractor is burning or how long it takes to do a job. So I'm going shit-spreading in the tractor. I'm looking forward to it.

CHAPTER 15

It'll only get messy if it barrel rolls

Remember Triumph were talking to me about the Nürburgring attempt and it went a bit quiet when the German track said 'Nein' to the whole thing? Well, after I agreed to ride with the Smiths Triumph team at the TT, Triumph started talking to Spellman again.

I felt the factory were thinking, 'You're riding for us now,' but I didn't see it like that. I'm riding for Smiths who are supported by Triumph, just like I'm riding for TAS who are supported by BMW. I'm not riding for BMW. I should like Triumph, because they're a family-owned British company, really British, not just a British name, but I haven't totally clicked with them yet. Anyway, I kept my mouth shut and not long after the Smiths deal was sorted, Triumph started talking about me trying to break the outright motorcycle world land speed record at Bonneville Salt Flats, Utah, in a Triumph streamliner.

In early March, me and Andy Spellman went to meet a couple of Triumph bods in a service station on the M1. Even though they were trying not to be too obvious, I felt from the start that Triumph only really wanted to know one thing: would we make the attempt into a TV show? I told them I'd rather not have it filmed and they stuttered a bit. I like to see if they want me involved because I'm a good man for the job, or is the main reason they chose me because of the TV? I'm not stupid, no other truck fitters are being asked to try and break land speed records at someone else's expense, but I don't want to be anyone's corporate poster boy. I weighed things up, and in the plus column is being given the chance to do stuff that no one in the world is going to do. So sod it, I said yes. The TV lot were happy too. I had gone from a hard line of only agreeing to do the Wall of Death programme and wanting to take a break from the TV, compared to how much I did in 2014, to doing this as well, but it's another once in a lifetime experience.

Triumph got on with organising a date for me to visit the bloke who'd built the streamliner, who was based out in Portland, Oregon. By now there was talk about me being the first man ever to do over 400 mph on a motorbike. As usual, I asked Triumph to make the trip as short as possible.

A flight was booked for Wednesday, 8 April, a few days after the Donington British Superbike round. I worked Monday and Tuesday, biked home Tuesday night, then went dirt tracking with Tom Neave and had a couple of big offs – during one of them Tom ran over me, but I was alright.

As part of the record attempt deal I arranged to be able to take someone with me whenever I have to fly to Portland. I travel on my own a lot and I don't mind that, but it's good to take people, so I had Tom's uncle, Tim the beef farmer, come to America with me for this first visit. I'll take someone different every time I have to go.

After dirt tracking we set off to Birmingham airport, getting there at two in the morning, and kipped in the van for a couple of hours before checking in. Then we took the short flight to Amsterdam and swapped planes for the much longer flight over to Portland, Oregon, on the north-west coast of America. James and Nat, the director and cameraman from North One, came out to do a bit of filming too. Spellman also arranged for me to fly business class, so we waved goodbye to Nat and James, who were in the normal seats, where I'd be if I were paying for myself. In business class the wine keeps coming and I got pissed on the flight. I was like a buckled wheel.

We landed in Portland on Wednesday dinner-time and were met by Matt Markstaller, the man who built the streamliner, the Triumph Castrol Rocket.

I had been filled in on some of the history of the project. Triumph USA had funded much of the $1.5 million, with sponsorship also coming from the oil company, but Matt is the bloke who designed and built the machine and he is not a messer. It sounded to me that because the Rocket had underperformed in its previous record attempts, both in terms of speed and interest from the public, Triumph head office in England got involved to get something more for their investment.

Triumph have a big history with land speed records. Matt explained that for 15 years, between 1955 and 1970, Triumph engines powered the world's fastest motorcycle except for a short 33-day spell when it was taken away, before a Triumph-powered machine won it back. Streamliners with great names like Devil's Arrow, Texas Cigar and Gyronaut X-1 set and broke the record time and time again, until the speed was up to 245.6 mph. One of the most famous names in the history of motorcycling, the Triumph Bonneville, is named after the dry lake bed in Utah where the records were set. The current world's fastest motorcycle is the 376.4 mph Ack Attack, and it is powered by two turbocharged Suzuki Hayabusa engines. The American Rocky Robinson was riding it for that record. His fastest speed was 394 mph, but to set the record you have to take the average of two runs within an hour.

It became obvious, very quickly, that Matt Markstaller knows everything about everything to do with this bike. He knew the answer to every question I asked, and doesn't have to check with anyone else. He's been there for every turn of the wheel his machine has made. Matt is precise, very intelligent, a slim fella, that looks to be in his early forties but is actually 52. He told me he had lived in Portland most of his life, but he mentioned he'd spent a couple of years working in Spain for his church. That put me at ease. I thought a religious man might be less likely to strap me into a death trap.

Matt didn't know much about me, except I'd raced at the

Isle of Man. He told me that knowing I was up for a race like that had filled him with confidence.

We went to look at the bike and get me measured up to make sure I would fit in it. I keep calling it a motorcycle, but it looks like a modern fighter aircraft without wings. It's a streamliner, a missile on two wheels. I sit in it, like a Formula One driver, with my feet in front of me, legs slightly bent, and instead of handlebars or a steering wheel the controls are two levers. I'll be strapped in with a five-point racing car harness and it's nothing like sitting on a bike, it's more like being in a top fuel drag racing car. When I'm strapped in, the crew fasten a canopy over the top, so I'm fully enclosed, just looking out of the small windscreen.

Matt got some cardboard, bent it and put some padding in the cockpit. I was in and out of the streamliner for a couple of hours – with a helmet on, with it off, canopy off, canopy on. The rider they originally designed it around is an American short circuit racer, Jason DiSalvo, and he's tiny, so there was a concern about whether I'd fit in, but I do.

The body of the Triumph streamliner is a full carbon-kevlar monocoque, meaning the skin forms the strength of the structure, instead of being panels fastened to a framework. The cockpit is designed to survive 30 g. It has a tailfin, like a jet plane, and the team can choose one of three different sizes depending on the stability needed and the conditions. The whole machine is 25.5 ft long, 2 ft wide and 3 ft tall.

It is powered by two Triumph Rocket III engines, from the company's huge cruiser. At 2.3 litres, the Rocket III has the biggest displacement production bike motorcycle engine, and physically it is a massive lump, but the maximum cylinder capacity for a land speed record bike, set by the land speed record people, is 3000 cc, three litres, so both these engines are sleeved-down to 1485 cc. In the Triumph Rocket III motorcycle, the engine looks massive, but they don't in this thing. And weight isn't an issue.

Carpenter Racing, a drag racing specialist, have built the motors. The easiest way to reduce an engine's cylinder capacity is to put smaller pistons in it. They could have shortened the stroke too, but didn't. That means they keep the piston speed up and the turbo spinning. The Rocket has MoTeC engine management and runs on methanol.

The engine arrangement, and the way they synchronise and drive together, is beautiful. The engines are fitted one behind the other but staggered, one hard to the left of the bodywork, one hard to the right, and both of them behind the rider's seat. The clutch is computer-controlled, working off the revs. The bike engines still have their standard gearboxes, that are synchronised to shift gears together. The output shafts feeds into a Porsche 953 gearbox.

Matt explained he had paid Goodyear $150,000 out of his total budget to have the mould made for the tyres. In the history of record attempts tyres have been pretty important, as you'd imagine. The streamliner has hub-centre steering, but Matt needed very specific front wheel bearings and could only find them in Germany at $8,000 per bearing and the bike needs two of them. So he bought them. He wasn't about to compromise or cut corners. At the other end of the scale, it has ABS from a scooter, so you can't lock up the back wheel. The brakes are carbon/carbon like a MotoGP bike's dry set-up.

The bike makes 1,000 bhp, nothing stupid, but it is more than four times as powerful as the Tyco BMW S1000RR TT superbike, and that'll do over 200 mph with the wind behind it over the Mountain.

Matt has done the maths and he reckons with the drag ratio of this streamliner you only need 300 horsepower to do 400 mph. But you'd need a lot of space to get up to that speed, that's why he's gone for 1,000 horsepower, so his Rocket accelerates quickly and still has time to brake in the given space. That is another limiting factor – a place big enough to get up to speed. In the very early days, Pendine Sands, where I broke the bicycle land speed record for the first series of *Speed*, was a site of land speed record breaking. More recently people have tried Australia, and the team behind the Bloodhound SSC car, that is hoping to break 1,000 mph, plans to use Hakskeen Pan, in the north-west of South Africa, but more records have been broken at Bonneville in Utah than anywhere else. The last official motorcycle land speed record to be set anywhere other than Bonneville was in New Zealand in 1955. Back then the record was 184 mph. You just have to hope it doesn't rain in the run-up to a Bonneville attempt, like it has the last couple of years. If it does, the lake forgets it's supposed to be dry.

If I ever get to 400 mph, Matt explains, I'll get rid of the first 100 mph, braking down to 300 mph, by using one of the parachutes, then I'll start feeding the brake on and use the second parachute. The bike needs an 11-mile run to complete a record attempt. That's five miles to get up to speed, one mile for the timed attempt and the final five miles to come to a stop. Five miles is Grimsby to Keelby! That's a long way, but at 400 mph I'd be travelling a mile every nine seconds. So, hypothetically, if I did get up to 400 mph and didn't back off, brake or run out of petrol, I could cover five miles in 45 seconds. That doesn't sound that quick to me, but I'd love to be stood at the side of the A46 and watch something pass at 400 mph. The most impressive thing I've ever seen with my own eyes was a top fuel dragster at a drag strip in Gainesville, Florida. You could see the pulses out of the exhaust, just watching those cars blurred my vision and I couldn't turn my head quick enough to follow them. They do 0–100 mph in 0.8 seconds and use something like 25 litres of fuel in one 3.2-second run. A drag car is all about brutal acceleration, the land speed record is all about top speed. Still, a drag car runs at 330 mph in 0.189 miles (305 m). They are mental.

So far, the quickest Matt's Rocket has ever been is only 236 mph and the record they're hoping to beat is 376. And now it sounds like everyone has set their heart on a nice round 400. Maybe I'll need a helmet bag full of rocks between my legs ...

The original rider, Jason DiSalvo, is not a messer, he won the Daytona 200 in 2011, but Matt told me it took him three days to be able to handle the bike without the training wheels. Obviously you can't stick a leg out if you think you're going to fall over, so it has stabilising wheels that tuck away into the bodywork when they're not needed. It must be a tricky beast, and I'm looking forward to giving it a go.

DiSalvo got to 230-odd, and, from what Matt said, it sounded like he didn't want to go any quicker and made some excuses. The team's official attempt in 2014 was rained off, but then they went and rented Bonneville for themselves. Matt explained that they were only given a permit to run at 200 mph, but it didn't really matter, they could've gone as fast as they wanted, and a blind eye would have been turned. That's when DiSalvo did 236. People like Englishman Jack Frost can go faster than that riding a turbocharged Suzuki Hayabusa on a Yorkshire airfield, and Frost is on a bike that doesn't look much different to a standard road bike, never mind a 25-foot long streamlined thing that looks like a nuclear missile.

During the time they rented Bonneville, the team made a load of little adjustments and asked DiSalvo to have another go, but it sounded like he was worried about the wind, explaining the Rocket didn't feel stable. Matt had the on-board camera and told me it looked totally stable. So they suggested another day to the rider, but he said he was racing. DiSalvo had just become the dad of twins, I think, and Matt Markstaller didn't believe his heart was in it. Which is fair enough. No shame in that at all.

The record attempt is planned for 23–27 August – just four months away. There are three or four serious contenders for breaking the 400 mph barrier, with two of the bikes, Ack Attack and BUB 7, both previously holding the outright motorcycle land speed record.

When the BUB and Ack Attack teams were going at it, between 2006 and 2010, they raised the outright record by over 54 mph. In 1990, the motorcycle land speed record was 322 mph, set by Dave Campos in a twin-engined Harley-Davison. Then the Ack Attack and a BUB leapfrogged each other, by 10 mph give or take each time. The legendary dirt track champion Chris Carr set a record in the BUB streamliner with a two-way average of 367.38 mph, then the Ack Attack, with Rocky Robinson in control, upped it to 376.4 in 2010. So it's not going to be easy, but when I hear Matt describing all the details I just thought, We've got this in hand. What could possibly go wrong? There's nothing to hit at Bonneville. It's only going to get messy if it barrel rolls.

Triumph asked if I wanted my skull and spanners and number eight on the side, and at first I thought, Nah, I want to be a bit more incognito about it – until I realised how cool it would look decades in the future, when it's sat in a museum with my skull and spanners on the side. But I'm getting a bit ahead of myself. We have to break the record first.

The streamliner is fascinating. It has a purpose-built trailer and purpose-built truck to tow it, and the bike is the business, so I'm honoured to be part of the project. I'm glad I didn't cut my nose off to spite my face, just because I got the feeling someone at Triumph was getting a bit corporate about things.

Matt Markstaller's bread and butter is running the research and development for Daimler Freightliner trucks. His sideline firm is called Hot Rod Conspiracy, and it was that business that built the Triumph Castrol Rocket. The whole trip was mega, but the highlight for me was visiting the Freightliner truck development workshops.

Matt had built a wind tunnel for trucks and that was beyond impressive. Even with all that, though, they're 20 years behind the truck job in Europe.

In America the scale of a truck business is massive, compared to Europe. Out there, a small fleet is 300 trucks, a big fleet is

8,000. In Europe there are only a very few companies that have over 100 trucks. In Britain it's not unusual for a driver to buy and run his own truck as a sub-contractor, so the person who is spending a big part of their life in it is making the decision. In America it is usually a company accountant who influences the decision to buy trucks and everything is about the price. So trucks don't have disc brakes or canbus electronic systems because these fleets can't afford them. And I don't think their emissions rules are as tight as ours and they don't have any of our fancy semi-automatic gearboxes.

It sounds like the American truck drivers are stuck in their ways, too. They like their air windows, a system where the windows go up and down with air pressure, not electric motors. And the trucks are all double-drive (both sets of rear wheels are driving), but we only need double-drive for 80–100-ton weights. It makes the truck heavier and uses more fuel. But Americans have them and they only pull 40-ton over there. I couldn't work it out, and Matt didn't have an answer for that either. I think it's just because they've always done it that way.

We had one night in Portland, and James and Nat went out on the town, but I backed off because I was racing that weekend. On Thursday, 9 April, in the afternoon, we flew back from Portland to Salt Lake City, and from there to Charles de Gaulle, Paris. We landed back in Birmingham on Friday afternoon, then it was a carry-on getting out of Birmingham and up past Nottingham on a Friday afternoon.

I had to rush home, because I had a busy weekend at Scarborough coming up.

I was interested in the whole record-breaking thing, especially the chance to do 400 mph, but meeting Matt Markstaller made me even more fired up. His passion gave me even more passion for the job. I was looking forward to August.

I was in Ireland for the bike job and made the time to do a bit of research for work. We're doing a truck up to concours standard and there's a company in Ireland that had one restored in Holland, that was very, very good. We're using it as a benchmark, so I went to have a look at it.

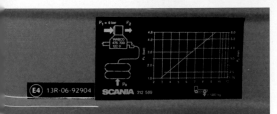

The North West 2015 was a waste of bloody time, except for a couple of things, one of them being a visit to McElvaney's truck yard to do more research on the Scania I'm restoring. This was the best one I'd ever seen. I liked the attention to detail of the load-sensing graph on the door and the reflective sticker.

Practising TT pit stops on Lady Helen's driveway in the Isle of Man, the day before the Superbike race.

My TT helmets, painted for me, as usual, by my mate Paddy.

(*Facing page*) In the back of the TAS race truck before one of the races. This high-tech bit of kit stops me getting arm pump. Easier than an operation and a few weeks off work to recover.

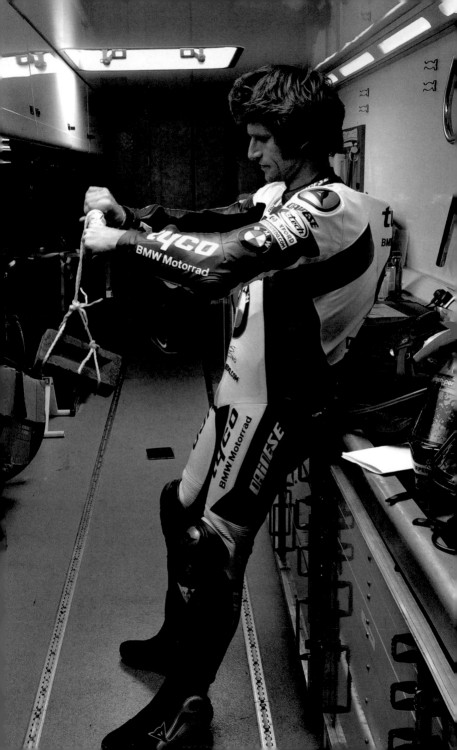

With Nige on the beach in TT practice week. Me and Spellman realised it was a £1,000 fine for not having him on a lead and spent half an hour chasing the bugger.

If I'm around and nothing needs doing I'm happy to sign a few things, but I don't deal well with people mithering me when there's racing to sort out. The support I get is great, though, and I know one day they'll all realise I'm just a lorry mechanic from Grimsby.

Catching up with all Nige's news after the Superbike TT.

First look at the Victory electric bike I rode to fourth at the TT, after two laps' practice. I told the boys they still burnt fossil fuels to get the batteries charged and electric power was all balls. That broke the ice but hats off, it's a work of art.

For the last few years, me and four lads from Hope have buggered off for my birthday. We always used to do a race in Newquay, but this year we made a change and rode a few trail centres in Wales and went out for a few beers. It was mint.

A photo from a week that would take some beating. I got the Sunday night ferry to the Isle of Man for the Southern 100, got there at six on Monday morning, practised that night, practised and raced Tuesday night, raced Wednesday night, raced Thursday afternoon and won the main race. Flew to Gatwick, stayed in a hotel (£95, broke my heart), then flew out to Munich where I met Jason, Lee, Sam and Tim, who had driven out in my van. Then we drove to Austria, got signed on for the Salzkammergut Trophy mountain bike race. We kipped on that football field. Up at five in the morning, raced till nine at night – it's only 135 miles but it's 24,000 feet of ascent and it's the toughest one-day race in the world. Finished the race, had steak and chips, got in the van and drove home to Lincolnshire straight after it. I was knackered.

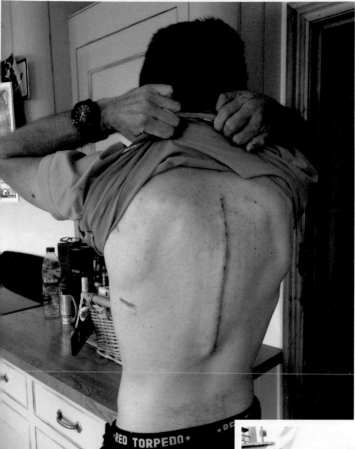

ust a week after the operation and the scar
ooked neat. They had to cut me open to
od my spine back together.

After the accident at the Ulster Grand Prix
I kept talking in my sleep. I don't know if
Sharon was thinking I was talking about
other women or this or that, but I kept
dreaming about this industrial parts washer
I'd seen at McElvaney's. That is literally my
dream parts washer. It's massive. That's the
back timing cover off a Scania in there, and
that part is three feet across.

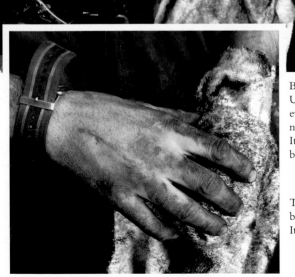

Back at work after the
Ulster accident. I'm sore, and
everything's a struggle, but I
needed to get back to work.
It was driving me crackers
being at home.

The scar from having the
bones in my hand plated.
It's still swollen in this photo.

CHAPTER 16

Racing in my anorak.
Not very corporate

I had a bit of a kip on the plane back from Portland, so I was set to drive straight to Moody's to see the lie of the land. From there I went to Sal's to pick the dog up, before driving to Wharton's for tea. He's the old fella who used to come to the odd race with me and share his wisdom. He's not been well.

I couldn't stay too long because I had to meet Mark McIvor, my TAS mechanic, to prepare the BMW race bike for the next day's race at Oliver's Mount, Scarborough. I'd brought the BMW superstocker back from Spain with an idea to do a couple of track days at Cadwell, but I hadn't had time. I had ridden dirt track and the Triumph, though. The bike was still in its plain white fairings, but Mark had brought the right bodywork, so we set to drilling and fitting it, getting done about ten o'clock.

I eventually remembered that when I go to places like Donington I have to turn it around and use it for my own amusement. Even so, my boss at the truck yard, Mick Moody, was sent more abusive text messages after the race, ordering him to call me an ignorant bastard next time he saw me. That's just what he wanted on a Bank Holiday Monday. Going to Scarborough to race is different.

Mark stayed at mine and the next morning we were up at half-five and out of the house for six, just 12 hours after getting back from Portland. We headed north on the drive to Scarborough. I went in my own van and Mark drove to the North Yorkshire track in a rented Transit with a roof-rack on the top. We looked like a couple of driveway tarmackers. As soon as we arrived we unloaded the BMW and grabbed my riding kit for it all to go through scrutineering.

I've raced the Spring National for the last three years. It's the first real road race of the year, because the British Championship round at Donington is a short circuit. It doesn't hurt to be in as many race situations as I can, but the feeling of the Spring meeting is different to the bigger Gold Cup weekend later in the year. The track surface is shitty, blathered in muck, because it still feels like the back-end of the winter, even in mid-April. It's cold and normally windy, but it gives you an idea and it's worth being out on the bike. Plus it's only 70 miles up the road from my house. The Spring National was always a one-day meeting, so every time I've done it with the Tyco TAS team I've taken the bike myself. This year it was a two-dayer. A lot of the teams, like Mar-Train and RC Racing, wouldn't traipse their trucks there for a one-day meeting, but they would for two days, so the organisers changed it.

I just had the one bike, the superstock that I'd ride in the Open class, so I didn't practise till ten. Sometimes there is a benefit in having the more powerful superbike over a superstock around Oliver's Mount, and I could've raced either in the Open class, but perhaps the superbike advantage isn't so big at that time of year on a slippery, slimy, cold track.

Both my 2015 superbike and superstock bikes are based on BMW S1000RR road bikes, but you can make a lot more changes to a road bike modified for the Superbike class than one that runs in Superstock. A superstock bike must have the same wheels, brakes and front forks that come on the standard road bike that anyone could buy from a local bike shop, though the fork internals, springs, damping or whole cartridges can be replaced with higher spec stuff. Superbike rules allow for far more engine tuning and component changes, too. Superbikes can run slick tyres, but superstocks have to have treaded, road legal tyres. Modern superstock tyres, like the Metzelers I use, are virtually slicks with a very minimal pattern cut into them, but they're still road legal. Modern road bikes, like the BMW and Kawasaki's ZX-10R, are so good, straight from the showroom, that there isn't the same gulf in difference between the two classes now, so it's not such a big handicap to be racing against superbikes if you're on a superstocker.

Because this was an Open class, and I chose to race a superstocker, I could have chosen to fit slicks, but I ran it on treaded tyres. I used the Metzeler cross-ply front the company developed from my feedback. That tyre is better when I want that last little bit of it while braking and leaning in at a corner. At Scarborough the bike was pushing on into the corners because of all the auto-blipping gubbins, and it still gave me the confidence to turn it in. The electronics are pretty sophisticated on the standard BMW, and the bike's engine management system, its computer brain, knows when the rider is changing gear and revs the engine to smooth the gear changes. It helps when you're hard on the brakes and have enough to concentrate on.

The quickest lads this weekend were Dean Harrison, Ryan Farquhar, Ivan Lintin and Lee Johnston. My Tyco TAS teammate William Dunlop didn't race there. I don't know why. He's better at some Irish stuff than I am, but I beat him more than he beats me around Oliver's Mount.

Dean Harrison's a good lad, in his mid twenties and he's the next in line for winning TTs. He's already won the Lightweight. I've spoken to him a fair bit, but he's a typical Yorkshireman, he knows it all.

Lee Johnston's a sound lad, people call him the General. He's from Enniskillen in Northern Ireland, right on the border, but you'd think he was from the south, because of his accent. He lives in North Yorkshire and rides for East Coast Racing. He's five foot bugger-all, a cool-looking dude with loads of tattoos and hair. You wouldn't be surprised if he was in a boy band.

I was only going to race twice each day, and was entered in the Open races that riders could enter on a superbike, superstock or 600. All of the fast blokes were on superbikes except me and Lee Johnston. My superbike wasn't finished, so

I had the superstock, and given the choice that's the bike I'd prefer to be on for this meeting. Johnston was on a superstock like me. I qualified on pole, but five seconds off the lap record, that I set a couple of years ago in better conditions.

In the first race the bike was shit off the line. It has launch control but I have always thought I can usually do a better job manually with my own throttle and clutch control. I learned that I can't with this BMW, it just wants to wheelie. I don't know if it's because the initial movement of the rear shock is too firm, so rather than squatting, it just wants to lift the front, but it wasn't good.

Launch control, traction control and anti-wheelie are all names for similar kinds of engine management systems. Keeping it as simple and basic as possible, a modern sports motorcycle is so powerful that it can wheelie or spin its back tyre in lots of situations. For road riders, buying bikes straight out of the showroom that are now making over 180 bhp, this is usually a bad thing, it can be too much power in a lot of situations and it comes in fast, so manufacturers are offering what are called 'rider aids', to try and stop their customers spannering themselves left, right and centre. The BMW S1000RR system is so good we can use it in races.

If a racer gives his bike a handful of throttle off the start line the thing will just wheelie. If the wheelie is too high you have to close the throttle, and that buggers up your run to the first corner. So you have to get the throttle, clutch and back brake just right – or you did before sophisticated wheelie and launch control. Different manufacturers' systems work different ways, but they measure the difference between the front and rear wheel speeds, and the extension of the front forks, to work out if the front wheel is off the floor, or if the back wheel is spinning. The biggest differences between the control systems is how they then reduce the power to bring the front wheel back down, or stop the rear spinning. In the past, systems I've tested would retard the ignition or cut a spark to one of the four cylinders, effectively reducing the power by 25 per cent. The BMW is more subtle. It closes the throttle openings no matter what the wrist on the twistgrip is doing, but it takes some getting used to.

After the relatively poor start, I was fifth or sixth going into the first corner, a left-hand hairpin that goes into a steep rise. The BMW wants to wheelie like buggery out of there, so I am living on the back brake to make it half-sensible. I never had that problem testing in Spain, but we get it to Scarborough, a track with big changes of elevation, and it's a bloody handful.

I know where I'm going around Oliver's Mount and know where I can overtake people. I usually do it along the back straight, at the top of the track, heading towards the left before the café. There is a kink in the straight, but if you get the right line you can pass.

I got past a few lads, but Farquhar was in the lead and he had made a break. He was riding well, especially as he hadn't raced a superbike for a couple of years. Fair play. He's always good round there. He's had 100 wins at Scarborough. I didn't get a chance to speak to him, but I gave him a thumbs up on the grid. I think there's mutual respect between us. He was my carrot and I got my head down and eventually passed him for the win.

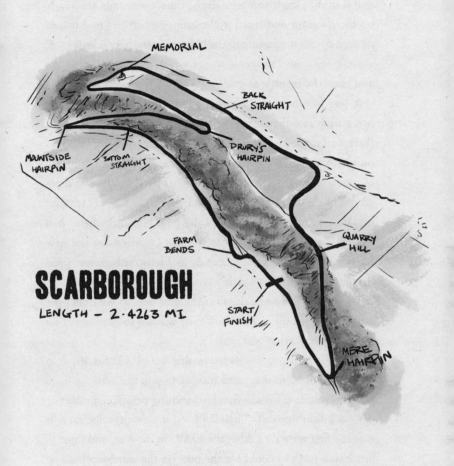

MEMORIAL

BACK STRAIGHT

DRURY'S HAIRPIN

MOUNTSIDE HAIRPIN

BOTTOM STRAIGHT

FARM BENDS

QUARRY HILL

SCARBOROUGH

LENGTH - 2·4263 MI

START/ FINISH

MERE HAIRPIN

The next race I got another terrible start. When I'm waiting for the lights to change, I have the bike just above tickover and feed the clutch and revs all the time. Some lads are nearly on the rev limit and trusting the launch control. I'm mustard when it comes to reacting to the lights, but the bike is unsettled, wheelie-ing, and I'm trying to get straight on the back brake and chop the throttle slightly.

It was like race one all over again, fifth or sixth into the first corner and then up to me to try and pass lads on the next three or four laps. Lee Johnston took some passing. He was on a BMW like me, but he was getting wild. He's not afraid of opening the throttle. I'd get close to passing, then he'd get all out of shape, so I'd have to back off so he didn't crash into me. It was cat and mouse, but I did pass him and when I had I didn't have the speed to catch Dean Harrison on the new Mar-Train R1. I was going as fast as I felt comfortable. I put that fastest lap in, but I didn't win.

There were a lot of delays on the first day, so we didn't get out of the track till seven. Mark only wanted to have beans on toast for tea, so that was easy.

The next morning I walked the dog before setting off, then Tim Coles came to mine and travelled up in the van.

It was mizzling for our Sunday morning practice, not wet or dry, so I didn't go out. Then it pissed it down for the race. It was the first time I'd ridden the BMW in the wet, and I got as much of a feel as I could for the bike on the warm-up lap and then went straight into the race.

The Metzeler wet tyres are good, but the bike needs to be set up differently to make the most of them. It needs to be more supple at both ends. When you're feeding on the throttle the suspension needs to give a fair bit more. In the wet you want the suspension to load the tyres gently and gradually. If it's too harsh, the tyre just spins. You adjust the suspension by backing off the preload, taking the tension off the spring in its static state, to give it a little more movement. It's a bit kinder to the tyre.

I changed the throttle maps on the dash. Just putting it in the rain setting gave me the best initial throttle response I've ever had. Bloody brilliant. And that's just customer stuff. It's a road bike, not a special race bike. Anything past that initial 10 per cent was brutal, and there was no feel higher up the rev range, but we've got something to work with. I had to keep giving it gears, to keep the thing settled. At 9–10,000 rpm it's probably only making 120 horsepower, but by 14–15,000 rpm it's making close to 200 bhp, so I kept it in the higher gears to tame it.

Everything's so good with the modern BMW engines that there isn't a lot of improvement you can make and still keep within the rules of the Superstock class. The team make sure the valve clearances are all perfect, take a few burrs out ... They're just tiny improvements.

The big race on Sunday was the second leg of the Spring National, the feature race. It was so cold that I went out on the warm-up lap with my Hope jacket over my Tyco leathers. Mark said, 'OK, but take it off on the start line.' He was there with me on the start line and could see how cold and miserable it was and can't have had the heart to tell me to take it off, so I raced in my anorak. Not very corporate, but the weather was minging. If he'd have told me to take it off I would have. Whatever Mark says goes.

The conditions were so bad I was considering pulling in rather than risk sliding off a bike that wasn't set up for rain, in a race that I was still only using as a test. But it wasn't hurting me to get a feel for the bike in crap conditions, so I stayed out and finished in fourth place.

I came in and told Mark it was only luck that the bike came back in one piece, adding there's not a lot being learned, but I'd go out in the second race if you want. Then someone told us my two results were good enough to win the Spring National class, so I was pretty chuffed that I hadn't pulled in.

I had learned stuff about the bike, and I always enjoy working and spending time with Mark, especially when we're working out of the back of a Transit. I don't need all the fancy race trucks, and racing like this is closer to what I really enjoy from a race. Even if it's so cold and wet I have to wear a jacket over my leathers. Racing at Scarborough hadn't answered the question of whether I should keep racing or not, but at least I enjoyed it.

I worked on Monday, then left that night to drive out to the Metzeler factory in Germany, to do a couple of days' filming for them. I drove there in a fancy Range Rover Sport that I was road testing for the *Sunday Times*. There isn't a lot of slack time at the moment …

CHAPTER 17

Fair play to him, he gave me a cup of cold coffee with ice cubes in it

At a race like Donington I'm not really enjoying myself, but I'm trying to achieve something and see the bigger picture. And I can amuse myself by looking at the people around me, dressed like they think a motorcycle racer is supposed to dress ... and just smile to myself. But I look forward to a race like the Cookstown 100.

Cookstown is the traditional start to the Irish road racing season, and this year was 24–25 April. I'd already done the Spring National at Scarborough two weekends previous, and Donington, so it wasn't my first real road race of the year and the British Superbike season was in full swing. Like all of the races in Northern Ireland, the main race takes place on a Saturday, for religious reasons, with a short practice and qualifying session and a couple of races scheduled for Friday. As usual, I'd had a busy week in the run-up to it.

The weekend before Cookstown I had been over in Northern Ireland at a custom show at Antrim Harley-Davidson. It's run by the same people who run the bicycle mail order company Chain Reaction Cycles and they wanted me to be part of their open day. They paid for my ferry, gave me some Shimano Di2 gears with electric shifting for one of my pushbikes, and I got to see Sharon for the weekend.

On Monday I was at Moody's from seven till seven, then the next day I was up at three o'clock to drive down to Chichester to go in the stunt plane – the day that had to be postponed when it clashed with the truck IVA test. I had to be there for eight, but the traffic was bad, so I was late.

Being a passenger in a Red Bull stunt plane was all part of filming for the Wall of Death programme, to show the effects of big g-forces. The pilot was trying to get me to pass out, but I didn't and I think he was a bit surprised. He let me take control of the plane and do some manoeuvres, and all. After we landed I had to do what the TV folk call 'a piece to camera', talking about the experience, my feelings at that exact moment and my thoughts about the whole thing. As normal, it's all off the top of my head. I've never had a script in any of the programmes I've done. I sit there and talk to the director, at the side of the camera. I can never look right down the camera and talk to the audience like most presenters. Sitting there, fresh out of the plane, I felt horrible and had to keep slapping myself on the face to try and shake myself out of it. I felt like I had the worst hangover in the world.

After the filming was done I set off driving home, but I was still feeling rough. I had to stop at one of those fancy coffee shops at the side of the road. It was a lovely April day, knocking on for 20 degrees. I was still slapping myself on the face when I walked in.

I looked at the menu above the counter and saw what I thought would work for me. It was one of those cold coffees that I know the name of but won't let my mouth say. I asked the bloke behind the counter for a cold coffee. He said, 'Do you mean a f_____?' I said, 'No, just a cold coffee.' He asked if I was sure. I told him I was, and, fair play to him, he gave me a cup of cold coffee with a couple of ice cubes in it. So I never had to ask for, or drink, a you-know-what. Anyway, it seemed to do some good and I got home safely at ten o'clock. I was still feeling rough, though, so I went straight to bed, knowing I was up at five the next morning. After a few hours' sleep I felt a million dollars. I even rode to work on my new Orange Five mountain bike, rather than my single speed.

The single speed is easier on the road, because it's lighter and has skinnier tyres, so there's less rolling resistance. It's built for speed. The Orange Five is a bombproof bit of kit, and light for what it is, a full suspension mountain bike, but much heavier than a road bike. I was still feeling good at the end of the day so I rode a right oddball way home, first heading down the docks, then Stallingborough; Killingholme; Habrough; Newsholme Woods; Brocklesby; Kirmington; back to Brocklesby; Searby Top; Searby Bottom; Howsham; North

Kelsey ... 35 miles in all. I even wrote in my diary, 'Best ride home ever'.

I worked Thursday, then cycled home again, rushed about to get loaded up and collected the dog from Sal, before driving the four hours to the night crossing out of Holyhead and back to Ireland for the second time in a week.

I got to the docks just in time to roll onto the ferry, no messing. They pretty much shut the door after me. Nigel slept in the van for the three-hour crossing to Dublin, while I read my book, *Look Who's Back*, a story of Hitler waking up on a park bench in 2011, that was a bestseller in Germany, then got forty winks. I got to Sharon's for one in the morning.

Sharon told me she wanted to come to the racing, but I wasn't keen. As far as I'm concerned, girlfriends and racing don't mix. She said she'd be no bother, and had some work to do for Skerries 100, so she'd be going anyway, so I wasn't about to tell her she couldn't go to the race. I love spending time with her, but not when I'm at a race. She said she'd be off for most of the day, so we set off on the drive north.

I had to be in Hillsborough, the bottom side of Belfast, for eight on Friday morning to do something with Ford. Trust Ford are sponsoring the Hillsborough Oyster Festival, and as part of this big family event there is a go-kart race, though they call it a soapbox race.

When Ford first got in touch, they asked me to be involved in the go-kart side of things and I said maybe, because I need a new van and I thought they could do me a deal on one. I asked them to give me a price on a new Transit. When they came back with a price it was only £200 less than I could get it for through Moody's connections, so I told them thanks very much, but no thanks. I gave it a miss and bought a Transit myself.

Then they came back and said they'd give me a van. This was after I'd already ordered one, so I'll give one to my sister, Sal.

On that Friday morning I have to do some photos for the promotion, then I have to turn up to the event, but it's all getting a bit tight because I have to fly out to Bonneville for the top speed job and it'll be touch and go getting back in time. It'll be right, I'm sure.

After doing the Ford stuff, we went on to Cookstown in Co. Tyrone, where I got signed on and waited around for qualifying. We were only going to get a five-lap session of combined practice and qualifying on Friday and another on Saturday morning before we were expected to race. That would be five laps of a place I hadn't seen for two years.

I had left home thinking that the BMW superstock was hard work around Scarborough, nearly lethal in the wet, so it would be even harder work around a track like Cookstown. After Scarborough I had told Mark McIvor I needed a few things changing. He'd got back to the TAS workshop and got Davey, the electronics man, who is also Philip Neill's brother-in-law, on the case, and they'd altered the chassis while they were at it too.

When the time to qualify came around I got on the bike, set off on those five laps and everything changed. I went from seriously considering packing in racing – no 2015 Isle of Man TT, no more serious racing – to thinking racing motorbikes was the best thing ever again. And that's at Cookstown! A track I like, but I'm not wild about. It's never been one of my favourites, but something clicked.

Everything's a bit ramshackle at a race like Cookstown. It's all run by enthusiasts and no one's making any money. Small Irish races like this one are sponsored by local companies who want to do their bit for the sport and the towns they're in. The kind of companies that support these races are family garages; mini supermarkets; the local council; plant hire firms and fuel companies. When I say fuel companies, I mean those that fill up your house's heating oil tank, not BP or Shell. It couldn't be more real.

More than half the Cookstown track is made up of roads that are so narrow two cars would struggle to pass each other, and there's cowshit all over the road, because of the farm traffic. I was coming out of the road-end corners and heading for hedge bottoms on the exit. It was the absolute bollocks. I hadn't seen the place for two years, but I knew I had to go hard straight from the off, because all the others go-ers would be there and if you're not in the top eight, you're going to struggle. Within two laps of getting on the bike, I was doing 185 mph down the cowshit-covered straight. It reminded me that the road racing experience is going to take some replacing.

The organisers try to get four or five races done and dusted on Friday night, to take the pressure off Saturday, but the weather buggered that up. Francis Everard, the clerk of the course, held the riders' meeting and told us the weather was likely to be wet for Saturday morning, and explained he was shuffling the race programme so the races for the fastest and most powerful bikes, the Open and the Supersport 600 classes, would be moved to later in the day when the weather was supposed to be better. That meant the less powerful bikes, that run on treaded tyres, would run in the morning. It was the sensible way of dealing with it, and the 125s and classics went out early with no complaints. The race classes at a meeting like Cookstown are different to British Superbikes or the TT. There are two classic classes; 125s; 400s; Supertwins; Supersport and Open.

The clerk of the course is the man the buck stops with at a race meeting. Francis Everard used to race and he can think on his feet, and comes at it from a racer's point of view. He did a brilliant job, with the support of the club behind him. On that Saturday race day they cut a lap or two off some of the smaller races, and managed to run 18 races in a day and still get the roads open for six. No messing.

I had been asked to practise on the Tyco TAS BMW superbike, that had just been built, on the Wednesday before Cookstown, but I couldn't make it over because I had to be at work. My team-mate William Dunlop tested it at Kirkistown and they had a mint day in great weather, so I was kicking myself a bit – but, as always, truck work is the priority.

So for Cookstown I decided to ride the superstock, that I'd raced at Scarborough, in the Open class. Having an Open class is the old-school way of doing it. You can enter anything up to 1300 cc, and a good rider on a 600 can go well on a tight Irish track, up against the 1000s. Like at Scarborough, I could have run slicks, but I chose treaded Metzeler Racetec RR superstock tyres.

By the time I was ready to get on the bike it was dinnertime. I'd spent the morning reading a book in the back of the truck. The main pits are in the pub car park, with another pit over the other side of the road. The start line is just outside the pub, the Braeside Bar. The weather had improved. There were still a few damp patches, but nothing bad.

The track is only about two miles long, but it's tricky enough and fast, with an average lap speed of 90 mph on the big bikes. I'd qualified fifth, on the second row, but I wasn't too bothered, because while I want to win races, I was still learning the bike.

I got a better start than I did at Scarborough, because I murdered it. I had to be cruel and I used some of the wheelie control. The BMW doesn't have cables leading to the throttle bodies, it has a potentiometer on the twistgrip that measures the movement and sends an electrical signal to the throttle bodies to tell them to open. Like I explained earlier, if the engine management brain senses a lack of traction it does the job of closing the throttle. At that stage of the season, the traction control was doing too much, so I didn't trust it. I felt the lack of traction too, so I shut the throttle slightly to find more grip, but then the traction control system would cut in as well, and that begins to cause problems with the chassis.

Anyway, I revved its nuts off from the start and was third, I think, going into the first bend, a right-hander called Gortin Corner. I passed Michael Dunlop into here and was behind Derek Sheils and Derek McGee, two fast Irish national racers, proper go-ers. I got up to second, then into the lead, when the race was red-flagged. The restart was the same, into third off the start, then I plugged my way through.

I was getting my pit board signals every lap. They said +1 second, then +0.5, then +0.2. It turned out to be Michael Dunlop catching me. I was going as hard as I felt comfortable with and he came past me over a jump. It was unexpected, but a safe move. He's bloody good round there and he rides hard. If he'd made this move when I was racing the Suzukis I would have had to watch him pull away, but on the BMW I could sit on his back wheel. And he was riding his Yamaha superbike on slicks. He was a bit faster through the smoother stuff, but I felt I was quicker on the rough stuff out the back of the circuit.

It's worth describing what a lap of Cookstown is like. You push your bike out of the pub car park onto the start–finish straight to line up for the race. On a flying lap, this is a 185 mph straight. We're only running two teeth more on the back sprocket than we do at the TT, so it's fast. From a standing start, I'll be reaching something like 150 mph in fifth gear, before the first 90-degree right-hander, and I change down from fifth to first gear. Every other lap it would be sixth to first. I'm hard on the throttle exiting, and up through the gears into second, then third into a left-hander, then back into first for a corner called McAdoo Bends, named after the famous team owner and sponsor from Northern Ireland, Winston McAdoo. He lives close to the corner. McAdoo's is tight enough, and it's a place I am asking the bike for 80 per cent throttle, but it would only give me 20 per cent. The bike's brain knew there was a difference in wheel speed and the gyro was telling the engine management system that it wanted to wheelie, but

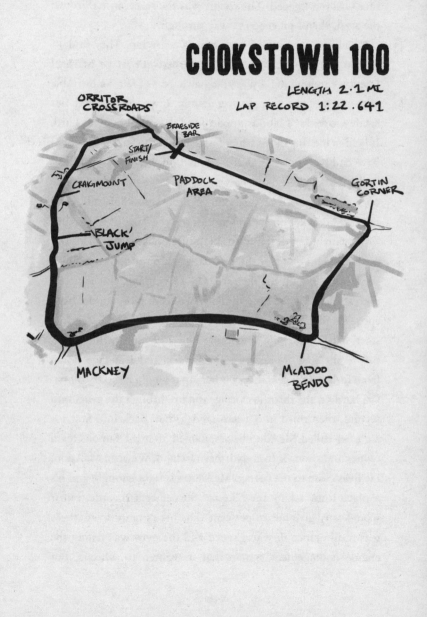

COOKSTOWN 100

LENGTH 2.2 MI
LAP RECORD 1:22.641

ORRITOR
CROSSROADS

BRAESIDE
BAR

START/
FINISH

CRAIGMOUNT

PADDOCK
AREA

GORTIN
CORNER

'BLACK'
JUMP

MACKNEY

McADOO
BENDS

I had it covered with my foot on the back brake pedal. The power delivery felt flat until I changed gear, then it would go like hell for a second till the anti-wheelie cut in again. It kept second-guessing me, trying to keep the bike under control while I was already doing it with my foot on the brake, like I always have done.

I roll around McAdoo's with a tiny bit of throttle, before going back to first gear for another 90-degree right.

From there it's up a steep hill, the hill that was covered in cowshit in practice. This is a place I'm virtually riding in the hedge bottom and where I thought, This is the best thing ever!

I'm giving the bike gears up the hill until I'm in fourth. I'm not revving it hard, because the hill is so steep that the bike feels like it wants to wheelie end over end. I don't have the throttle at 100 per cent open, I'm just in fourth gear, instead of the top of third, to keep the bike settled. At the top of the hill, I roll the throttle, staying in fourth gear. There's a wall on the right. I get close to it as I line the bike up for a jump that turns left. At these speeds, you have to line it up just right.

I must be doing the thick end of 140 mph when I hit the jump. The road doesn't drop away much, so the bike isn't far off the floor, like it is at some other Irish road circuits. Still, I'll be jumping a good 20 feet or more, which is enough as I'm trying to turn the bike in mid-air by leaning it on its side, a bit like a motocross scrub. When I'm on the right line, I'm apexing the corner in mid-air. I'm good through there. Which is just as well, because if you're on the wrong line at 140 mph with both wheels off the floor, you're in big trouble. So I tilt the bike a bit in mid-air and land. My BMW is dead settled.

I'm stood up, with all my weight on the footpegs, none on the seat. The bike is still in fourth gear and I'm onto the throttle for something like half a second, just 20–30 per cent throttle, before getting hard on the brakes and back to bottom gear for a very tight 110-degree right-hander, called Mackney. It has a hedge as an apex and I have my shoulder in the hedge.

I'm in first for the corner, then I short-shift into second as I exit for a right and slack left. I start getting on the throttle through the right and accelerate through the left to get the drive down the back straight. This is the straight with another jump in it. This one is called Black Jump and it's the one where Michael Dunlop passed me twice in the first race. The leaders are hitting the jump hard in fourth, so north of 140 mph, but it's dead straight, so there's no art to it. When you land you chuck the bike straight into Craigmount, a really fast right, still in fourth. There's a bloody big stone wall on the left and the temporary grandstand on the right. A couple of boys have been killed hitting the wall on the left when I've been racing here.

I roll off the throttle in fourth, then get back on it towards another jump. There are walls on the left-hand side, where the meatwagon parks, and a telegraph pole on the right-hand side. The telegraph pole is the apex even though it's not a corner, really. When you jump, you sort of aim for the pole, because if you jumped straight you'd end up in the wall.

When I land I go back two gears to second, for another 90-degree, road-end right-hander with a steep adverse camber. I have to make sure I'm off the brake when I tip in or it loads the front tyre and makes the front end want to wash out. On the exit I run right out to the kerb and change up to third, before going back to second for a 90-degree right-hander. The camber is in your favour through this bend and I'm grinding through the toes of my boots.

Next it's up to third and round a dead rough sweeper, called Orritor Crossroads, with Heras galvanised steel mesh fencing on the outside, placed tight to the track. Then we're back onto the start–finish straight, and up to 185 mph. My bike's telemetry, which is the data the bike captures, is saying I'm going from 100 to 50 per cent throttle before I'm braking for the first corner, Gortin, because the track is quite steep downhill into that bend and the bike just wants to wheelie. If I didn't feather the throttle before getting on the brakes I would just lock the front wheel. And that's a lap of Cookstown. It's short, tight and busy.

Back in that first race, Michael Dunlop had passed me over Black Jump, but I got back in front at Gortin, and then ran tight lines for the rest of the lap, that didn't let him get his nose back in front, but it was a close finish. My bike wasn't 100 per cent sorted, but it was ten times better than it had been at Scarborough. I've never been the king of the late brakers, but the BMW is so stable on the brakes and the bike even blips the throttle for you when you're going down the gears.

The winning margin was half of fuck-all, 0.114s, because Dunlop was trying to get the run on me, but he wasn't riding like a dickhead or anything. I was first, Michael Dunlop second, Sheils third. William was fifth. He won both the 600 races, though, by a fair margin too, on Chris Dowd's Yamaha R6.

I had a few hours between my two races, so me and Davey got our heads together to talk about the electronic settings. He had been sent some information by the Germans at BMW headquarters telling him a load of stuff. When I raced the British Superbikes in 2008, for Shaun Muir's Hydrex Honda team, I used to sit and look at the graphs on the computer screen, but I haven't done it much since, not even at the TT. Now, because we're developing a bike that is new to me and the team, we're learning a lot by really studying it and it's helping me go faster.

Even though the bike I was racing is a superstock bike, the BMW has a GPS tracker on board as standard, and it can trace the racetrack and show where the engine management system is closing the throttle, because of lack of traction, and where I'm closing it. It's showing my throttle trace and the actual throttle opening on the same graph, so we could see that I might be asking for 50 per cent throttle, but it's saying, 'Nein, you only need 40 per cent.' The Suzuki didn't do that. Even the no-expense-spared TAS Suzuki superbike was a lot less sophisticated, but I'd get around it by controlling the bike with the back brake, when I felt it needed it.

The more I learn about the BMW, the more I think it's mega. At some points, in first gear, I'm asking for 80 per cent, but only getting 20 per cent, because it wants to wheelie. On any other bike I'd be hard on the back brake to keep it settled, and I still am at times, so I need to learn a different way of riding or back the traction control right off. As we were talking, Davey said he thought I could improve my starts if I just got out of first gear quicker. We spent hours looking at the lap-top screen, and this was data from a bloody superstock bike! That just shows how advanced road bikes are getting, that they have all this technology – stuff race teams are not allowed to add to superstock bikes if they didn't come like that from the factory to the showroom. The Suzuki had been left years behind.

Eventually we went for beans and sausage on toast with Hector, the team boss, and Mark and Denver from the team. We were in the Braeside Bar and people were still asking for stuff signing, but they seem more polite in Ireland. Not everyone in England or at the TT is rude, I'm not saying that, but no one ever sends text messages to my boss, calling me a See You Next Tuesday, after I've been racing in Ireland.

For the second race, I was fifth on the grid again and this time I went into the first corner in second place. I'd listened to Davey and got it out of first gear early, so I was short-shifting at 6,000 rpm, when the thing will rev to 14,000. Derek Sheils was ahead of me again, but I got past him. It was a hard enough move. I ran in a bit hot into the right-hander called Mackney and had to go around the outside of him. It wasn't dangerous, but when I was ahead of him I put my foot out to say, 'Sorry, mate.' Still, I had to get past him. It wasn't a parade lap. Dunlop got past too, and my pit board was showing +0.2, then +0, +0, +0 every lap. I could hear him behind me for four or five laps. Because of the weather, a lot of the races had been cut in length, so they got everything in before the roads opened again, and I think this Open class race was a ten-lapper.

The Yamaha sounds different to every other bike, so I was pretty sure it was him, but I wasn't looking back and he wasn't trying to get me on the brakes. He was trying to pass me over the jump, though, where he had in the first race, but I'd learned a bit and was going faster, giving him less chance to make a move. I knew that neither of us would get away from the other, so I was riding a line that was giving him every opportunity to get past at the slower road-end corners. I wasn't braking early, but I wasn't running a defensive line either. He passed me on lap six, but I didn't fight back, choosing to sit behind and see where he was quick. He passed me about two-thirds of the way around the lap, leading into the smoother part where he'd been quicker in the first race of the day. We went over the start–finish line and he'd already pulled four or five bike lengths on me, but by the time we were in the rough stuff I'd caught back up and he'd have been able to hear my exhaust.

We got to the Mackney corner, where I'd passed Derek Sheils to take the lead, and Dunlop low-sided in front of me at 50 mph, no speed at all really. He had too much lean and too much throttle, something had to give and his Yamaha's rear tyre let go. He skidded up the road on the front of his helmet and I nearly ran over him as I steered between him and his bike. It wasn't a big crash, but by the time I got around three more corners the red flags came out.

We were halfway through lap seven of what was going to be a ten-lap race, and after a lot of umming and ahhing, they decided not to have a restart, but to count back to the end of the last lap, and gave the win to me. The team looked pleased and I was happy for them.

Sharon was true to her word and I didn't see her till everything was done. She wasn't trying to congratulate me after the races, or hold an umbrella or carry my drink and helmet. I didn't know where she was and I preferred that. She understood I didn't have a problem with her, it's just the way I'm used to doing things at races and I don't want to change it, if I can help it.

On the ferry home, I was thinking about the bike and decided I want the traction control to be switchable, so as soon as I'm on the back brake it turns the system off. It wouldn't have been possible to race the Suzuki at Cookstown, like the BMW had let me. The BMW in superstock specification, with minimal tuning, is faster than my full-on superbike was last year. The BMW still needed more work, and I hadn't been on the superbike yet, but it was looking good. I would be back over to Northern Ireland for the North West 200, in a few weeks' time. It's not my favourite racetrack, but hopefully I would get the same buzz I got from racing at Cookstown.

CHAPTER 18

Bored to back teeth of riding through bloody chicanes

I wasn't looking forward to the 2015 North West 200. I think if I really put my foot down the TAS team wouldn't make me go, but I didn't force it this year. Everyone thinks that you have to go to the North West for preparation if you want to put a good show on at the TT and perhaps I was just following that thinking. Now, having been, I couldn't give a damn. It's a week off work to ride for a couple of hours on Tuesday, same on Thursday plus a couple of races that evening, then the races on Saturday. Cookstown fitted as much racing, if not more, into one night and one day. I know they're two very different races, but things could be tightened up at the North West. It is Ireland's biggest race, and one of the largest spectator events in the whole of Northern Ireland, and it's set up to bring money into the local economy, so it makes sense to string it out to keep fans in the area.

The main man is Mervyn White, and he makes a good job of organising a big race meeting, but from where I'm looking, he doesn't seem to want to delegate responsibility, so every decision is on him. That means the organisation becomes bloody painful at times. I don't mean it's badly organised, because it isn't. It is a massive event, held over a large area – the track is 8.97 miles long and touches the outskirts of three towns. Tens of thousands of fans all watch, with who knows how many more watching it on BBC Northern Ireland's feed on the internet. What I mean when I say it's painful is how long it takes to get a race off, from leaving the pit, to actually starting the race. You go out on a warm-up lap, then you're sat on the grid for another ten minutes while it feels like someone somewhere is making their mind up. At Cookstown, or my favourite race, the Southern 100 on the Isle of Man, they get through the races one after another, no messing. But I'm comparing the North West 200 to an Irish National race, when Mervyn and the other folk who run the NW200 want it to be compared to the TT. That's fair enough, a few years ago the NW200 was seen as a bigger race in a lot of people's eyes, including those who were running *MCN*. And, as always, I'm only talking for myself. It might suit all the other riders and teams to be away for a week just a few days before they have to go to the TT for a fortnight, but it's not good for me.

The NW200 organisers all mean well, there is no doubting that, and it is bloody difficult trying to organise any real road race, never mind one the size of this one, so I want to make it clear they do a great job in tough circumstances.

The weather's not been kind to the North West the last few years and they've have had a few big crashes and even deaths. There were no fatalities in 2015, but my mate Stephen Thompson, a Northern Irish lad and a really funny bloke, had a bad crash. It happened at the fast kink after the first-gear York Corner on the way up to Mill Road Roundabout. Stephen, Dean Harrison and Horst Saiger were all involved, but Harrison was lucky to get away without injuries. Stephen had the worst of the injuries and his arm was badly damaged, then I heard it became infected, and surgeons decided it was best to amputate it after a couple of operations couldn't mend it. A spectator was hit by a flying bike and it wasn't looking good for her either, but she was on the mend when I wrote this.

So, obviously it could have gone a lot worse for me, but I still didn't enjoy much about the racing this year. I liked being in Ireland, though, and I made the most of the Wednesday and Friday, days you do nothing at the North West. On the Wednesday, a mate of mine called Glyn Moffitt took me around the Crosslé car factory in Holywood, County Down, near Belfast City airport. Crosslé have been making race cars since 1957. My mate Glyn is a proper signwriter and he does some work for them. Crosslé were once at the cutting edge, winning Formula Ford races and championships around the world, and now they're still making the trick, classic-looking race cars. They're proud to say they're 'the longest surviving customer racing car constructor in the UK'.

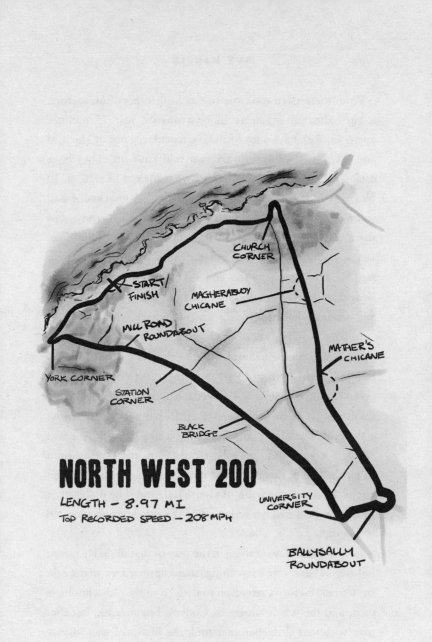

START/FINISH

CHURCH CORNER

MAGHERABUOY CHICANE

MILL ROAD ROUNDABOUT

MATHER'S CHICANE

YORK CORNER

STATION CORNER

BLACK BRIDGE

UNIVERSITY CORNER

BALLYSALLY ROUNDABOUT

NORTH WEST 200

LENGTH – 8.97 MI
TOP RECORDED SPEED – 208 MPH

From there Glyn took me to Cooke Brothers Engineering, a big industrial engineers in Newtonards, just 15 minutes away. Cooke's have a lot of the big machinery out of Harland and Wolff when the shipyard has sold stuff off. They have a massive engineering shop, with what looked like 20 or 30 blokes working on the shop floor. I was gobsmacked. I had some right interesting conversations with the lads there, but there was one fella who will stick in my mind a long time. He was shorter than me, and not built much heavier than me. He was knocking the end off a hydraulic ram with a sledgehammer. The end is threaded on, but it gets stuck fast and needs a whack to free it. A hell of whack.

Anyone working in the truck game needs to know how to swing a sledgehammer, and I like to think I do, but the way this lad went at that digger was the most committed I've ever seen anyone with a 4 ft sledgehammer. And it wasn't a small one. It must have been a 20 lb hammer. I can swing a sledgehammer, but I couldn't swing it like he could. He was taking two steps in to get a bit of a run-up, and timed it right to hit the end of this hydraulic ram dead-on. He had a target about the size of the palm of your hand, and if he didn't hit it square on he'd make a write-off of the ram – costing a good few grand.

You would not want to be in the way of that man. He meant business. There were a few things that impressed me that week: the Crosslé factory's attention to detail and the old-schoolness of it, and the whole set-up of Cooke's Engineering, but that man with that sledgehammer took the biscuit. I was Sunday league compared to him. He was the man.

Back at the track, the organisers wanted me to do something for the BBC Northern Ireland telly coverage of the race, so I did that. They had me driving up and down the beach in a nice John Deere tractor talking to a presenter lass, so that was alright and everyone was happy.

Then, during practice, I came in after a lap and Stephen Watson, the grid presenter, asked how I was getting on. In the heat of the moment I told him I was bored to back teeth of riding through bloody chicanes and that I had no interest. Up to top gear, back to bottom gear for a chicane. Up to top gear, back to bottom gear for another chicane. Now, perhaps I shouldn't have said it, but I genuinely felt it at that moment, and still stand by it now. It upset a few people, but I was still revving from being on the bike at 200 mph. I didn't have the peace of mind to remember my mum's advice: if you can't say anything nice, don't say anything at all.

I stayed with my mate, Paul Dunlop, who lives not far from the track, and on Friday I drove down to Rostrevor, on the border near Newry in County Down, where I rode my mountain bike on my own for an unsociable four or five hours. After that I crossed into the Republic, picked Sharon up and went for an ice cream and some tea on Skerries seafront. From there we went to McElvaney's truck yard. Moody had told me he'd seen a restored Scania 143 at Truckfest, the big truck show in Peterborough. He reckoned he'd never seen anything like it. It was about the time we'd just started restoring a 143 for a customer. Moody doesn't get excited about anything, so it must have been good, for him to tell me about it. He didn't know whose it was, but I tracked it down to McElvaney's, the official Scania dealer for the south of Ireland, who are based in Monaghan. There used to be an Irish national race in the same town, and it was one of my favourites.

The boss, Mr McElvaney, knew I was keen to see the 143 because Patrick, a truck fitter I'd met at Cookstown, had been in touch with him. So through this fella and that fella I got to meet them at about nine at night. And it was worth it. It was a 143H, the heavy-duty chassis. Nearly everything in the UK is a 143M – the motorway chassis, but Scania Sweden wouldn't send the M to the Republic because the state of the roads was so bad. The restoration work was more than impressive and this 1996 truck was the best I'd ever seen. It's a bold statement, but the 143 we're doing for a customer is going to be even better. The 143 500 is a legendary truck and boys in the haulage game want them for shows. They're into their trucks like some motorbike shop owners are into old bikes.

McElvaney's yard must have made an impression on me, because months later I was literally dreaming about his industrial parts washer. I've got to get a grip.

That night we went back to Paul's ready for the races the next day. By this time I'd had a practice at Kirkistown on the superbike and that had all gone well. Even saying that, honestly, it never entered my head that I was in with a chance of winning at the North West. For the last few years I've used it as a means to an end to prepare for the Isle of Man, but I don't see it like that any more and it's become a pain in the arse. It didn't help that I was made to say sorry to this man and say sorry to that man in front of the TV cameras about my thoughts on the chicanes that I'd come out with. It had made the back pages of the local papers and it shouldn't have done. The stories should be about whoever is doing the winning, not me spouting my mouth of. Perhaps that's a reflection on the quality of the racing. If they're having to talk about what I said, there's obviously nothing better to write about.

Mervyn White wasn't happy with me, but if they're not happy with what comes out of my mouth they shouldn't allow the TV bods to come and stick a microphone in my face the second I come in from practice when I'm all revved up after being on the bike. I don't know if people want the riders to have opinions or not. I think they just want yes men and I'm not one of them. If you're not happy with my opinion, then don't ask for it. If you want someone to say everything is fantastic, when it isn't, then ask someone else. I thought honesty was the best policy, but obviously not in TV land.

I like being with the team, Phil, Denver and Mark, wherever we are, but riding round that track isn't fun for me. Philip Neill, the team boss, was even telling me to just get through the week in one piece and get to the TT. The year Conor Cummins rode for TAS, 2012, he got taken out at Mather's Cross chicane, broke his wrist and buggered his TT up. He didn't ride a single race at the Isle of Man TT because of it, and that's the biggest race of his year. Once you're at the TT no one even remembers what happened at the North West. Plus you get good short circuit lads, like Alastair Seeley – who was racing the TAS BMW – who go bloody well at the North West, but then they're not worried about the TT. Seeley's big race of the year is the North West. He's a very good short circuit Superstock and Supersport rider too, but I'd say the

NW200 is what earns him decent prize money and helps get him signed to teams for the following year. He doesn't do any Irish national stuff or the TT – this is his only road race.

I started the Superbike race from the fourth row, and didn't even know where I finished until I checked when I was writing this. I came in eighth, one place behind William Dunlop. TAS rider Alastair Seeley won it and came second to Lee Johnston in the Superstock race that I didn't finish. I didn't enter the Supersport race that the big crash happened in, because the Smiths team didn't travel to the race. Maybe that was a stroke of luck.

I left Northern Ireland thinking I'm not going back to the North West 200 – and I have to up my sledgehammer game.

CHAPTER 19

Blacking out is going to be the only problem

When I agreed to do the Wall of Death record attempt and visited the Fox family to start my training back in February, I also agreed to catch up with them during the year for more training and time getting used to riding on their wall. Even while I was agreeing to it I was wondering how I was going to fit it all in. And that was before the Triumph streamliner thing had cropped up. I know Ken was expecting to see more of me, but I've been too busy and he understands that.

Months after that day with the Foxes I was doing a BMW press day in Germany. It was something Philip Neill, the boss of the TAS racing team, had asked me to do. TAS don't ask me to do many press or sponsor days any more, so I made sure to fit it in. The event is a huge BMW do in a mountain resort called Garmisch-Partenkirchen, on the Austrian border. It's been going ten years and they reckon 40,000 BMW owners from all over the world come to it. They have ride-outs, custom shows and stunt riders, and there was a Wall of Death there. I got talking to the German bloke, Donald, whose wall it was. I told him I'd ridden a bit with Ken Fox. Because I hadn't had time to see Ken, I asked Donald if I could have a go on his wall. He said, 'Ken Fox? He's my hero. You can have a go if you want.' So I did. And it very nearly went pear-shaped.

I hadn't tried to ride like that for months, but because I'd been taught by Ken and I'd made it up onto the wall for 40 laps on my own the last time I did try, I thought I could go straight into riding this wall. I learned pretty quickly I couldn't, but I was on the wall doing 30 mph by that time. And, like all the Wall of Death riders, I was riding without a helmet, just in my jeans, T-shirt and trainers. If anything had gone wrong it would've been a bomb scene.

I nearly came out of the top of the wall, then I made a tiny correction, and nearly crashed into the bottom. It's a vicious circle. I didn't crash, but Donald could see I was struggling. He gave me a bit of advice, but he didn't have time to really go back to basics and tell me what I was doing wrong because he was there to entertain the crowd that had turned up and was just letting me have a go in between shows. I had four goes then gave it a rest. I felt like I'd pushed my luck.

Word got back to Ken that I'd been riding on someone else's wall and he hit the limiter, telling the folk at North One that if I didn't practise exclusively with him then he didn't want anything to do with the programme. That would scupper the job, obviously, so I needed to smooth it over with Ken next time I saw him.

The live programme needs pre-recorded sections to give the background of the training and to build up the story. For one part we went to RAF Henlow air force base, in Bedfordshire, for a g-force refresher course with a group of RAF fast-jet pilots, just me and all these Typhoon men. They were very intellectual blokes, very precise, very British and upper-class, like you'd imagine fighter pilots would be.

I listened while they were reminded how to deal with g-forces in their job and told about new methods of handling it. The pilots gave me some tips, pointing out that it was really tricky to deal with big g-forces. It takes your brain and heart ten seconds to recognise positive g and get a grip of what's going on, so it's dead important to cope with those first few seconds. You do it by blowing against the inside of your mouth and tensing your legs and your whole lower body. After that your body is doing all it can to deal with forces it's being put under by raising your heart rate.

But there is positive and negative g-force. Positive g is what you feel when a plane accelerates for take-off, pushing you back in your seat. Negative g is when the plane brakes after landing and you feel you body pushing against the seat belt as you slide forward. The pilot training day explained that the human brain and body are better at instantly dealing with negative g.

While I was there I had a really thorough medical, checking everything, just stopping short of a greased finger up my backside. The RAF doctor noted my resting heart rate and was surprised how low it was, asking if I did a lot in the gym. I just told him I did a bit of mountain biking.

A few days later I got a letter from the doctor. He explained he'd been concerned that I seemed to have an abnormally low heart rate, so he'd checked with another doctor for a second opinion. He said he wanted me back for another ECG scan, or electrocardiogram, because the heart rate shouldn't be that low and he was worried something was adrift. The ECG picks up the smallest electrical changes on the skin caused by the heart. The letter was dead confidential, the TV bods didn't even know, and I didn't tell them. It's not going to stop me doing the Wall of Death programme.

I was still struggling to find time to go and see Ken Fox, with all the time I had spent at the North West, the TT and my work at Moody's. I was also due to go to Bonneville Salt Flats to have my first practice in the Triumph Rocket Streamliner, but then that was cancelled because it had rained and flooded the salt flats. An hour of rain at that place buggers the salt for weeks. Every cloud has a silver lining, because even though I could do with getting to grips with the streamliner it now meant I didn't have to go to America and I had a free week. I spent a few extra days at Moody's and arranged to meet up with Ken at a music festival called Beat-Herder in the Ribble Valley, Lancashire, to get myself back in his good books.

The first thing I did when I saw Ken was apologise for the thing in Germany and explain that I was just trying to get a bit of practice in. He understood, but he told me that I still needed his advice. And he was right. I hadn't ridden the wall for six months, except for that short session in Germany, and that didn't fill me with confidence. Road racing is what I do, riding the Wall of Death is what Ken does, so whatever he says, I do. If he wants me to ride the bottom for 20 minutes, then that's what I do.

Without asking me anything, Ken went right back to the beginning, showing me all of the steps, but ten times faster than the first lessons. My brain must have remembered how to deal with the sensation of being on the wall, because I wasn't anywhere near as dizzy and Ken had me back on the wall within a couple of hours, even after having six months off.

I was reminded that I had to have my head tilted right back, looking where I'm going. You're looking 180 degrees round the wall. You can't just look right in front of the front wheel, because that's when you make mistakes and over-correct. So it was lots of 'Look at the wall, look at the wheel, look at the wall ...'

I rode loads that day, then I rode again the next two days at Dirt Quake, where Luke was set up with the other wall. Dirt Quake is a dirt track event held at King's Lynn speedway and run by *Sideburn* magazine. I went in 2014, raced a Harley-Davidson chopper on the dirt and had a great time, so I sponsored the event the following year, Spellman organising for the Wall of Death to come along as part of our sponsorship. Sal was there selling woolly hats and T-shirts; me and Sharon slept in the Transit and a few mates came. I got to race both my dirt track bikes on Friday night, my 2015 Honda CRF450 and framer with the Honda CR500 two-stroke engine. It's a handful. The next day I raced the same Harley chopper, that

Krazy Horse in Bury St Edmunds let me use. They'd put longer forks on it to make it harder to ride, but I still managed to win on it and had a great time.

After three days of regular riding on the wall I was getting straight on it, and right near the top. I'm enjoying it and feeling safe. It left me thinking it's going to be easy to do 80 mph. The blacking out is going to be the only problem, and while it's still the biggest thing I've done in my life, my brain is getting used to it, and as it does I'm less daunted by the whole thing.

But I can't take anything for granted. The next weekend Luke had his wall set up at a cliff-top festival in Norfolk and Ken Wolfe crashed and put himself in hospital. Ken Wolfe, not to be confused with Ken Fox, has been riding the Wall of Death, week in, week out, for over 20 years and even he can make a mistake. It was during the section where three riders are all on Honda 200s, the same bikes I'm learning on, and they're all on the wall at the same time, racing each other. It sounds like Ken clipped the back wheel of Danny Danger when he was only a metre from the top of the wall. He crashed hard and was out cold for a short time. He broke his collarbone and his cheekbone and needed metal plates in his cheek to put it back together. The accident happened at two in the afternoon, and Luke says they were performing again, without Ken Wolfe of course, at five the same day. The show goes on.

My wall is being built in a hangar on an air base in Lincolnshire, and I've got the use of it for two weeks to practise and suss it out before the live TV programme. I'll get on the wall in the morning before work and I'll go back at night. The attempt is a few months off, but the bike I'm building isn't taking shape. It's still a bare frame on the old sofa in my shed, but it's not a worry. It'll be done. It'll be a purposeful-looking machine, no paint or bugger-all. It'll have dirt track handlebars and the suspension has to be solid, but I still want it to look trick. I want a Weslake look to the exhausts, so they come straight back from the engine under your legs, on either side.

The problem is, I have a date to work to and I know roughly how long it'll take if I go hard at it, so even though I'd really like to have it finished and sat in the shed ready and waiting to go, that's not going to happen. It'll become the priority when it becomes the priority. When I'm in the middle of the road racing season, with races in Ireland and the Isle of Man coming thick and fast, it's hard to get much else done.

Riding this massive wall is a journey into the unknown. No one has ever done it before, and it won't be until I get in the middle of the wall that I'll have a real idea what it's like. Even Ken and Luke have no idea what it's going to be like. The wall is going to be made of 50-odd 20-foot shipping containers, lined out with wood. It's easy to be sat here thinking it'll be a piece of cake, but it might be a different story when I climb into the world's biggest ever Wall of Death.

CHAPTER 20

Turning down the biggest job in TV

After the way I've treated North One, the television production company I've worked with since 2010, I would have thought they'd have nothing to do with me by now. I've dropped them in it a few times, because I couldn't get away from work, or chose not to, but they keep wanting to work with me. Sometimes I reckon I could organise a beetroot jar opening contest and they'd want to come and film that.

I don't have any big secret that makes them want to keep making programmes with me. I'm not trying to be like anyone, or be anything; I'm just trying to be true to myself, which is why I sometimes end up seeming like a bit of an arsehole, from their point of view. I'm not purposely trying to be an arsehole, but my core belief is, Don't forget where you come from. Sticking to that sometimes means I leave the folk at North One in the lurch at the eleventh hour. I'm not testing them or seeing how far I can push my luck. When I let them down I do genuinely feel bad for messing them around, because they're nice people. I like them a lot and enjoy doing stuff with them. Plus I know they're only trying to do their jobs and earn a living.

There is a hardcore group of directors, cameramen, soundmen and researchers that I work with and have since the beginning: Ewan Keil, James Woodroffe, Nat Bullen, Andy Chorlton, Tom Norton, Amy Roff, Sarah Swift and Dani McGirr. And in the same way as I am with the TAS Racing team, I'm happy to work with the people I know. I'm not always looking for the next opportunity. Being a TV presenter is not one of my goals in life, and I know that if they ever did get sick of me and tell me to eff off I'd be alright, because I've never lived like a rock star. If it all stops tomorrow I'd be in at Moody's the next day, as usual. I don't owe anyone anything.

At the end of 2014 I said I was going to lay off the telly side of things. I thought it was taking up too much of my time, and I stepped right back for the first half of 2015, just doing the odd day here and there for the Wall of Death programme. Then the land speed record attempt came up and I had to fly to Oregon to make sure I'd fit in the streamliner, and a couple of the film crew, James and Nat, came along on that. That was killing two birds with one stone, though.

When Triumph asked me to attempt the record I said I'd love to, but I'd prefer it if we just did it and didn't try to make a TV programme out of it. When I said that, the Triumph people started saying, 'Well ...' and 'Ah ...' They were only asking me to be involved because I can get it on telly. And I knew that. I'm not sure they knew that I knew.

Andy Spellman doesn't see it like this, and the fella at Triumph, who is organising the press side of things, keeps saying that's not the case, but Triumph hasn't come to me because of any particular skills I might have, so let's not bullshit each other. Still, where or when was I going to get the chance to ride at 400 mph if I turned this opportunity down? So I agreed and North One is making a show about it for Channel 4.

I am a lot more comfortable making the programmes now, but the best thing in the world, as far as I'm concerned, would be to make all these shows and for them to never be broadcast.

I'm certainly more comfortable in front of the camera and talking to people while I'm being filmed, and I'm getting better at dealing with the attention. Well, that's not really true, I'm not better at dealing with the attention, I'm just better at staying out of the way. I don't put myself in positions where I think Brian the chimp is going to go off on one. I try and keep out of the way as best I can. North Lincolnshire is pretty good for that. I'm not going to red-carpet events in London. Still, I can't avoid the attention completely.

I went out for a curry with Tim Coles, and a fella came up and said, 'Sorry to disturb you ...' I came straight out and told him he wasn't sorry, but go on. He was trying to make out he knew me, because he knew my Uncle Rodders (who isn't my uncle), and said, 'Remember me to him next time you see him.' He was just trying to show off in front of his mate or summat, but why do it when I'm just trying to have a quiet curry out of the way?

Another time a woman searched out Moody's phone number and rung him up, out of hours, to complain that she'd hung around for something to be signed, but his scruffy truck fitter rushed past and wouldn't sign it. It has nothing to do with Moody, but people still think they can ring him up and get me in trouble. He wasn't having any of it and pointed out it was people like her who make me want to pack in racing.

What else is going on in someone's life when they feel the need to do that? You obviously don't know anything about me. I'm not there to sign autographs. If everything's going right and I have five minutes, I'll sign stuff, but otherwise I'm there to practise or race, especially if it's a bike I haven't ridden before and a track I've not been to for years. I'm not going to tell anyone to sod off, but I'm going to keep on walking. I don't know what some people expect me to do.

But the attention isn't all bad.

The week before I went to Pikes Peak I was out having a short road test on the Martek, to check the last few bits and bobs, when it chafed through an oil hose and shit all its oil out. I was about seven miles from home and there wasn't much to do but sit and cry or start pushing the bike home. I got about halfway home, and the weather was coming in, when a woman pulled up and said, 'Do you want a lift home, love?' I propped the bike up against a tree (it doesn't have a sidestand), jumped in the car and was taken home so I could fetch my van and collect the bike. It was all spot on.

Then, a few months later, just before Christmas, someone knocked on my door. I didn't recognise the woman at first, but she reminded me that she was the one who picked me up when the Martek broke down and I remembered. She explained she did some volunteering at the local grammar school, and asked if I'd go and hand out the Duke of Edinburgh awards. I told her, no bother, one good turn deserves another.

At that point I didn't think all young 'uns were useless buggers, but we'd had a couple of apprentices at work and they're always too busy looking at their telephones to be interested in what you're trying to tell them. So I could have been guilty of tarring them all with the same brush.

Then I found out how much these pupils were doing off their own bats to win a Duke of Edinburgh award. No one is telling them what to do, but they're doing a load of different stuff, like three-day treks across the Brecon Beacons; getting involved with the community and the church; dealing with people and putting themselves out of their comfort zone. All the kids that were up for awards had done things like this and I was well impressed, because it was all voluntary, not part of their exams or daily lessons. The school couldn't get the Duke of Edinburgh to hand out the awards that year, he must have been busy, but I felt quite honoured to be asked to do it. I gave out 60 or 70 awards, and they're not easy to win. It made me reassess my views on modern youth.

This was the second time I'd been to Caistor Grammar School. For some reason my mum thought it was a good idea for me to take my eleven-plus to try and get into grammar school. I know it sounds like something from the 1950s, but they still have it, even now, in Lincolnshire. She should have known better, though. I didn't pass.

Spellman tells me about all sorts of emails that come through every day inviting me to weddings and birthday parties all over the world. I'm asked to cheer up people who've fallen into threshing machines or crashed their bikes. Again, I don't know what I'm supposed to do, but I'm not about to turn up at a random wedding like a performing monkey so someone can take a picture with me. Who would do that?

Things got even more daft in the summer when all the Jeremy Clarkson stuff kicked off and it became clear he was getting the boot from *Top Gear*. Loads of rumours started that I was going to replace him. It was all a load of rubbish at first, just bookies putting out odds to get gullible people to part with their money, but then Chris Evans got involved with *Top Gear* and Spellman got a phone call from some gadgie at the BBC, saying that Chris Evans wanted to talk to me and that I could do one show, do all the shows, do what I wanted as long as I was involved in *Top Gear*.

I didn't say no straight away, but the more I thought about it the more I knew it wasn't right for me. For one thing, if I did it I'd always be compared to Clarkson, whereas the Channel 4 programmes are me doing my own thing, I'm not filling anyone's shoes. Another reason not to do it was because the BBC man said it was the biggest TV show in the world. How many presenters would turn down one of the biggest TV jobs in the world? Not many of them, but I did. I'm not being cocky, but I can turn down the biggest TV show in the world, because TV work is not my big picture. I'm whinging about the amount of attention I'm getting at the moment – imagine how bad it would be if I were on *Top Gear*. I couldn't go and race a Harley-Davidson chopper at Dirt Quake on a quiet weekend, could I?

Top Gear might pay squillions of pounds, but what do I want all that for? I can earn enough money for the life I want fixing trucks and doing a few other bits and pieces. If someone has loads of money they go down in my estimations. I don't think more of them because they're loaded; I have to look harder at them and try to drag something good out of them so I can like them, something that makes me think, 'Oh, that makes him alright.' People who are just mad for earning aren't my kind of people. When money becomes their all, then it's a problem. Don't chase the money.

When Spellman told me about the *Top Gear* phone calls I asked his opinion and he said he'd think about it and call me back. An hour later the phone rang and he told me he didn't think I should do it. He reckons that as I am now, the tail isn't wagging the dog. If I don't want to do something I don't have to. I know he looks out for me, but that put him further up in my estimations. He gets a percentage of what I earn and he'd be quids in if I was doing *Top Gear* and everything that went with it. I reckon most managers or agents would have snapped the BBC's hand off, but Spellman knew it wouldn't suit me. He's looking at the big picture too. We're doing our own thing and North One are on our wavelength now. They're the only production company I've worked with, and the Wall of Death attempt is the best idea they've ever come up with. It's the best idea anyone's come up with.

Not long after the *Top Gear* stuff was dying down, Spellman and the top bods from North One had a meeting with the folk who commission programmes for Channel 4. They choose which production companies make what programmes to fill the time. The gist of the meeting was that Channel 4 would take anything I wanted to make, which is bloody unusual, I'm told. Still, it doesn't make me think I should go mad and fill my boots or stick a load of noughts on the end of what I'm being paid. I have the same attitude I had from the start: if someone comes up with an idea I like the sound of, I'll do it, and if they don't, I won't.

An example of that is when North One offered to put me through flying lessons so I could learn how to fly a Spitfire. I turned it down for a few reasons. For one thing, I'm probably not clever enough. Then I thought, how long would it take? And though I would like to be able to fly a Spitfire, there are loads of other things I want to do and I don't have time to do everything. As great as it would be to say I've flown one, it's not going to change my life. I'm looking for things to change my life, but not too much ...

CHAPTER 21

If he says pork scratchings are the fuel of champions, I'm listening

The week before travelling out to the TT was as hectic as normal. We had a day's filming of the g-force refresher course and medical at RAF Henlow, that I shouldn't really have done, but Spellman reminded me I'd taken the money so I had to. Even so, I was still drying my teeth thinking about it. You know, when you take your car into a garage and the mechanic pulls his lips back and sucks in air to show it's much worse than you hoped it was.

I was meant to do two days' filming, but I got it down to one. The second part of the pilot's refresher course was to go in the centrifuge at Farnborough for assessment. This is the thing you might have seen in the James Bond film *Moonraker*. It's where a person is strapped into a seat in a pod on the end of an arm, a bit like a fairground ride, and spun around faster and faster. The pilots are all wired up and monitored to make sure they are still fit for the job.

I told Moody about two days of filming and he said I couldn't do both, so I had to duck out of the second day, because I had a truck coming off the boat on Friday morning for an MOT, and then I had another to get ready for an IVA test, before I left for the TT that night.

Honestly, I wasn't too bothered that I missed the centrifuge, because it was right before going out to the TT and I felt that rough after being in the stunt plane, even needing a cold coffee on the way home, that I didn't want to risk having my brain scrambled before going out to the Isle of Man. But me forcing the TV lot to change their plans was a bit last-minute and it caused a load of trouble, of course. I rang Danielle, who does all the organising, but she was away, so I spoke to another lass, Gemma. I told her it was my fault, explaining that I thought the wagon was coming in earlier in the week. North One make it sound like Armageddon when I drop them in it like this, and it mucks everyone around, but it always gets sorted. They don't call me an arsehole to my face, but I'm sure they do when I hang up the phone.

The TV lot know the truck job comes first, and Moody knows trucks come first, but perhaps he thinks they need reminding. It would be better for everyone if I were a bit better organised some of the time.

So, after filming on Thursday, I was up at five on Friday, and drove into Grimsby instead of biking to work as I normally would, because I knew I'd be rushing about to get to the ferry. I was in work for half-five, servicing the truck that had just come off the boat. I got the MOT done, and the truck passed, then I was onto a load of other jobs because I was going to be away for a fortnight. Still, I got away from work half-handy, drove home and sorted out all my riding kit and everything else I needed for the TT.

I packed all the dog's stuff in the van, because Nigel was coming with me this time. I ended up forgetting the hand-held hoover to clear up after ourselves, though. I stay in a barn conversion at my mate Gary's and it's always very tidy, with cream carpets, so I wanted to make sure we didn't leave a mess. But if that's all I forgot, then I wasn't doing too badly.

Paddy had painted me another helmet – he's the mate I mentioned in the Pikes Peak chapter, who painted my Martek. Even though he's self-taught and only does a few helmets a year, he does a mint job. This latest helmet was dead subtle, carbon and battleship grey. It still had the outline of the martin bird on the top and the skull and spanners on the sides, but it also had Nigel on the back, hidden in my number eight. Paddy has also done me a new blue and pink Britten tribute helmet, after Brian had helped me batter the other one when I (we? he?) crashed the go-kart on Mont Ventoux. Both helmets looked so good that earlier in the season I had done a few races in the standard plain carbon-fibre AGV Pista, like it comes from the factory. I didn't want to risk scratching them.

AGV are the Italian helmet company owned by Dainese, who have supplied me with kit since 2010. Dainese want the riders they support to wear Dainese leathers and AGV helmets, not Dainese leathers and helmets from another company. They make a few exceptions, but that's the way they prefer it, explaining that they design the leathers and helmets, boots and gloves all to work together. They've been good to me and the kit is trick, so I have no problems about wearing AGV and Dainese. And it makes things easier dealing with just one group of people.

AGV have made replicas of my helmet to sell through dealers. I still think that's mad. When I was an apprentice riding my Kawasaki AR50 to John Hebb's Volvo, companies only made replicas of the helmets worn by grand prix stars like Mick Doohan, proper legends. To think one of the most famous helmet companies ever would want to make a replica of one of mine, and that people would buy it, still amazes me. When I did get out to the Isle of Man, I saw loads of folk riding around in the black and yellow replicas.

I met Stewart Johnstone, the TAS team's chassis engineer, at Ferrybridge services on the M62 at seven o'clock. He wanted me to take a load of stuff out to the TT because he was flying out. Stewart's brother Steve got in with me. Steve works for TAS, but he doesn't do all the road races, just the TT and all the British Superbike races. From there me and Steve went to Cammy's, just off the M62 in east Lancashire, and had our tea. His missus makes a good lasagne. Cammy, who you last heard of in the Pikes Peak chapter, was working for East Coast Racing, who Lee Johnston (no relation to the Johnstone I had in the van) is riding for. I was happy giving Cammy a lift over, so the three of us jumped in the Transit, Nigel in the back, and drove to Heysham for the 1am ferry crossing. Nigel slept in the back of the van again, and I was in a cabin.

We docked at about six on Saturday morning and I dropped Steve and Cammy off at the pits, then drove over to Douglas Head, overlooking the ferry port, and let the dog out. He had a sniff about, then followed a walker and was gone out of sight, but I wasn't worried. This was his first time on the Isle of Man, but he always manages to find his way back to me, so I just fell asleep. An hour later there was a knock on the window and the same walker asked, 'Is this your dog, mate?'

Later that day we had a rider briefing and signing on. It's a pleasant experience, because everyone involved with the TT racing is so helpful, even though I'm always slack when it comes to sorting out my TT licence. Then I went to see my friends Craig and Lisa, who I've known for years. I introduced them to Nigel, because they were going to look after him while I was on the bike.

Saturday is the first practice day, but it's only for the newcomers, the Lightweight class, that is for 650cc supertwins, and sidecars. They were all classes I wasn't involved in. The rest of us don't get out until Monday, but then that was cancelled because of the weather, so I didn't get on till Tuesday night. That means I'd been on the Isle of Man from first thing Saturday morning, and didn't get a run till Tuesday night, when the Superbike practice started at half past six at night. It's no one's fault, but it's a lot of hanging about when I could be getting on with a hundred other things.

With not much else to do, on Sunday and Monday I rode my mountain bike and walked the dog. One morning

Nigel went off like a rocket and I fell off my bike up on the mountain while I was chasing him. My front wheel got cross-rutted and I went down hard enough that I heard my hip go 'CLONK' when I landed. Not a bad clonk, just like the air had gone out of it. I thought it was alright, but by the time I'd got to the bottom my knee was sore and had swollen. Luckily a specialist physio called Isla, from a local practice called Scott Physiotherapy, comes to a lot of the big races to sort out pains, injuries and niggles riders are suffering from. She sets up in a tent in the pits and she had done that for this year's TT. The riders don't even have to pay; all the Scott Physiotherapy folk volunteer their time for two weeks, and a charity, the Rob Vine Fund – founded and named in honour of a racer who died at the 1985 TT – pay for the supplies of tape and stuff they get through. So I gave Isla a call and arranged to see her.

The 2015 TT was the first time I'd ever raced for two different teams, meaning I'd have to ride both teams' bikes during a single practice session. When I first raced at the Isle of Man the bikes were my own. Since then I've raced for teams that run bikes in all the classes I was competing in. It's not been the same for every racer. John McGuinness will usually race the Superbike for Honda's official team, then Superstock and Supersport for another Honda team, like Padgett's, so you see him racing two different colours of bikes and in two different sets of leathers. Now, because TAS are running BMW and the Germans don't build a 600cc supersport bike, I'm racing for TAS in Superbike and Superstock and for Smiths Triumph in the Supersport 600 class.

That Tuesday night I did four laps in the time we had: one on the TAS BMW superstock; two on the TAS BMW superbike and one on the Smiths Triumph supersport. All bikes feel a bit shit when going as slow as you do on the first couple of nights of practice, so that first session is just about getting back into the place and trying to get up to speed. You can't go flat out after not seeing the track for 50 weeks. It takes a while for you to get your eye in and remember just how hard you can push.

The superbike felt especially slow, because its electronic systems were trying too hard. The anti-wheelie and traction control were both cutting in too much. I think I did a 127 mph lap that first night, but the bike felt a bit wild. For people who don't know much about the TT, that's an average lap speed, so I'm doing close to 200 mph over the mountain to make up for the slow first gear corners where I'm only doing 30 mph. Still, when you're going that slow, or comparatively slow, it does make the big bike feel wild. The faster you go, the smoother it feels and you're even using less petrol, because you're carrying more speed through the bends. You're not braking into corners and accelerating hard out of them to get back up to speed. That means you're using a more constant throttle and keeping your momentum. That's what the TT is all about, momentum. I just need a few laps to get my brain up to speed and to build my confidence up to where it was in race week of the previous year.

All of practice week I had been waking up at four, so I would take the dog for a walk, have a cup of tea, watch a bit of a DVD of a TV show called *Utopia* that I'd been loaned, then jump in the van, drive over to the other side of the island

and have my physio in Isla's tent, at eight in the morning. It was bloody brilliant.

Isla's husband Ben is another physio with Scott Physiotherapy, and he's a hardcore athlete. He gave me a medical research report about the way some endurance athletes are training using a high-fat diet. It was fascinating. Every man and his dog thinks fat in a diet will kill you, but this report says the opposite. A part of Ben's staple diet when he's racing is pork scratchings, so I brought him a box of Mr Porky's. He worked out that they have the best ratio of calories to weight, which is important in the kind of event he competes in. Ben does well in 180-mile running races, like the T184 where he's running for 59 hours and grabbing less than four hours' sleep in that whole time, so I'm not about to argue with him. If he says pork scratchings are the fuel of champions, I'm listening.

I had another five laps of practice on Wednesday night. One on the superstock, two on the superbike, two on the supersport. When I'm having two laps it's two flying laps. I'm not coming in to adjust anything after the first lap, because there's not enough time. You need to sit down when the session's all over to make a decision from what you learned in those two laps about which way to go for the next day.

I think Rebecca Smith, the boss of the Smiths team, would rather have me ride their bike in black leathers, but I didn't have time to change out of my white and blue BMW suit. If I changed leathers it would mean missing a lap, and it was more important to practise than have the right leathers on. I'd wear the right ones for the race.

On Wednesday night the news broke about Michael Dunlop jumping ship from the team he'd started the season with. He had signed with my old team boss, Shaun Muir, to race the Milwaukee Yamahas, but he left the team in the middle of practice week and started riding his own BMW, that he'd raced the previous year. It was announced that the Hawk team he had raced for in 2014 were coming over to the Isle of Man to spanner for him.

Part of me thought fair play, if he's on a bike that he doesn't think is good enough to win, then fair enough; but another part of me thought you can't do that. You made your bed, you've got to lie in it.

Those Yamahas were running at the sharp end of the British Superbike championship, so they seemed to be right bikes. And racing is Dunlop's job, it's not like he's a full-time milkman, so walking out on a team might catch up with him. It's not like Michael is in the last year of his career either, he's only in his mid twenties. You get some good years, you get some bad years. For a short while I thought you can't do what he did in such a small world as road racing without knackering your future chances of getting signed to ride decent bikes, but I wouldn't be surprised if he ended up riding for TAS in 2016. Philip Neill is dead keen on him, even though he's done that to the likes of Yamaha.

But I don't know all the ins and outs of Dunlop's situation. There might be loads of things that forced him to make that decision, and a little bit of information is dangerous. I do know he was Milwaukee Yamaha's only rider, so they packed up and got the ferry home. It was a bit of a disaster for them.

After Wednesday night's practice I sat down and spoke to Stewart Johnstone, telling him the bike's doing this here and that there. He took it all in and made some changes, including softening the forks in the initial part of the travel.

We were out again on Thursday night. There was a lot less feel from the superbike after the latest round of changes, but when I opened the throttle in a corner it would go where I wanted it to, so that was better.

I didn't have the 'this is it' feeling that I'd experienced earlier in the season in those first five practice laps of Cookstown – until the last session of practice week on Friday night. Stewart had translated my gibberings into what I wanted and the bike felt great. Earlier in the week the superbike would drive well off smooth bends, but when I was accelerating hard and under g-load it wasn't handling right. By being under g-load I mean when the road was coming at me, either because of the camber or I was going up a hill. It was collapsing the tyre, but I thought the suspension was too soft and was bottoming out, meaning the suspension had no more travel and had compressed until it was solid. It felt like this was making the tyre compress and deform too much. But Stewart is far cleverer than me. He looked at the telemetry and said actually the suspension was too stiff and the tyre was collapsing before the suspension moved. He softened the front and rear suspension right off and it was a different bike. We leaned the fuelling off too, because the fuelling wasn't great on a closing throttle.

Next time out I'd only gone half a mile and I knew the bike was better. After ten miles I thought, This is something like, I can push now.

On Friday the superbike was running hot, 100 degrees, when it should be 70. We changed the engine and put a bigger radiator on it, and it went back to high 60s. Maybe the head gasket was leaking slightly. Something was up.

There was another problem too. At the North West I had trouble with the bike finding false neutrals – going into neutral instead of the gear I selected. There's a little spring in the gearbox, and it would jump the other side of a pawl and create these false neutrals. It happened on Friday too, making me miss the corner at the end of Sulby Straight, one of the fastest parts of the track, and run into someone's driveway hard on the brakes.

During practice week I was putting more effort into setting up the superbike than the superstocker, because you can copy a lot of the set-up from one bike to the other. The Smiths Triumph 675 was something completely different. It has plenty of power and we just kept adjusting the gearing because it could pull a bigger and bigger gear. It was impressive. I was doing fewer gearchanges per lap on that than I am on the big bikes, and that's unusual because on a 600 you're normally up and down like a fiddler's elbow. The smaller supersport bikes don't have the same spread of torque as a superbike, so you have to constantly change gears to try and keep the bike making peak power. If you let it drop too low in the rev range a supersport bike feels sluggish. The Smiths Triumph didn't, though. And the suspension felt so good that I didn't make any changes to it.

I felt genuinely confident going into the race week …

CHAPTER 22

I don't want another podium

As practice week for the 2015 TT ended, we made a few more very slight changes to the superbike before the first race, the Superbike TT. They were a bit of a gamble, and involved making the forks' valving softer, but keeping the same fork springs, then adding more oil to stop them from bottoming out. Really we were just moving a little bit further in the same direction. Every time I spoke to Stewart Johnstone I could see his gears turning. Next time out on the BMW I thought, You are the man. He had transformed it and the bike was spot on. Taking nothing away from the other lads in the team, but Stewart is the Messiah. If he said, 'Put pumpkins in as wheels, it'll work,' I'd do it. By now, my superbike was handling as good as the previous year's Suzuki, but the BMW had 30 horsepower more.

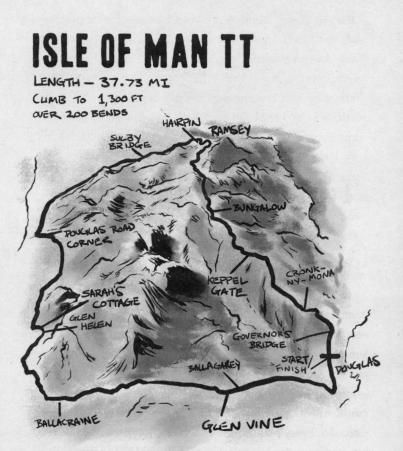

ISLE OF MAN TT

LENGTH — 37.73 MI
CLIMB TO 1,300 FT
OVER 200 BENDS

HAIRPIN
RAMSEY
SULBY BRIDGE
BUNGALOW
DOUGLAS ROAD CORNER
KEPPEL GATE
CRONK-NY-MONA
SARAH'S COTTAGE
GLEN HELEN
GOVERNORS BRIDGE
START/FINISH
DOUGLAS
BALLAGAREY
BALLACRAINE
GLEN VINE

Isla the physio had sorted my knee so it wasn't a problem and, like I said, I genuinely felt confident. I had been doing a bit of signing outside the TAS pit, but I didn't have to do anything for sponsors with 200 people all queuing up, and I preferred that. I had the dog to walk before and after I was on the bike, so I felt I had something constructive to do. Nigel went missing so many times it confirmed that he knows his way back to me. I think he went chasing pheasants. He'd come back, absolutely drowned. Where the hell he'd been I do not know, but he looked like the happiest dog in the world, bending himself in two because he was wagging his tail that much. Then he ate my phone.

It had been decided on Friday that Saturday's Superbike race would be put back a day because high winds were forecast, but I was in the pits early on Saturday morning anyway, ready for a final lap of practice on the superbike at 10.40. This was to make up for the practice we missed on Monday. Then the news came through that a helicopter had crashed near the 33rd, very close to the track. The pilot was killed and with that accident and the strong winds, reckoned to be one of the causes of the helicopter crash, everything was put on hold. Eventually, the practice lap was rescheduled and we were hoping to get it in at 6.45 that night, but it was also cancelled because the wind still hadn't dropped and it was bad on the Mountain.

Sunday was the same routine. I dropped Nige off at Craig and Lisa's and went to the pits early. I wanted to stay out of the way, so when it was time to race I turned up as close as possible to the start time, because I didn't want any mither, but there was still time to do a couple of interviews while I waited in the long line of bikes on Glencrutchery Road.

Then, finally, it was time to race. I had chosen number eight again, so I set off ten seconds after Gary Johnson and ten before Ian Hutchinson.

We had tweaked the swingarm pivot position; rear suspension linkage; shock valving; spring ratio; steering offset … I started the race knowing that the bike was spot on, and it felt good, even with a full load of fuel, but it didn't last long. Not even three miles into the 226-mile race the bike conked out. It was like I'd hit the kill switch, except that four letters and a number stayed on the dash. I can't remember what it said, except 68° – the temperature was still showing.

I just thought, Shit, shit, shit, shit, shit! Then a panicked Fuck! – I realised I was at the top of Glen Vine and there was a bike ten seconds behind me. It's got to be one of the worst sections of track to break down in. You go from one side of the track to the other, and I was in the middle. I was coasting, with a dead bike, and just had to get somewhere. I saw a gateway with a marshal stood by it and he opened the gate as I rolled through it. It could've been messy, but it wasn't.

Just as I was climbing off the bike some bloke was trying to take pictures of me, so I angrily told him to fuck off. I turned the bike off and on again and it started. I'd lost at least 30 seconds, but I asked the marshal if I could go off again, but he made a face when I did and said he'd have to check. He rang through to the chief marshal or the head of the section. The reason he had to check was because I'd have to accelerate from standing still, when other bikes were coming through at 150 mph, so I could understand his thinking. I just wanted to get back to the pits, not be stuck out on the track for the length of the race and more, because that would be well over two hours in total. On the other hand I didn't know why the bike had stopped and I was also worried that it could do it again at an even more inappropriate time or place, so I went and sat behind a hedge and started winding myself up.

I was swearing and angry, but I wasn't directing it at anyone, it was just the frustration. I had taken my helmet and body armour off, and Brian was going mental. He said to me, 'That fella who was taking photos of you was smiling at you.' That's the gist of it, but there was a lot more swearing involved. Then Brian told me to go sort him out. I walked over to the photographer and told him to give me the camera before I stuck it through his skull. Then I paused and added, 'So I can see the white of your brain!'

Something had broken inside me and the photographer was shocked. He started saying he'd delete the photos. The marshal, who'd opened the gate for me, was walking behind me. I turned to him and said, 'I'm not a violent man, but you do not do that.' I was raging. I've never been like that. If the photographer had said anything smarmy back, I think I'd have done something that would have put me up in front of a judge. Brian was off the leash and out of control. Then the marshal put his arm around me, while I kept saying to him, 'You just don't do that.' And he agreed, but in a calm way.

I walked back to the tree, sat down and reminded myself to breathe. Half an hour later the photographer reappeared with a flask of tea and an apology. We sat and talked for an hour. I could hear the bikes going past, but I didn't give a stuff about what was happening in the race.

His name was Les and he was the nicest bloke. He wasn't a professional photographer, just a local amateur. He said he was sorry and that he loved all the TV stuff. He added that his missus thought I must be alright because I have a dog that looks happy.

Les adopts greyhounds. He told me he was retiring in March and doesn't enjoy his job much. He visits South Africa for a month every year and the Yorkshire Show for a week. I explained to Les about Brian, but I didn't call him Brian, just the chimp. I told him about the book, *The Chimp Paradox* by Dr Steve Peters, and explained that I knew why I reacted the way I did and I apologised. I do think Brian had every right to go off his trolley, though.

After the race finished I wanted to make sure there was no rage left in me, so I started pushing the bike back to the pits along the road. I thought I'd treat Brian like I treat Nigel. If the dog is being mischievous and ripping things up I take him for a long walk to get it out of his system. I got my head down and started pushing. I had only got a mile down the road when the team van pulled up with Steve, Phil and Denver inside.

I think I could've been in the running in that race, because no one did the best race ever, but there isn't a lot of point in thinking like that. Bruce Anstey won and he obviously deserved to. I was thinking that if we'd have got that practice lap yesterday we would have had the problem then, not in the race.

We got the bike back in the pits and the team left all the windows in the truck's awning covered. By the time I was out of my leathers the Germans from BMW headquarters were there, plugging laptops into the dashboard to download the information it had logged. No one said anything to me. Hector Neill, the team owner and Philip's dad, shrugged. What could anyone say? I had already been thinking, Should I get on the ferry tonight? It had been in my mind that if I won that race I'd have gone home that night, not done another race at the Isle of Man. Not trying to be cool about it, just 'Job done, move on'.

When I told Les, the nice bloke who I had threatened to brain with his own camera a few hours earlier, that I might just go home, he'd said, 'You could do that, but you'd regret it, wouldn't you?' And he was probably right.

The Germans were stumped. They couldn't replicate what had happened out on the track, so it was a case of changing everything. Obviously no one's whooping or high-fiving, but no one was sheepish or walking on eggshells. It means nearly as much to the team as it means to me. William finished in fifth, and by now all my rivals had another six laps of practice on me.

The race had been red-flagged on the last lap, with six riders already over the line, because Michael Dunlop hit a bike – a backmarker who had crashed in front of him. It sounded like Dunlop was on a real flying lap, perhaps on for a podium, when he hit this bike at the Nook just before Governor's Bridge, and pretty much within sight of the finish line. From what I was told there was nothing Dunlop could do to avoid the bike, and he hurt himself. That meant only six people finished, so the organisers counted back the results for those who didn't cross the line, but Dunlop was excluded from the results.

By now my bike was starting first time every time. When the Germans and the TAS team were looking at the data that the bike had recorded, they could see when the bike cut out, but there was no clue why. It could be the tilt switch, a failsafe cut-out that stops the engine if the bike falls completely on its side in a crash, but they'd expect different initials to come up on the screen if it was that. They decided to just change every electrical component. I sat and stripped the loom to see if I could see anything, just for my own peace of mind. There was a tiny nick in one wire, but I don't know if it was enough to cause the problem.

Because this race had been put back to Sunday it meant I would be back on the bike in another race the next day, instead of having a day off in between. So there wasn't much opportunity to brood, when normally there's a lot of time to think too much during a TT.

That night we all went to Lady Helen's house for a team meal. She is a friend of Hector's, dead posh, and the whole team goes every year. We also use her driveway for practising pit-stops with the TAS team. It's long enough to get a lick on, before stopping on a mark and going through the process of filling the tank, changing the back wheel and my helmet visor, then pushing me down the pit lane. We'd go through it two or three times just to blow the cobwebs off before the first race. The TAS team doesn't compete in any other races that have pit-stops, so it's a good refresher.

On Monday we were originally supposed to be running the Supersport TT in the morning, and Superstock in the afternoon, with sidecar qualifying in between and practice sessions for Lightweight and TT Zero, the electric bikes class, on the same day. With all the hold-ups on Saturday and Sunday it was shuffled to allow the first sidecar race to slot in. Then it was changed again, to have the Superstock first, but on Monday morning, minutes before the roads were supposed to be closed at 10.30, there was a bad road accident, which meant there was another change.

The Superstock race was postponed till Tuesday and the first Supersport race finally got underway at 6.30 on Monday night.

Denver, from the TAS team, did my visor for the Supersport races. He's been doing my visor so long now that he can change it without fiddling no matter how much pressure is on, so he helped out the other team. I came into the pits and Denver told me I was running fourth, and gave me the facts. My dad was doing one of the pit boards, and when I passed him, on the third lap of the four-lap race, I saw it showing I was fifth, but I knew the pit-stop hadn't been slow, so I couldn't understand what was happening. The next man on the road was Gary Johnson, who set off ten seconds ahead of me, and I caught him on the last lap. I'd spent the two laps after the pit-stop scratching my bollocks off and I was still in fifth place. I was wondering, am I doing something wrong here?

When I pulled in after the race I was told I'd been done for breaking the pit lane speed limit, like I had done in 2010, and it all made sense. It was a 30-second penalty, but I didn't shout or scream because I genuinely wasn't bothered. The Smiths team had set the limiter and tested it beforehand, I pressed it at the right moment, but the team reckon the tyre expanded and that put it over the speed limit. There's no margin for error and that was the explanation given to me. There was no point in getting revved up. The team said they'd set it at 55, when the speed limit is 60, and it was still over, but the team are mega and I didn't say anything. I wouldn't have won the race, but I was in fourth at the end of the second lap and felt I was on for second or third. Hutchy won the race.

The Smiths Triumph felt spot on, but different to the Suzuki. Looking back, I know I could have spent more time on the bike at the British championship rounds, but I didn't want to go to them. It was as simple as that.

Earlier that day we had another lap of practice and William Dunlop crashed his TAS BMW superstocker at Laurel Bank and broke a rib, putting him out of the rest of the TT.

Tuesday's Superstock TT started well. We'd made a couple of changes set-up wise and the bike was a handful from the off. It wasn't bad, but it was moving around a lot. The bike wasn't bouncing from kerb to kerb, but it was getting excited. I had to relax and let it move about beneath me. It was the kind of race where the bike was having wild moments and I would have to check the brake pads hadn't been knocked back away from the discs, by pumping the front brake lever to make sure they were ready when I needed them next. I did a 130.304 mph lap from a standing start, putting me in third behind Michael Dunlop and Hutchy. That's a bloody good lap on a superbike, never mind a less powerful superstocker, and the second lap was good too.

I was still in third when I came in for a pit-stop and my bike wouldn't start. I lost summat like 35 seconds in that pit-stop, because the battery was flat. I had dropped to seventh by the time we got it going. Some people ask if it makes me lose faith in the TAS team, but it doesn't at all. It's a new bike to us and they put lightweight batteries in a place you'd think they'd be alright, but because they put them above the engine they got too hot. The team didn't know that when these batteries got to a certain temperature they don't put out the same amps and it couldn't crank the engine over. When I came in after the race it wouldn't do anything, it was completely flat. Then we left the bike for half an hour and it started first time. I didn't even know where I finished till I checked when I was writing this, a few weeks later. I was seventh.

Hutchy won again, his second win of the week, and had made an impressive comeback. He rode bloody well. Anyone who is winning nowadays is going well. No one gets handed a win.

When I was out walking Nige that week I wasn't going over what had happened, beating myself up about anything. I was just thinking about what's likely to happen in the race, and deciding where I could push a bit harder or try a different line. I've come full circle with how I work with teams. I used to want to know every detail about every change and why the mechanics had done it, but now I tell Stewart what the bike is doing and he chooses the direction for the bike set-up and what changes need to be made. I don't really need to know what's happened any more, but he gives me the basic details. Now I say, 'It's doing this and I want it to do this,' instead of me deciding, 'I want this changing and that changing.'

I got a podium on the Triumph in the second Supersport race. Hutchy won again and Bruce Anstey was second. The race was pretty much the same as the first Supersport 600, just without the 30-second penalty for breaking the pit lane speed limit.

I was rubbish on the first lap. I've tried different styles of riding on the first lap and it doesn't seem to make a difference. I've tried scratching my balls off to get to Glen Helen and I've tried riding like a granny and I'm still rubbish, but by the second lap I'm alright. I can get it off the line, but I'm not as fast as some of the other boys on that first lap, even if I'm faster than them later in the race. I've tried pedalling for 20 minutes on the turbo trainer in the truck to get a bit of a sweat on and raise my heart rate before I get in my leathers, but it hasn't made much difference.

I used to struggle with arm pump in races, too. The medical name for arm pump is chronic exertional compartment syndrome. In a race your arms are holding on and supporting your bodywork under braking, and if you're going at it from stone-cold you're asking a lot of those muscles. The blood rushes to the muscles in your forearms to oxygenate them, but it gets trapped in the muscles and can't flood out, so your forearms go solid and that takes the feeling away from your fingers and palms of your hands. That means you can't feel how hard you're pulling on the front brake lever or gripping the handlebars.

I'd get arm pump in the second lap of a race and then it would stay, but I've got around that now. Lots of racers suffer from it and have operations to stop it happening. I was going to have the operation to cure it, but that would mean having a month off work and I didn't want to do that. Instead I tie a bit of rope around a piece of broom handle, that's been cut down to about 12 inches in length. The other end of the rope is tied around a house brick. With both ends tied, the rope is about three foot long, so when I hold the bit of brush shaft out in front of me at about chest height the brick is just above the floor. Then, with my arms straight, I wind the broom handle in my fists so the rope is wrapping around it and lifting the house brick up towards my hands. When it gets near my fists, I wind the rope down so the brick is going back to the floor. I do it ten times, ten ups, ten downs, and it works. It's not masking the arm pump problem, it's cured it.

With William out because of his broken ribs, I was asked to stand in for him and ride the Victory electric bike in Wednesday's one-lap TT Zero. The race is for bikes that are 'powered without the use of carbon-based fuels and have zero toxic/noxious emissions'. I won't get into the whole subject about how green the power stations were that made the electricity that charged the batteries, because the technology has to start somewhere.

Victory Motorcycles are an American manufacturer that has been in business since 1998 and are owned by the massive Polaris company. They also make snowmobiles, all-terrain buggies and electric golf buggy-type vehicles, and they own Indian Motorcycles.

The electric race bike was a trick thing. It was originally developed by Brammo, but Victory bought them out. I got one lap of practice on it and the race only lasted one lap. Lee Johnston was on the other Victory and the favourites for the race were the Mugen Shindens ridden by McGuinness and Anstey.

The first Zero TT was in 2010, but there was a race called the TTXGP, basically the same thing, in 2009, and these bikes are so much quicker now, just five years later. Rutter did the first ever 100 mph lap of the TT on an electric bike in 2012, winning himself £10,000 put up by the Isle of Man government. This year McGuinness did 119 mph on his way to the win. I managed 109.717 mph on the Victory, and Lee did 111.620 mph and was third behind Bruce.

Racing an electric bike is a very different experience, because the electric motor doesn't need gears, so you're not involved as much, you're just steering it and braking. And there is next to no noise from the motor, just the drive chain and tyres on the road, until you brake – then I realised how noisy brakes are. But it was a good experience and the Victory lot were good folk who taught me about neodynium rare earth magnets, that work with the fancy new AC motors this bike was powered by.

The final race of the 2015 TT was the Senior, for all the same bikes that competed in the Superbike TT earlier in the week, the race I lasted three miles of. The starting order is the same, with any riders who were injured or unable to race missed out and any newcomers who had high numbers, but had proved themselves to be fast, moved up the order. William, who had been number six, didn't line up, but no one took his number.

The BMW felt like the best bike I'd ever ridden, but then Hutchie caught me, taking ten seconds out of me, so fair play, and I chose not to start battling with him. The TT is different. It's a time trial, so if he had caught me, he was ten seconds quicker than me, and I wasn't about to start screwing up his race by trying to pass him back, even if there were places where I was still faster than him. I sat behind him and I could see that he was quicker in some places and I was quicker in others.

In the last lap he slowed right down, or at least compared to what he was doing, and I knew he was having trouble with his bike, but I didn't want to muck about passing him, if he was on for a win, so I stayed sat behind him, when perhaps I shouldn't have done. I heard later that his exhaust was falling to bits and sitting behind him wasn't the right thing to do. I don't think I'd have won it, McGuinness had got the jump from the off, he's mustard from the start and won, with James Hillier in second.

When I was told I had finished fourth, less than eight seconds behind Hutchy in third, I honestly wasn't bothered. I would rather have fourth than second or third. If I can't win I don't want another bloody podium. I only want to do all the bullshit of the podium and the press conference if I've won. But I didn't purposely finish in fourth, I was trying my balls off and did a 132.398 mph lap, faster than the outright lap record set in 2014 by Bruce Anstey, so I wasn't hanging about. McGuinness went even faster, though, and raised the record to 132.701 mph. Setting my fastest ever lap didn't mean a thing to me. I want to ride my bike as hard as I can, and I did, but it didn't make any difference that I got this lap time or that lap time.

Following Hutchy gave me something to think about, because if I hadn't been behind him I'd have thought my BMW and the way the team had set it up was the best thing ever. I could see that I broke a record in one of the sectors because the bike is so strong, but that has made it bad in other areas. The section I was fastest in was from the Bungalow to Cronk-ny-Mona, four or five minutes of riding. The Bungalow is where the tramlines cross the road on the Mountain, then you've got Hailwood Rise, Brandywell, 32nd, Windy, 33rd, Keppel Gate, Sarah's Cottage, Creg-ny-Baa, Brandish, Hillberry and Signpost, where the section ends. I could see where and why Hutchy's bike was better in other areas. Sometimes a bike can be a bitch below a 130 mph lap (that's a lap average, not a top speed), then at about 130 mph lap speed it's alright, and you find a sweet spot, but then when you get to 132 it can be a bitch again. So the BMW is still the best superbike I've ever ridden, but I can see where and how it could be improved.

The racing was over and, like normal, I wanted to get home as soon as possible, so I headed for the boat straight after the race. I just had enough time to call at Craig and Lisa's to pick up Nige, then call in at Steve's, who sorts the ferry out for me.

It felt like an uneventful TT, summat and nothing, but it was the first one I'd enjoyed for a while. I had the dog there and that seemed to make a big difference; the bike was working well, and I wasn't put in the position where I had to sit and do signings, so except for threatening to stove Les's head in with his Nikon, Brian had stayed quiet and I could come and go as I pleased.

Tim Coles and Cammy came back in the van with me. I dropped Cammy off at his place, then got back on the M62 before taking Tim to his farm. I eventually got home in the early hours of Saturday morning. I had a few hours' sleep and went into Moody's over the weekend, so I knew what I was going back to on Monday morning.

For a while I was thinking that I wouldn't go back next year, that I would have a year off from it. I'm hopefully going to sort it with TAS that I can do all the races I normally do except the North West and the TT. I don't know what they'll say to that, but I want to enter the Tour Divide bicycle race, that's held at the same time, then maybe go back to the TT the year after. I'm only 33. Look at Bruce Anstey, he was 45 in 2015, and John McGuinness is 43.

Ian Hutchinson won three races when plenty had thought he'd never be on the pace again after nearly losing his leg and having dozens of operations to sort it. He has dedicated his whole life to winning TTs, but I realise I can't do that. From 2004 to 2009 the Isle of Man was the focus for me, but then the TT and the North West started demanding press days, and telling riders to be here at this time for these photos and that time for this thing, when I just wanted to ride my bike. The press events didn't feel constructive in any way, I was just being asked the same questions by the same journalists, sitting there wondering, Aren't you sick of asking me those same questions? – wishing I was somewhere else.

Sharon knows me well enough, and she says to me if I did just try to focus on the TT now everything else would have to take a back seat, it would drive me so mental that I probably wouldn't be in the right frame of mind to win a race when I got there. It's a catch-22. That's Hutchy's life, fair play, but I can't focus on that one race, and that alone. It's not in my nature, it's not my sole purpose and there's too much else I want, and need, to do.

CHAPTER 23

I don't have time to be having a week off work with a broken back

The Ulster Grand Prix is up there with the Southern 100 and Armoy as one of the races I most look forward to and enjoy, because they're all good meetings with good organisation and held on good tracks. Plus I don't feel like I'm there for a lifetime. I get there, get the job done and get back.

I went to work at four on Wednesday morning, and left at ten to drive to Gloucester to pick up the Triumph TT bike I'd bought from Smiths. I needed it because I'd entered to race it at the Ulster. Now I've got it I can do what I want with it. I can ride it myself or stick a lad on it. It's a mega bike and Rebecca gave me a new 675 road bike as part of the deal.

From there I drove straight to the ferry, to get over to Northern Ireland in time for Wednesday night practice, but the weather turned out to be horrible so I only went out in one session. The schedule for the Ulster is practice on Wednesday; qualify on Thursday, then race the Dundrod 150 that night; Friday is a day off and then there's a load of races on Saturday.

The track is called the Dundrod and there used to be two different meetings held on this road circuit, the Ulster Grand Prix and the Killinchy 150. The Ulster was always the bigger, International meeting, and the Killinchy was an Irish national meeting, at the end of June if I remember rightly, where they ran the Dundrod 150. They merged the two meetings and now the Killinchy's big race is on the Thursday of the Ulster, in August.

I covered my new Triumph's fairing with white sticky plastic, to mask the names of sponsors that are nothing to do with me. It looked rough when I'd finished, but it's a brilliant bike. I only rode it once at the Ulster and qualified third, and that was the first time I'd sat on it since the TT. The bike showed its quality because I qualified third and I wasn't even pushing it. I also qualified on pole on the TAS BMW superstock and the TAS superbike.

The Dundrod is an open race, so riders can choose what they want to ride, within reason. I chose to race the superbike, because I wanted the fastest bike possible. My team-mate William Dunlop, and another BMW rider, Lee Johnston, both prefer the BMW superstock to the superbike, but I don't. The superbike is a handful, but it makes more power. A superbike is always going to be a bit of a handful because it's

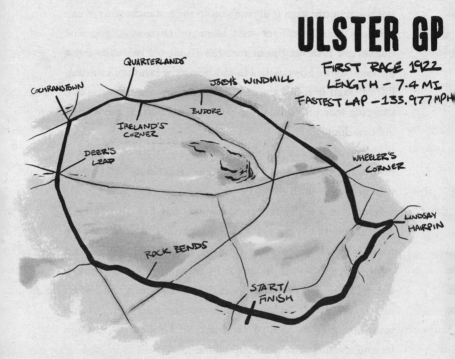

ULSTER GP

FIRST RACE 1922
LENGTH - 7.4 MI
FASTEST LAP - 133.977 MPH

COCHRANSTOWN

QUARTERLANDS

JOEY'S WINDMILL

BUDORE

IRELAND'S CORNER

DEER'S LEAP

WHEELER'S CORNER

LINDSAY HAIRPIN

ROCK BENDS

START/ FINISH

always pushing the boundaries of something – tyres, power, aerodynamics, suspension, or the track. As soon as technology improves in one area it allows you to push it in another area.

I didn't get a brilliant start from my front row, and was fourth and fifth for the first couple of laps. Eventually I got through all the boys, with Hutchy being the last man I passed. I'd followed him for a couple of laps and knew I was faster, knowing that he wouldn't be able to come back at me when I did pass him.

I planned to come up the inside of him on the exit of Budore on the run to Windmill. I could take it flat out, but Hutchy was struggling with it.

Budore is a really fast right-hander that I've always been good through. On the exit you run right out to the left of the road, where it drops away into the gutter. I set the pass up on the corner before, Ireland's. I knew not to come through Ireland's balls out, because I was right with Hutchy and when he backed off for Budore I'd risk running into him, because we're using every inch of the road. So I rolled off through Ireland's, letting him get a gap on me.

On the exit of Budore, Hutchy was out of the seat, fighting his bike, but I could turn tighter and come up the inside. You've got to be committed to do it, and I'm not showing off, but I'm good through there.

When I was past him I knuckled down for two or three laps to try make a gap, but my pit board was saying +0, +0, each lap. I'm not a big one for looking behind me, but I knew someone was coming with me and I didn't think it would be Hutchy. I had a quick look and saw Bruce Anstey, right there.

When I'm on it at the Ulster there is only one man who manages to stay with me and that's Bruce. From 2006 on, when everything's been right with me on a superbike, I get out in front and no one comes with me. It's been the same on Yamaha, Honda or Suzuki. Supersport and Superstock races have been a bit different, but the Superbike races are my thing. It's just knack. That was until 2014, when everything was good and Bruce still came with me. I beat him twice and he beat me once. So I guessed it would be him before I even looked back. Going onto the last lap, I knew he was going to try to pass me, and I had a good idea where it would be. Bruce was right on me when we crossed the finish line to go onto the last lap, with me leading. The BMW is strong into corners, where I was weak last year, but I knew I couldn't give him a millimetre. Then I caught a backmarker in a bad place, lost a bit of momentum and realised that would give Bruce some encouragement. Now I had no chance of dropping him on the last lap. I was pressing hard and he had come with me.

Catching the backmarker though Deer's Leap made me start thinking I had to be 100 per cent everywhere – in the ditches, on the white lines, everywhere – but I like riding like that.

I was in sixth gear into Deer's Leap, then back to fifth to accelerate down the hill, still in fifth, using all the road, and into the downhill right, Cochranstown. Next I'm back two gears for Quarterlands, where my elbows and knees are in the grass, the superbike's tyres just on the very last bit of available tarmac. I still felt I had it all covered, because I knew I'd get a good run out of Ireland's and my BMW is every bit as good as Bruce's Honda, so he wasn't going to pass me up there.

I accelerated out of Quarterlands in second, just getting the light on the dash to change gear. I was driving hard, going from 20 per cent to 100 per cent throttle without even thinking about it. Exiting the next corner, Ireland's, I felt the back tyre slide a little bit, at about 130 mph. It was nothing I would normally panic about, not even something I would've corrected, I'd have just let it slide – then the next thing is I'm looking at the tarmac, thinking, Oof!

I've always been good at crashing and not hurting myself as badly as other riders, because I don't tense up, but I didn't have a choice with this one, because I was knocked out. If I had been killed I'd have been none the wiser, but I woke up in hospital. When I opened my eyes there were a lot of people looking over me. Nobody was panicking, but they were busy.

I started getting a bit of an idea of what was broken because the doctors were listing the breaks: 'There's fractures in your spine, your sternum's broken, this is broke, that's broke.' I asked about my hand, because bones were stuck up, but I couldn't feel them because everything was aching. I could poke at the bones that had been broken and shoved out of place, so they said they'd have a look at them. It turned out I'd broken a metacarpal in my hand, between my knuckle and wrist, and they had to pin it.

The worst of the injuries were to my back. The T4 to T9 vertebrae were broken and had unstable fractures. The crash happened at something like 6.30 on Thursday evening and the next day I was operated on. They locked my spine together with a metal rod. They did my hand at the same time. There was nothing they could do about my broken sternum or ribs.

This was my biggest ever crash, no doubt about it. It was the daftest crash, but the biggest one. I can't say for sure, but left to my control I reckon I'd had saved it. I've had slides like that before and I let them develop. Well, she developed. I don't look back and think, I shouldn't have been going that hard. I don't think I had done anything wrong. It might have turned into a highside, but with this crash I knew nothing about it. I reckon the bike's traction control had shut the throttle for me, when I'd have kept it sliding more. And when it shut off it gave the tyre a chance to grip again and caused the bike to buck me off over the highside. I saw the video and it's such a strange crash.

After the operation all I was thinking was, Get out of hospital, get back to work, get better. I felt I had to be back at work for Monday morning. I was hurting, but I had a man in my head saying, 'No, no, you said you were putting that engine in first thing Monday morning.'

My blood pressure had been dropping further and further, and the hospital put it down to dehydration. My body had gone through all sorts. I don't know about my head, because the white of my right eye was completely black. The more drips they put through me, the better it got. Everyone at the hospital, the Royal Victoria in Belfast, were bloody brilliant.

The surgeon who operated on me wasn't much older than me, and when he spoke I listened. Well, I listened when he said they couldn't stop me checking myself out of hospital. I wasn't listening when he advised me against doing just that. He told me they needed a load of X-rays to make sure all the metalwork was alright. They X-rayed me on Monday night, but there was no one to check them, so I had to stay till Tuesday morning.

My dad had come over to watch the racing and stayed with me. Sharon wasn't at the race, but she flew over on Friday, arriving while I was being operated on and then stayed with me too. My dad had his camper van, so when I did get out of hospital I lay in the back of that for the journey home.

Brian the chimp had been quiet through all this until I got back home. He was getting riled when I couldn't get to sleep and annoyed about not being able to get in and out of the shower easily. I went in the shed at 7.30 on Thursday morning trying to do a bit of work, something easy like turning my Triumph T150 valves down on the lathe. They are going in the engine of the Wall of Death bike. I did a couple, but I was knackered and had to go and sit down. The chimp was reacting to that too, until my human brain caught up and Brian backed down. Still, come hell or high water, I was going in to work on Monday, a week and a half after the accident.

Andy Spellman visited me and said we should move the Wall of Death back at least a month, and that we had to decide that it wasn't happening on the original date right away, so people could start changing their plans. James from North One had come over to Ireland while I was in hospital. He was being friendly, but I think he wanted to see how bad I was with his own eyes, because they've got a fair bit riding on me. He said for years they'd been paying a fortune in insurance to cover me and they were finally getting something back for it.

Never say never, but I think that's it for me and road racing. I've got too many other things to do: the Wall of Death, the land speed record attempt, mad pushbike races ... I'm laid up here, eight days after the accident at the Ulster, I've already had a week off work, and I'm probably going to have another half a week. As much as I love my motorbikes, I'm not getting enough buzz out of it to warrant all this time off. It's not the worst pain in the world, but it's a pain to have to miss work, so I've got to stop putting myself in that position. I don't have time to be having a week off work with a broken back.

Earlier in the book I mentioned that I might be interested in doing some world endurance racing, like I had at Le Mans, but not now. I might do some oddball races, but my focus is the 2016 Tour Divide. It's a self-supported mountain bike race; that means you carry everything you need, and it's 2,745 miles south from Banff in Canada to Antelope Wells, New Mexico – the length of America, top to bottom. It'll take two weeks of cycling 20 hours a day. Anyone attempting it is going to be completely broken day after day, but it's how you come back from it. And that's what I'm interested in. It fascinates me that the injuries and bones I broke at Ulster will mend and I'll come back stronger than I ever have been, then I'll go to the Tour Divide and break myself again and repair from that. I like breaking myself. Even lying here, broken sternum, broken back, broken hand ...

I'm not trying to prove a point to anyone. I just know my body can do it. It's not giving me any satisfaction. It's hard to explain, because it's not about proving anything to anyone. I just need to do it.

One night I was lying in bed and every fourth heartbeat a really sharp pain went through my heart. I didn't have a phone,

Sharon had gone out to fetch me something, and I thought I had a heart attack coming on. Then I realised I wasn't sweating, so I didn't think it could be that. The hassle of the situation made me realise there's more to life than racing motorbikes. I already knew that, but this crash has highlighted it, underlined it, drawn a ring around it and added an exclamation mark. I was right all along. I enjoyed racing this year, but not enough to warrant this. This is all my decision. Sharon's been brilliant. She isn't saying I should do one thing or another, and that means a lot.

The only reasons I can think of to keep racing are the TAS team and the relationship with BMW. But those aren't proper reasons to race. The reason to race is to go and be competitive. Road racing has given me a good life, and I'm not being cocky, but I've brought something to racing too. We've been good for each other, but I've done it for 13 years. I'm 33, I've still got my limbs, they're a bit sore at the moment, but they'll fix. It's time for the next job, because, as my grandad Voldemars Kidals always said, 'When you dead, you dead.'

Acknowledgements

Gary Inman for translating the untranslatable; Andy Spellman for keeping the train on the rails; Lorna Russell for putting her balls on the line with the books; Neil Duncanson for the interesting TV jobs; Dobby, The Maws, Tim, Paul, Cammy, Adrian and Shorty for giving my brain peace and for being Brian's friend; Mark McIvor, Mark McCarville, Denver, Phil, Philip and Hector for making the racing happen; Craig, Lisa, Isla, Gary and Jane for looking after me on the island; Jason, Alan, Francis and Forbes for all the push biking; James, Ewan, Tom, Nat, Sarah, Amy and Jess for the entertainment and the trickest Risbridger; The Fox family for the teaching and that curry; Moody and Belty for being constants; Dad and Mum for rearing what you're reading; Sal for being a proper grafter; Nigel for being the best dog in the world; Sharon for being Sharon. Thank you all for managing the unmanageable.

Index

Ack Attack 216, 221, 222
Action Truck Parts 179–80
AGV 18, 89, 144, 198, 278–9
AKP (Arundel Kerr Produce) 193
Al Jazeera 116
Alford Motorcycle show 132
Almeria, Spain, testing at 184, 187–92
Anstey, Bruce 292, 298, 300, 301, 303, 308, 309
Archers, The (radio programme) 187
Armoy 153, 305
Armstrong, Lance 126–7

Baker, Brad 98, 100, 101, 103
Baker, Matt 50, 51, 52
Bayliss, Troy 101, 102
BBC 50, 116, 191, 253, 257, 273, 274
Bell, Mark 48–9
Belli, Marco 97
Belty (friend) 126, 175, 176, 316
Benny (friend) 107, 108–9, 110, plate section 2
Bimota 500VDue 185
Birtwistle, Alan 100, 102
Blazusiak, Taddy 100
blood doping 126–7
BMW 102, 114, 156, 158, 161, 164, 172, 183, 186, 188, 190, 192, 198, 204, 211, 213, 225, 226, 229, 230, 232, 233, 239, 242, 243, 245, 247, 248, 251, 259, 261, 262, 281, 282, 283, 284, 287, 293, 296, 301, 302, 306, 309, 314; S1000RR 157, 164, 219, 227, 228, 229, 230, 232
Boast, Peter 96–7, 98, 102, 103–4
Boat That Guy Built, The (television programme) 58
Bonneville Salt Flats, Utah 30, 214, 216, 219, 221, 222, 239, 264
Brammo 300
Brands Hatch 27, 106
Bridewell, Tommy 188
Brindley, Ollie 100, 102, 103
British Superbikes (BSB) 95, 106, 121, 171, 188, 193, 196–205, 214, 235–6, 241, 248, 284; Donington Park 196–205, 214, 226, 235; Oulton Park 204
British Supersport 188, 196, 198, 202
British Superstock 188
Britten 110–11, 112–14, 115, 120, plate section 1, plate section 2
Browder, Bill: *Red Notice* 191

BUB 221–2
Bundla Tea Estate, India 69

Cadwell Park 18, 87, 89, 91, 165, 225
Caistor 192, 206–7, 272–3
Caistor Grammar School 272–3
Campos, Dave 221
Carlile, Andy 163, 164, 165
Carpenter Racing 218
Carr, Chris 222
Cavendish, Mark 80
Chadwick, Sarah 207
Chain Reaction Cycles 236
Channel 4 33, 45, 48, 53, 166, 270, 273, 275
Chimp Paradox The (Peters) 40–1, 79–80, 292
Clarkson, Jeremy 273
Climb Dance (short film) 13
Cohen, Sacha Baron 181
Coles, Tim 32, 38, 88, 91–2, 96, 97, 127, 129, 132, 133, 134, 135, 137, 184, 188, 199, 210, 215, 232, 270, 303
Contractor, Hafeez 70
Cooke Brothers Engineering 256
Cookstown 100 235–6, 239–51, 252, 253, 258, 285
Cooper, Dan 170
Crosslé car factory, Holywood, County Down 254, 256
Cummins, Conor 259

Dainese 18, 86, 87, 102, 198, 278–9
Davey (TAS) 239, 248–9
Daytona 18, 220
Denver (TAS) 259, 292, 295, 315
Dirt Quake, King's Lynn Speedway 265–6, 274
dirt track 16, 32, 74, 76, 84, 88, 90–104, 154–5, 184, 210–11, 214–15, 221–2, 225, 265–6, 267; plate section 2
Dirt Track Riders Association championship 95
DiSalvo, Jason 217, 220, 221
Dixon, Darren 202
Dixon, Jake 202
Dobby (friend) 192–3, 194, 210
Donington Park 197–9, 200–4, 205, 214, 226, 235
Doohan, Mick 69, 279

'downhill soapbox' (world gravity racer speed record) 29–44, 89, 139; plate section 1
Ducati 101, 184, 185
Duke of Edinburgh Awards 272
Dundrod 150 306
Dungait, Forbes 128, 130, 132, 184, 315
Dungait, Francis 128, 132, 184–5, 186, 187, 188, 191, 192, 315, plate section 2
Dunlop, Michael 157, 242, 243, 246, 247, 249, 250, 284, 293–4, 296
Dunlop, Paul 13, 257
Dunlop, William 156, 157, 188, 191, 228, 241, 247, 260, 296, 299, 300–1, 306

Eaton, Lee 127–8
Evans, Chris 50, 273
Everard, Francis 240, 241
Ewals, John 23

Farquhar, Ryan 158–9, 228, 230
Fendt 210–11, 212
Ferguson, Trevor 158
Five Tens (biking shoes) 134
Fleet Factors 179
Ford 238–9; RS200 plate section 1; Transit 32, 39, 84, 87, 96, 98, 128, 137, 166, 168, 184, 193, 201–2, 226, 234, 238–9, 265, 279–80; Trust Ford 238
Forsyth, Keith 135, 136
Fox family 142, 143, 144, 145, 146, 147–9, 152, 261, 262–3, 264–5, 266, 267, 316
Fox, Ken 142, 143, 144, 145, 146, 147–9, 152, 262–3, 264–5, 266, 267
Fox, Luke 142, 144, 145, 146, 147, 149, 265, 266, 267
Free Soul Riders 59, 61–2
Froome, Chris 31, 80
Frost, Jack 221
Frost, Sloan 110

Goa, India 72–4, 75, 77
Goodwood Festival of Speed 112
Goodyear 218
Gowland, Graham 197
Grant, Kevin 112, 113
gravity racer speed record, world 29–44, 89, 139, plate section 1
Griffiths, Jason 193–4, 315
Grimsby 14, 18, 52, 55, 174, 181–2, 220, 278
Grimsby (film) 181

Hallam University, Sheffield 33, 35, 44, 147, plate section 1

Harley-Davidson 16, 58, 221, 236, 265–6, 274
Harris, Shaun 105
Harrison, Dean 228, 232, 254
Hawk 157, 284
Hayden, Nicky 93
Head, Douglas 280
Hero Honda 58, 59, 61
Hewer, Nick 52
Hewitt, Gary 83
Hillier, James 301
Hillsborough Oyster Festival 238
Holden, Robert 118
Honda 91, 114, 161, 168, 266, 281, 309; CB200 142, 145, 148; CBR600 Supersport 168, 208; CR500 engine 265; CRF450 94, 95, 96, 102, 265, plate section 2; Hero Honda 58, 59, 60, 61, 63; Hydrex Honda 132, 196, 248; NSR500 Grand Prix bike 60
Hope (mountain bike company) 41–2, 193, 233
hovercraft speed record 29, 139
How Britain Worked (TV series) 14
Hoy, Sir Chris 80
Hunt, Hugh 141–2, plate section 2
Hutchinson, Ian 290, 296, 297, 298, 301, 302, 303, 304, 308
Hydrex Honda 132, 196, 248
Hynes, (née Martin) Sally 'Sal' (sister) 8–9, 49–50, 52, 77, 186, 195, 206–7, 225, 238, 239, 265, 316, plate section 1, plate section 2

Iddon, Christian 100–1
Independent Vehicle Assessment (IVA) 177, 178, 179, 194, 236, 277
India 53–78, 116, 127, 140
Indian Motorcycles 142, 299; Scouts 142, 143, 144, 145
Indianapolis 500 12, 18
Ingsoc 181
Inman, Gary 95–6, 102, 199, 200, plate section 2
Ireland 9–10, 105, 117, 173
Isle of Man TT 10, 12, 17, 18, 20, 23, 27, 62, 83, 87, 104, 111, 112, 114, 117, 121–2, 151, 152, 153, 154, 155, 156, 157, 158, 159–62, 164, 165, 166–7, 172, 189, 197, 198, 205, 213, 216–17, 228, 239, 258, 259, 267, 276–86, 287–304, plate section 3

Jama Mosque, Delhi, India 62–3
Jenkins, Dave 147
John Hebb Volvo 108, 109, 173, 279

John Trigger 167, 200
Johnson, Gary 166, 171–2, 290, 295
Johnston, Lee 228, 229, 232, 260, 279, 300, 306
Johnstone, Stewart 172, 188, 279, 285, 287, 297
Jones, Alex 50
Jones, Jason 200

K-Tech 16
Kaaden, Walter 187
Kalka, India 67–8
Karol Bagh, Delhi, India 57–8
Kawasaki 156, 161; AR50 77, 83, 108, 279; 650 158; ZX–10R 27, 227
Kelsa 167
Ken Fox Wall of Death 140–2
Kidal, Voldemars (grandfather) 10, 314
Killinchy 150 306
Kirkistown, Northern Ireland 183, 190–1, 241, 258
Kirmington, Lincolnshire 108, 206, 237
Krazy Horse, Bury St Edmunds 266

Lady Helen 294
Laverty, Michael 188
Layt, Matt 95, 96
Le Mans 24-Hour motorcycle race 129, 154, 313
Lincolnshire 19, 30, 49, 73, 97, 101, 104, 125, 170, 184, 187, 209–10, 211, 266, 270, 273
Lintin, Ivan 169, 228
Lockerbie bomber 116
Loeb, Sebastien 13–14
Lorenzo, Jorge 93

Mad Nige 9
Mahad, India 72–3, 75
Manx Grand Prix: 2012 158; Newcomers 2014 117
Manx Norton 121
Mar-Train 227, 232
Markstaller, Matt 215, 216–17, 218, 219, 220, 221, 222, 223, 224
Márquez, Marc 92, 94, 95, 98, 99, 100, 101, 103, 114, 158
Marsh, John 122
Martek 14–18, 23–4, 26, 36, 83, 87, 96, 151, 164, 192, 271, 272, 278; plate section 1, plate section 2
Martin, Guy: Brian the Chimp and 79–89, 139, 198, 199–200, 270, 278, 291, 292, 303, 312, 315; crash and injuries, Ulster Grand Prix 310–14, plate section 3; dirt track riding 16, 32, 74, 76, 84, 88,

90–104, 154–5, 184, 210–11, 214–15, 221–2, 225, 265–6, 267; fame 45–52, 268–75; Fendt 9-series tractor 211–12; fitness 124–5; g-force refresher course and medical, RAF Henlow 276–7; gravity racer speed record attempt 29–44; hovercraft world speed record attempt 29; India trip 53–78; Maw family and 206–12; motorcycle racing *see under individual race and racing category name*; motorcycle world land speed record 214–24, 264, 269–70; mountain bike racing 124–38, 194; North Lincolnshire and 209–10; Nürburgring Nordschleife, motorcycle record attempt at 162–6, 213, plate section 2; pre-season testing motorbikes 183–95; retirement 311–14; tandem 24-hour distance record 29; truck fitter 52, 173–82; TV career 29–52, 53, 54, 94, 133, 139–52, 164, 166, 177, 178, 179, 211, 215, 219, 236–7, 262–3, 268–75, 277, 312; Wall of Death, speed record attempt plan 139–52, 214, 236, 261, 262–7, 269, 274, 312
Martin, Ian (father) 17, 49, 83, 85, 88, 97, 106–7, 108, 109–10, 116, 117, 123, 127, 128, 132, 133, 151, 173, 180, 193, 194, 206, 207, 209, 210, 295, 312, 316
Martin, Rita (née Kidals) 10, 53, 78, 107, 116, 194, 206, 207, 208–9, 257, 272, 316
Martin, 'Sal' (sister) *see* Hynes, Sally
Maws family 36, 70–1, 207–9
McCarville, Mark 188–9
McElvaney's truck yard, Monaghan 257–8, plate section 3
McGuinness, John 159, 161, 281, 300, 301–2, 303
McIvor, Mark 188, 200, 225–6, 232, 233, 234, 239
Mees, Jared 98, 100, 101, 103
Mehew, Chris 115
Metzeler 26, 121, 162, 163, 164, 165, 166, 190, 211, 227–8, 232–3, 234, 241
Miles, Jason 8, 29, 88, 133, 135, 193, 194
Mitchell, Austin 181, 182
Moffit, Glyn 254
Molnar, Andy 121
Molyneux, Dave 17
Mont Ventoux, France 31–7, 39, 89, 139, 278, plate section 1
Moody International, Grimsby 8, 31, 36, 86, 126, 167, 168, 174–81, 182, 184, 225, 236, 264, 269, 271, 303
Moody, Mick 8, 86, 146, 167, 168, 174, 175, 177, 179, 180, 181, 182, 226, 239, 257, 271, 277, 316

MoTeC 15, 218
MotoGP 14, 94, 99, 101, 103, 137, 157, 219
Moto2 17, 99, 100
Moto3 99, 100
Motorcycle News 198, 253
motorcycle world land speed record 214–24, 264, 269–70
Mr Porky's Pork Scratchings 192, 283
Mugen Shinden 161, 300
Muir, Shaun 157, 248, 284
Mumbai, India 69–72, 74

Neave, Tim 92, 95, 100, 101, 102, 210
Neave, Tom 92, 95, 100, 101, 210, 215
Neill, Hector 188, 249, 293, 294, 315, plate section 2
Neill, Philip 153, 156, 161, 162, 188, 239, 259, 261, 284, 293, plate section 2
New Zealand 105–23, 124, 127, 186, 219
Nigel (labrador) 8–9, 87, 89, 170, 180, 186, 195, 208, 238, 278, 279, 280, 281, 289, 292, 297, 302, 316, plate section 1, plate section 3
North One 31, 40, 41, 47, 48, 49, 53, 54, 164, 166, 177, 178, 179, 211, 215, 262–3, 268–9, 270, 274, 275, 277, 312
North West 200 13, 154, 188, 204–5, 251, 252–60, 264, 286, 303
Northern Ireland 13, 183, 190–1, 210, 228, 235–51, 252–60, 305–14
Norton: Manx 121; Monocoque 111
Nürburgring Nordschleife, motorcycle record at 162–6, 213, plate section 2

Oliver's Mount, Scarborough 88, 225–34, 235, 239, 241, 242, 247; Gold Cup 88, 89, 226; Spring National, 2015 198, 223, 225–34, 235, 239, 241, 242, 247
One Show, The (television programme) 49–52, plate section 1
Orange: Clockwork 132–3; Five 237–8; Gyro 132–3
Orwell, George 182; *Animal Farm* 26, 116; *1984* 116–17, 182, plate section 2
Oulton Park 204

Paddy (friend) 17–18, 179, 278
Palampur, India 68–9
Penrose, Spencer 12
Peoria TT, USA 102, 155
Performance Bikes 112
Peugeot 13
Phil (TAS) 259, 292, 315
Pike Jr, Zebulon 12
Pikes Peak International Hill Climb,

Colorado, USA, 2014 7, 8, 12–28, 29, 31, 36, 83, 87, 96, 105, 151, 154, 164, 271, 278, 279, plate section 1
Pirelli 121, 190
Plastic Fantastic 111–12
Polaris 299
Proper online shop 46
Purves, Libby 48, plate section 1

Rabat, Tim 99
Racefit, Derbyshire 15, 18
Radio 2 49
Radio 4 116; *Midweek* 48–9, plate section 1
RAF Henlow 263–4, 276–7
Rancho Canudas, Spain 98
Red Bull stunt plane 236–7
Redding, Scott 99
Redmayne, Billy 117
Rider Mania, India 74–6
Rob North Triumph 83
Rob Vine Fund 281
Roberts Sr, Kenny 92–3
Roberts, Steve 111–12
Robinson, Rocky 216, 222
Rossi, Valentino 92, 93, 97, 122, 165
Rourke, Jason 147
Royal Enfield 57–60, 61, 62, 63, 67, 73, 74–5, 76, 77, 114
Ryan, Mike 25

Saiger, Horst 254
Scania 48, 146, 167–9, 174, 176, 178, 194, 257–8, plate section 2, plate section 3
Scarborough: Gold Cup 88, 89, 226; Spring National, 2015 198, 223, 225–34, 235, 239, 241, 242, 247
Scott Physiotherapy 281, 283
Second World War, 1939–45 32, 187
Seeley, Alastair 188, 259–60
Sharon (girlfriend) 9–10, 36–7, 56, 209, 212, 236, 238, 251, 257, 265, 304, 312, 314, 316
Sheene, Barry 92
Sheils, Derek 242, 247, 249, 250
Sideburn 95, 265
Singh, Lalli 59
Smith, Alan 170–1
Smith, Bradley 99, 100, 102
Smith, Rebecca 167, 170, 171, 196, 197, 200, 202, 204, 283, 305
Smiths Triumph 167, 168–9, 170–2, 196–7, 200, 202, 204, 205, 213–14, 225, 281, 282, 283, 286, 296, 305
Southern 100 153, 154, 253, 305
Speed (television programme) 29–44, 45,

48, 50, 89, 94, 133, 139–52, 219, 236–7

Spellman, Andy 46–7, 48, 49, 50, 52, 53, 102, 164, 178, 179, 211, 213, 214, 215, 265, 270, 273, 274, 275, 276, 312, 315, plate section 1

Spencer, Freddie 93, 102

Spitfire 48, 275

Spring National, Scarborough 198, 223, 225–34, 235, 239, 241, 242, 247

Stoner, Casey 93

Strathpuffer 24-hour solo mountain race, 2015 124–38, 194

Sunday Times 170, 234

Superbikes 14, 16–17, 26, 95, 101, 106, 110, 121, 122, 156, 157–8, 159, 161, 164, 168, 171, 185, 188, 193, 196–205, 214, 219, 227, 228–9, 230, 235–6, 241, 243, 248, 251, 258, 260, 279, 280, 281

Supersport 100, 161, 164, 166–7, 169, 171, 196, 197, 198, 201, 202, 241, 259, 260, 281, 282, 283, 286, 295, 298, 309

Superstock 110, 114, 156, 159–61, 171, 188, 189, 190, 192, 204, 225–9, 233, 239–40, 241, 248, 249, 251, 259, 260, 281, 282, 283, 286, 295, 296, 297, 306, 309

Superprestigio, Spain, 2014 95–104, 105, 127

Suzuka 8-Hour, Japan 154

Suzuki 14, 17, 139, 155, 156–7, 161, 164, 243, 248, 249, 251, 287, 296, 309; GSX-R600 156, 162, 197; GSX-R750RR 17; GSX-R1000 14, 110–13, 114, 120, 156, 189–90; Hayabusa 216, 221; RMZ450 94–5; Swift 118; TS50X 193; 1271 cc engine 164; XR69 60

TAS Racing 14, 15, 26, 46, 94, 102, 153, 154, 155, 156, 157, 158, 161, 162, 164, 172, 184, 188, 189, 197, 200, 204–5, 213, 225, 226, 228, 239, 241, 248, 251, 252, 259, 260, 261–2, 269, 279, 281, 282, 284, 289, 294, 295, 296, 297, 303, 306, 314, plate section 2, plate section 3

Taylor Lindsey 169–70

Team Sky 79–80

Ten Kate 168, 169

Texter, Shayna 100

Thompson, Stephen 254

Times, The 154

Top Gear (television programme) 179, 273–4, 275

Toseland, James 168

Tour de France 31, 80, 126

Tour Divide, USA 117, 137–8, 303, 313

Toye, Jeremy 27

Track Electronics 15, 23

Transit, Ford 32, 39, 84, 87, 96, 98, 128, 137, 166, 167, 184, 193, 201–2, 226, 234, 238–9, 265, 279–80, plate section 1; plate section 2

Triumph 164, 165, 166, 169, 213–14, 215–16, 222, 269–70; Castrol Rocket (streamliner) 214, 215–22, 264; Daytona 675 164, 165, 169, 286, 305; Rob North Triumph 83; Rocket III engine 217–18, 219, 220; Smiths Triumph 167, 169, 170–2, 196–8, 200, 202, 204, 205, 213–14, 225, 281, 282, 283, 286, 296, 305; Speed Triple R 193–4; Tiger 1200 25; Triple 83, 151, 164; TT bike 305, 306, 312; USA 215

Twitter 28, 82

Tyco 205, 219, 226, 228, 233, 2

Ulster Grand Prix 7–8, 112, 152, 153, 305–12

Unser, Al 18

Unser, Robert 'Bobby' 18–19

Vatanen, Ari 13

Vehicle and Operator Services Agency (VOSA) 177, 194

Victory Motorcycles 299, 300, plate section 3

Walker, Mark 14, 17

Wall of Death speed record 139–52, 214, 236, 261, 262–7, 269, 274, 312, plate section 2

Wanganui Cemetery Circuit, New Zealand 105–23, plate section 2

Watson, Stephen 257

White, Mervyn 204–5, 253, 259

Whitman, Matt 171

Whitworth, Cameron 'Cammy' 18, 19, 23, 279–80, 303, plate section 1

Wiggins, Bradley 80

Williams, Peter 111

Wolfe, Ken 142, 266

Wood, James 96

World Cup 24-Hour solo race 24, 127–8

World Endurance Racing 154, 313

World Rally Championship (WRC) 13

World Superbike 101, 157–8, 168

World Supersport 168

Wright, Steve 48–9

Yamaha 60, 157, 161, 284, 309; FS–1E 108; R1 147, 165; R6 247, 250; TY80 trials bike 77